1973
W. B. SAUNDERS COMPANY
PHILADELPHIA / LONDON / TORONTO

William John Turtle, M.D.

Consultant – Pediatric Social Medicine,
Boston Hospital for Women;
Former Instructor in Pediatrics,
Harvard Medical School;
Associate in Medicine, Emeritus,
Children's Hospital Medical Center

With the assistance of
Lydia Pope Turtle

Dr. Turtle's Babies

W. B. Saunders Company: West Washington Square
Philadelphia, Pa. 19105

12 Dyott Street
London, WC1A 1DB

833 Oxford Street
Toronto 18, Ontario

COVER ILLUSTRATION

Mother and Child by Mary Cassatt. (Courtesy of The Art Institute of Chicago.)

Dr. Turtle's Babies   ISBN 0-7216-8938-8

Print No.:   9   8   7   6   5   4   3   2   1

Preface

When, six years ago, I retired from the practice of pediatrics, I cast about for some way to keep my hand in part time — some way to pass on what I had been learning over the years. "Write a book," I was advised. But book writing was quite outside my experience — for me, completely out of the question. Rather, I was tempted by a project that had been for some time simmering in the back of my head — the possibility of setting up prenatal talks and discussion groups for young expectant mothers.

Luckily for me, round about this same time, our children having married and left home to set up homes of their own, Mrs. Turtle was also, in a sense, retired. Having stuck by me throughout those busy years of practice, taken care of our growing children, made a home for us; having listened not only to my theories, dreams and gripes but, through manning our home phone, having also listened to countless anxious and harried parents and done her best to reassure and tide them over till such time as I showed up, she too was convinced of the need for and enthusiastic about the possibility of just such a project.

Out of the ideas and incidents, out of the welter of material that had accumulated over my years in practice, over the next months she helped me organize and outline the talks that were to form the basis for the discussion groups. Once they began she came to them all, kept records of attendance, kept track of questions, chatted with young people before and after the talks, listened with them, observed their reactions. After each session we would discuss, reappraise, rework our material. When the talks went on television, once again we revised our material. In the course of all this, inevitably and, as I see it, importantly, her slant, her point of view as a woman, and her experience as a mother and grandmother crept into and added flavor and breadth to the substance of the talks. After four years of this, we discovered that, quite unintentionally, we had in our hands the makings of the very book I had earlier refused even to consider. Here is the book—the result of many happy years of combined effort. This has been a joint venture and a lot of fun.

William J. Turtle, M.D.

Acknowledgments

In itself this book is an acknowledgment of all the help that has been coming my way over the years — first and foremost, from parents and babies and youngsters who came and kept coming, rounding out my clinical training, sharing in and shoring up my experience in the practice of pediatrics — so many of these, young and old, now grown to be good friends. Second, my thanks go to all the young people who sought out and steadfastly attended the prenatal talks, reinforcing my belief that there is a real hankering among parents-to-be for just such education, and also to the three sporting couples who stood by me and weathered with me "baptism" under the television lights.

To single out and give due thanks to all the nurses, secretaries, friends, and members of our families it has taken to keep me rolling is out of the question. Specifically, however, I do wish to acknowledge assistance in the writing of this book from those medical colleagues who have so generously offered their advice and criticism in their fields of specialty: in dentistry, Dr. G. Earl Thompson; in pediatric dentistry, Dr. Paul K. Losch and Dr. Lennard T. Swanson; in nutritional dentistry,

Dr. James H. Shaw; in ecological dentistry, Dr. James M. Dunning; in pediatric orthopedics, Dr. Arthur W. Trott; in pediatric psychiatry, Dr. Veronica B. Tisza; in ophthalmology, Dr. Richard B. Pippitt; and in the Poison Center of Children's Hospital Medical Center, Dr. Frederick H. Lovejoy. Also and very particularly, for her grasp of the aim of this project and for her canny guidance, I would like to express appreciation to Margaret I. MacLeod, a producer at WGBH-TV.

Above all I wish to extend especial thanks to four good friends for their encouragement and unfailing support: Dr. Duncan E. Reid, Dr. Langdon Parsons (my friend of the "Gray Zone"), Dr. John W. Chamberlain and Dr. Joseph W. Gardella. Their support and encouragement has stemmed primarily from our common preoccupation with clinical medicine and education —that is to say; the complete, the well-rounded care of the patient.

Lastly I would like to thank the staff of the publishers, W. B. Saunders Company, who have been so courteous, helpful and perceptive in the production of this book.

W.J.T.

Contents☙

Part Two
Postnatal Views

Introduction

I'm writing this book for you—you young couples who are thinking about starting a family, or whose first baby is already on the way.

"Good heavens," you say, "not another book on baby care! Aren't there already about as many books as babies? Haven't countless young mothers been sustained by Dr. Spock? And isn't his the last word on the subject?"

Well, with all due respect not only to Dr. Spock's fine books but to other excellent books on the subject, I think not. There will always be room for a new and different approach to a subject as universal, as personally meaningful and as complex as what I think of as the fundamentals of baby care. So, having enjoyed 33 years in the practice of Pediatrics, working along with parents and their babies, having at the same time enjoyed a home and three growing youngsters, and being currently registered in and enjoying a refresher course given by seven grandchildren, I writing this book for you mother-and-father-to-be. I know both of you are excited and anxious at the thought of having a baby, and that you are determined to do a good job of bringing it up and raising a family of healthy, happy, sound youngsters.

I know from experience that there are more young women just like you working hard at the job of being a good mother than at any other single occupation, and doing so with very little previous education or training for the job. It's rather appalling to think that you can't become a teacher, a stewardess, a nurse, a designer, a secretary, a librarian, a sales manager, a dietitian, let alone enter a profession such as law or medicine, without weeks, months or even years of training and education — you can't even drive a car most places without "driver education"; yet you are expected to care for and bring up your baby, a job that means more than almost any other, not only to you but to the community and the world-at-large, on a combination of instinct and common sense!

I know you can pick up a lot about baby care from baby-sitting jobs, from observing your friends, from your own family experience — some things to do along with a lot of things you'll "never do when you have a baby!" I know you read magazine and newspaper articles and books, but these aren't always helpful as far as you are concerned because they are primarily intended for the mother who already has a baby. In my experience all these bits and pieces added together — this hit-or-miss sort of education — just isn't enough. I happen to believe that to do any job well and to prevent mistakes it is important, *before you start,* to have a clear picture of just what is involved and where you are headed. It is this clear *beforehand* picture that I hope to give you in this book.

In the field of Preventive Pediatric Medicine tremendous strides have been made in a relatively short time as far as immunization and treatment of disease are concerned. When I was an intern at Children's Hospital Medical Center in Boston I used to see children and babies die of tetanus and diphtheria. When I began practice I used to try to help parents struggling with that miserable disease, whooping cough — three weeks coming, three weeks with you and three weeks going — think of the sleepless nights! But you couples won't have to worry about these diseases for your baby. You can see to it that early in life your baby is immunized against them, and against measles, mumps, polio and German measles as well. During my early years in practice the only treatment for pneumonia was bed, liquids, and drugs to keep the child comfortable. *Your* doctor, with the help of antibiotics, will be able to treat and cut down on the severity of the complications of colds for your youngsters. Medical research has made remarkable progress in an amazingly short time! However, as Dr. Janeway has pointed out, the bulk of a practicing pediatrician's time is devoted to the psychosocial aspect of his practice*; and certainly, while I used to do physicals and check-ups, give shots and boosters and take care of sick babies and children, the greater part of my time was spent trying to help parents deal with handling and behavior problems: What to do about:

    a. the baby that is still on the two o'clock feeding at six weeks of age;
    b. the baby that appears to stop eating;
    c. the baby with diaper rash;
    d. the baby that cries constantly to be picked up;
    e. the baby that struggles and kicks when you're trying to change its diapers;
    f. the baby with colic;
    g. the baby that falls out of its crib;
    h. the baby that at a year of age is practically ruling the roost.

These are the kinds of questions I used to be asked time and again by mother after mother — and I suspect the same ones have been asked repeatedly for generations. Mothers would come into the office struggling with these and similar problems primarily, it seemed to me, because no one had helped them to recognize and understand the *normal behavior* of a baby. All too frequently mothers' unenlightened, misguided responses to their babies' normal behavior is reflected in misbehavior on the part of their babies. Mothers and babies are still very much of a piece, a single entity, in the first months following delivery: action in one begets reaction in the other. Thus handling prob-

---

*Janeway, Charles E.: Some Shortcomings of Medical Education in a Free Society. Acta Paediat. Scand., Suppl. 172, 1967.

lems over this period are, in a sense, shared problems. And, just as it is so much easier to prevent polio and whooping cough than to treat them, so, I assure you, it is much easier to prevent these early handling problems than to deal with them once they have taken hold and become behavior problems. Babies are going to cry, they are going to suck their thumbs, they are going to lose their appetites, they are going to do all manner of things! The important thing is to prevent these manifestations of normal behavior and growth from becoming problems — to apply preventive medicine to handling and behavior problems.

How to tackle this aspect of preventive medicine? This had bothered me throughout my years in practice and when I retired I wondered if there wasn't something I could do about it. To accomplish anything, it seemed to me, some sort of pre-natal education should be offered girls. The question was: Do girls want it or feel the need for it? I asked the opinion of a colleague and was told, "Don't be crazy, Bill! You know perfectly well you can't talk to a girl about her baby before she's had it! And besides, what is there to talk about?" Well, I had my own ideas: I couldn't disprove the first part of his statement, but I *did* know that there was an awful lot to talk about. In practice, whenever I could, I used to have a talk in the hospital with each new mother, and it always seemed to me that that talk left a lot to be desired. There was so much ground to be covered that a half-hour talk — all that a girl could be asked to take at such a time — was hopelessly inadequate. Therefore I decided to do what came most easily out of my experience and what I enjoy most: talk to young girls about their babies, only this time to do it prenatally.

For three years I ran a series of discussion groups for the wives of students, graduate students and young faculty of Harvard and M.I.T. I started rather gingerly with afternoon discussions for a few brave but obviously interested girls who were expecting babies in the near future. Before long, at their request, the discussion groups were switched to evening when girls who were working daytimes could attend. The big surprise came when husbands began showing up with their wives, and their presence opened up a wonderful opportunity to talk not just about mothers and babies but about mothers and fathers, about parents and babies, about homes and families. I repeated the series of discussions three times in the course of the academic year. By the third year each of the series of discussions was attended by 65 to 80 or more young people — mainly couples — and these couples came repeatedly, week after week, in growing numbers, to listen to me talking about such things as breast- and bottle-feeding techniques, bubbling, rashes, poor appetite, coaxing, thumb-sucking, colic, prevention of accidents, when to call a doctor, overpossessiveness, training, schedules, discipline, and education.

During these sessions it became apparent to me that *prenatally* couples tend to think of the problems of their future baby in a detached and objective way that is difficult for them to achieve once they have a baby and have become emotionally involved. Furthermore, the questions and observations of these young people served to strengthen the theories and point of view I had developed over my years in practice; and their attendance and attentiveness convinced me that not only girls but couples — couples just like you — are eager to get information, prenatally, about the fundamentals of baby care. Repeatedly, at the end of each series would come the question: "Dr. Turtle, when are you going to write a book?"

During a fourth year the talks were given and once repeated over educational TV, and the interest and response of young people was the same and the same question about a book kept popping up. So here is the book, written for you parents- to-be in the hope that it will help to start you off caring for your baby with confidence and with as much information as possible about how babies grow, develop and behave.

Before we start to talk about your baby, let's take a minute to consider the home you two are offering it. I'm not thinking of the physical set-up — babies are extremely good-natured and adaptable and make themselves at home in igloos, split-levels, projects, bamboo huts, dormitories, any place you can think of the world around. What I'm thinking of is home atmosphere — in a sense this can be a real problem of pollution — here babies are more sensitive.

Throughout this book I'll be discussing responsibilities that fall to you as parents but I'd like here to draw your attention to a responsibility you have, right now, to each other, and one that the two of you will have to your baby: the responsibility to keep on your toes and anticipate and prevent behavior problems — your own as well as your baby's — and in this way to cut down on misunderstanding, friction and constant bickering; in other words, the responsibility to do your best to create a warm, happy, stable home. This isn't something easy, this isn't something that just happens, and it isn't a bit too early for you to start thinking in long-range terms about what is involved here. There is a challenge here for you to offer your children the opportunity to grow up in a home environment which, if all goes well, when they are fifteen or sixteen years of age will not prove to be unhappy, unstimulating, empty or confusing so that, groping for something home doesn't provide, they join the unfortunately large group of home-dropouts. It takes a lot of forbearance, a lot of determination and a good sense of humor to do this. I might add that you will get a great assist if, right now, between the two of you, you establish an honest and efficient communication system, a system into which as your youngsters are coming along they can tune in, a system that will help you and your children bridge that much talked of generation gap.

I'm limiting the period covered in this book to your baby's first year — I do so for two reasons:

First, because so much happens in this year that is basic to your baby's future growth, development and education that I feel it is impossible to overemphasize the importance of a good start.

Second, because this is when you parents establish attitudes and approaches to the care and handling of your baby that remain with you as you raise your children.

Babies in the first year grow very rapidly: the average baby doubles its birthweight in the first six months and triples it by the end of the year — a rate of growth it will never duplicate the rest of its life. If, however, you parents begin this year unprepared for the normal but subtle changes in development and behavior that inevitably accompany this rapid growth, you can so easily and unwittingly make mistakes — little mistakes that can lead to problems, the very handling problems you planned to avoid. The mite of a baby you were almost afraid to hold when the nurse first placed it in your arms can, in 12 short months, have you parents right in the palm of its little hand. So, let me stress once more the importance to your baby and to you of having some idea ahead of time about what the job of a parent involves so that you will not miss out on the opportunities this first year has to offer.

It is always a comfort to know that you are not entirely on your own as you tackle a new job, and so your preparation for parenthood should include an understanding and an appreciation of the extent to which nature will help you. I shall refer frequently to nature, so I want to be sure you understand what I mean by the term. A useful definition is "the inherent, the vital power that maintains and sustains life and over which we have limited control." As a maintainer and sustainer of life, nature has a very real stake in your baby's well-being. Those of you whose baby is already on the way have learned to respect what nature does in conception and I am sure you are also impressed by the way she has arranged to care for your baby in utero: protecting it, seeing to it that it gets all the nourishment it needs, and to a certain extent safeguarding it against infection. These are things over which you have relatively little control. Your respect for what nature does will be increased at the time of delivery.

Fortunately for you, after your baby is born nature goes

right on carrying out her part of the job, and it is important that you learn to recognize, understand and respect the way she does this, that you learn not to interfere, that you learn not to dissipate your energies trying to do what she will do far better. With a little mutual respect you and nature and your baby can make a good show.

As you can see I've done the usual—referred to nature as "she"—but literature and art offer plenty of precedents and even science, in the field of meteorology, accords hurricanes and typhoons girls' names—a rather dubious compliment, it seems to me. Also, I've sometimes used masculine, sometimes feminine pronouns to refer to babies: in all instances, pronouns of either gender, obviously, equally apply.

Now a little bit about your baby. At this point there is one thing of which you can be certain: your baby isn't going to be like any baby you have ever known before. He will have made a selection—judicious or otherwise—from among all the looks, traits, brains, dispositions and abilities of long lines of progenitors on both sides of the family and come up with—*himself*. And he should at all times be handled and respected as just that—*himself*. Moreover you parents, the two of you—your personalities, your backgrounds, your situation—are your own selves and provide your baby not only with a unique inheritance but with a unique environment as well. But while, on the one hand, all babies are different and their own individual selves, on the other hand, all normal babies, from Kamchatka to Capetown and from Singapore to Sandusky, proceed physically, developmentally and behaviorally along very similar lines. In the course of the first year they all:

    a. Hold up their heads and look around;
    b. Become aware of and accustomed to their surroundings and the people caring for them;
    c. Roll over (watch out for the first time!);

    d. Get an assortment of teeth;
    e. Learn to make their wants known;
    f. Grasp at things and hold on to them;
    g. Respond to your promptings and encouragement.

They do all these and many, many more things in common but — and this is important — because every baby is its own individual self, living in its own environment, there are tremendous, often hard-to-believe variations as to the time at which they start to do these things, the way they do them, the degree to which they respond and the degree to which they assert themselves. All of which means that, while there is obviously no one way to bring up babies, there is a very broad, basic pattern of growth, development and behavior against which you and I can look at your individual baby.

    Now, how am I going to give you couples a glimpse of this baby of yours before you even have it? How is this book designed to give you, prenatally, a picture of your baby, growing, developing, behaving and misbehaving during its first year? Well, to give you this picture and to provide you with plenty of perspective from which to examine it, I am going to offer you a two-angled shot at it — one view from high in the stands, as it were, and one from right down on the playing field.

    In the first half of the book I shall give you a picture of just what is involved in the job of being parents — the fundamentals: what they are, why they are and where they are heading.

    First, I shall take up the six areas of responsibility in the care and handling of a baby: the Treatment of Infections, the Feeding, the Prevention of Accidents, the Training, the Discipline and the Education. These aren't things you can afford to put off thinking about until your baby is several weeks or months old. These are the responsibilities that will be delivered along with your baby and will remain with you in one form or another all through your child's growing years. These are things you will do well to start thinking about right now, so you won't be caught napping.

Second, I shall take up the question of feeding your baby: whether to breast-feed or bottle-feed, the mechanics of breast feeding and bottle feeding, the mechanics of bubbling. This is information that will help you develop the simple but necessary skills that will ensure feeding going smoothly not only for your baby but for the entire family.

Third, I shall take up a few specific problems in care and handling that will inevitably crop up as you tend your baby, things like circumcision, hiccups, rashes, pacifiers, and masturbation, among others. These will be based on the questions I have been asked over and over again by the mothers of new babies.

Fourth, I shall make some suggestions that may help you add to the efficiency and safety of your nursery set-up — ideas I've picked up visiting in homes over the years.

In the second half of the book I shall get down to the practical application of these fundamentals to the daily care of your baby during its first year. I shall go over exactly the same material covered in the first half of the book, only this time I shall deal with it chronologically, starting before you and your baby leave the hospital, and going on to when your baby is six weeks old, four months, eight months and a year of age. I shall draw on the earlier material that relates specifically to each of these periods, sometimes expand it, sometimes refer you back to it for a fuller explanation. I shall then go on to consider the changes that will take place in the interval between these periods — deceptive changes whose significance may so easily be missed, leaving the average, unsuspecting parents caught way off base. The theme of this book is *prevention*. As I see it, understanding and foresight in the first year offer the best means of checking the unhappy, often insidious sequence of small mistakes becoming handling problems, handling problems turning into behavior problems and eventually growing into the resistant behavior problems of adolescents and young adults.

Those of you couples who read, as I hope you will, the second half of the book before you have your baby may find it repetitious—indeed it is repetitious—it is so intended. But when, possibly, you reread it in the hospital, having held your baby only a few times, having fed it only a few times, and are suddenly faced with taking it home, just you two parents, I would like to think you will find this second half familiar and reassuring. I would like to think you will find it begin to take on a new and greater meaning, that it will offer you understanding, encouragement and confidence.

So much for the way this book is designed to give you the "beforehand picture" I referred to earlier of what is involved and where you are heading as you begin to think of yourselves as parents. However, I feel it is only fair to warn you, right now, that from time to time I am going to turn the camera squarely on the two of you, so that you parents may also catch a glimpse of yourselves—growing, developing, behaving and misbehaving in the course of your baby's first year. Your baby isn't going to grow in a vacuum. In fact, I used to find it unsatisfactory and incomplete to consider a baby, to examine it, without, in a sense, at the same time examining its mother and, more likely than not, its father as well. You and your baby are going to grow up together, and I hope this book will help you, at the same time, to have fun with each other, to learn from each other, to love and respect each other and gradually to develop confidence in each other.

Now, before we get going, I want to be sure two points are perfectly clear: first, in this book I am considering only normal babies; and second, this book in no way takes the place of routine medical care and check-ups for your baby.

Part One

A Prenatal View

Pastel by Mary Cassatt. (Courtesy of The Butler Institute of American Art, Youngstown, Ohio.)

Chapter One

*The
Six
Areas
of
Responsibility*

1 – The Six Areas of Responsibility

.

Let's consider the six areas of responsibility in the care and handling of your baby in its first year:

Treatment of Infections
Feeding
Prevention of Accidents
Training
Discipline
Education

The idea of these separate but at times overlapping areas developed over my years in practice as I observed parents and their successes and failures, as I tried to come up with some simple, helpful and workable explanation of what parents' responsibilities are. It used to seem to me that the reason parents sometimes got into trouble was because they just plain didn't know what they were supposed to do, what their job consisted of. I know perfectly well that when you two become parents you will want to do everything you can for your baby. I also happen to believe that if you can be helped, ahead of time, to understand that there will be things *not to do* as well as things *to do* — that part of the responsibility of bringing up your baby will fall to nature and part to you — things will go more smoothly all round.

I pointed out earlier that nature has a very real stake in your baby's well-being. I think you can see that it is quite logical that, as a "maintainer and sustainer of life," nature should assume responsibility in the first two areas: *Treatment of Infections* and *Feeding* — that is, for the health and nourishment of your baby. To carry out her responsibilities she will need your assistance, but in these two areas hers will be the principal and yours the supporting role. Yet I have known mothers to waste an unconscionable amount of valuable time trying to push food and more food into their babies — definitely a thing *not to do* — nature assumes responsibility for the amount of food a baby eats.

However, nature isn't going to take over the whole show — she's not about to do it all for you by any means! The primary responsibility in each of the remaining four areas will fall squarely on the shoulders of you parents. Again, when you stop to think of it, this is quite logical: these are responsibilities involved in helping your baby adjust to living happily in the world with other people — first with you parents and, as time goes on, with others. Many parents find it difficult to believe that Prevention of Accidents, Training, Discipline and Education are responsibilities that have to be considered right from the start. Yet I assure you that if you learn early to integrate these responsibilities into the daily care and handling of your baby, you'll greatly increase your opportunities to do everything you can for your baby.

Now, let's take up, one by one, the six responsibilities that make up your job as parents.

Nature's Areas of Responsibility

Treatment of Infections

Your baby will come into this world with a natural ability to fight infections — that is why this area of responsibility falls primarily to nature. You parents will be able to carry out your supportive role more effectively if you understand how nature works. I don't for one second wish to minimize the importance of the "tender, loving care" you will give your baby when it is sick, but you should realize that even a doctor's role in sickness is largely supportive. Nature assumes the principal responsibility.

I am going to deal mainly with the common cold because

this is the infection with which you will be faced most frequently during the first year. It is usually a fairly mild infection but at times it may be the forerunner of a more serious one.

How do babies catch colds? Colds in babies are almost always the result of contact with someone who either has or is coming down with a cold. Therefore the best way to keep your baby's colds to a minimum is to try to prevent them by being as careful as possible about your baby's contacts:

    a. Especially in winter, when more people have colds;
    b. Especially with children who, as you know, have frequent colds and assume no responsibility about spreading them;
    c. By avoiding, as much as you can, taking your baby into crowds.

All this means judgment and common sense on both your parts. You mothers have to go shopping in supermarkets and department stores but with a little planning a father can, on occasion, stay home and cultivate his talent as a baby-sitter, or, with a good shopping list, he can do surprisingly well at the market.

Visitors sometimes require considerable tact on your part — they want not only to see your baby but to hold it. Unfortunately some people just don't seem to realize that what for them is only a "scratchy throat" or a "stuffy nose" may prove to be a full-blown infection to the baby they hover over or pick up and hug. Do your best to limit the guest with an obvious cold to a peek at your baby through the bedroom door. Parents, too, have colds but a father can stay away from the baby for a few days, and a mother can do her best by using a mask — it may help. Once again, where your own colds are concerned, your best bet is prevention: getting as much rest as possible and keeping yourselves fit.

I have stressed the fact that babies almost always get their colds from contacts. But when babies come down with colds, frequently mothers blame themselves for not having dressed their baby warmly enough or for having failed to replace the blanket that was kicked off. I assure you that babies rarely catch colds in this way, from exposure. This was brought home to me most forcibly one day, a number of years ago.

> The mother of a little patient of mine called up one winter's morning to ask if I was going to be on hand that day. Her two-year-old had wandered off after breakfast and couldn't be found. He was in his snowsuit but it was a bitter cold day, the temperature hovering around 10 degrees above zero. The neighborhood had turned out and a search was on but the mother wanted to be sure I would be available when he was found. Naturally I was relieved when, in the afternoon, she finally called. The boy had been found, curled up in a dog kennel— someone had happened to hear him crying. When I arrived he was whimpering and shivering and very pale—his rectal temperature was down to 92 degrees F. We got him warmed up—he hungrily gulped down a cup of warm milk laced with a spoonful of brandy which his father happily supplied—and before long the boy's color began to improve. He grew cheerful and wanted to play. When I left, his temperature was back within normal limits. For several days his mother kept me posted, and each day the boy was fine—no sign of a cold.
>
> Six weeks later I heard from her again. Her boy had a temperature of 105 degrees. A few days earlier her husband had had a slight sore throat, but not even enough to keep him home from work. Well, the little fellow was laid up for a time, and when I stopped in to check him over for the last time, his father stood at the foot of the bed and said ruefully, "Here he was, lost for most of a day and almost frozen to death and nothing happens; then I come home with a little cold and the poor kid has pneumonia—I just don't get it!"

No, babies seldom get their colds from exposure; it's almost always the result of contact.

Early Warning Signs

In spite of your efforts at prevention, your baby is more than likely to have a certain number of colds during her first year. Just as soon as a cold begins, however, nature responds with countermeasures, and these, if you are watchful and fortunate enough to notice them, can serve as the "*early warning signs*" of an infection. These countermeasures are nature's way of getting treatment of your baby's cold started:

1. *Your baby may become listless*—want to sleep all the time. He may fall asleep at unusual times or in unusual places such as the pen or highchair. (Babies need rest and sleep to fight infection.)
2. *Your baby may lose his appetite*—couldn't be less interested in food. (Babies need fluids, not food, to help combat infection.)
3. *Your baby may become fussy*—you just can't seem to do anything right! He wants constant attention—wants to be held! (Babies need comfort and warmth and tender care to combat infection.)

A baby may exhibit all these signs or any combination of them. But babies are all so different—in some these warning signs will be much more apparent than in others. Some babies, more frequently boys, go right on eating regardless of what they may be coming down with. Sometimes a mother is just plain too busy to notice. However, if one or more of the signs are present and you observe it or them, you will have the opportunity to get treatment of your baby's cold started 24 hours sooner than the mother who happens to miss the warning. As an added suggestion: if your baby has had a *known contact* or a *suspected contact*—a family gathering or any exposure to a crowd—you might start looking for the early signs after about three days (the average incubation period of a cold). If, *thanks to nature's early warning,* you can get treatment of your baby's infection started right off the bat, you have a good chance of cutting down on the severity and the duration of the infection.

Early Treatment

What is the early treatment of a cold—how do you support and carry on with the measures nature has already begun?

1. *Keep your baby warm and as quiet as possible.* This does not necessarily mean in bed, but wherever it's quietest.

You can always put a blanket over the baby that's fallen asleep in an unusual spot.

2. *Let your baby sleep as long as it wants to,* completely disregarding its schedule.

3. *Respect its loss of appetite! If your baby is getting solids you might omit them*—certainly don't push them.

4. Whenever your baby is awake *offer fluids frequently*—water or dilute fruit juices.

5. *Watch your baby's bowels*—if the movements become hard offer dilute apple or prune juice. You don't want your baby to become constipated.

6. *Feel free to spoil your baby!* (This is one time you should allow yourself to do so.) When it gets well you'll have a bit of a problem on your hands, but never mind! I remember a call from a mother whose baby had been ill for quite a time and was beginning to get better. The mother wanted to know if the time had come to start "unspoiling" her baby.

This early treatment of yours is simply a matter of creating the environment in which nature works best. Suppose your baby just had an off day and you started treatment but no cold developed—there's nothing lost. A good day's rest never does a baby any harm!

When *later signs of infection* appear, such as *a runny nose, a high temperature, vomiting, diarrhea* (frequent, watery, definitely green stools) or *pain,* continue or start the same treatment as for the early signs:

Quiet;
Sleep;
Cut back on solids;
Offer liquids frequently;
Watch bowels;
Feel free to spoil baby.

While you're carrying out your part of the treatment you can be sure nature is tending to hers.

How does nature respond as the infection progresses?

1. She usually pushes up the white count.
2. She produces antibodies in the blood stream to fight the substances causing the infection.
3. She usually elevates the temperature — she works more efficiently in the presence of heat.
4. Slowly she builds some immunity in your baby so that as time goes on he doesn't pick up every cold he happens to meet.

These aren't thing you can do! These aren't things a doctor can do! These are the things nature does in carrying out her responsibility for the treatment of infection.

So often parents say, "Isn't there something more we can do than just these simple things?" *Don't worry — by providing nature with the proper environment in which to work you are contributing a great deal!*

One thing you should be able to do is take a temperature. So often in practice when I would inquire about a baby's temperature his mother would say, "I don't know how to take it," "I'm afraid to take it!" or, "I'll have to wait till my husband comes home; I can't read a thermometer!" Let me suggest that now, before you have your baby, you get a *rectal thermometer* and the two of you get accustomed to reading it and shaking it down. Being able to take a temperature will help you gauge the severity of your baby's infection and, should you need to call a doctor, he too will want this information. The temperature should be taken rectally — under the arm or in the groin isn't very accurate. After a newborn has passed its first bowel movement — which consists of meconium, a black tarry substance — this is a perfectly safe procedure. Maybe I can make some suggestions that will enable you to realize how easy and safe it is.

1. Use a rectal thermometer. Check it to be sure the reading is well below the arrow — shake down if necessary.

2. Lubricate the thermometer with Vaseline or baby oil.
3. With baby on his back (they like to see you and they like to see what's going on), holding the baby firmly with one hand, slowly insert the thermometer in the rectum.
4. Put it in about an inch—don't worry, a little farther will do no harm.
5. Hold on to the thermometer and keep it in the rectum a couple of minutes. Rest the hand holding the thermometer comfortably against the baby's bottom so, should the baby move, your hand and the thermometer will move with it.
6. Remove and, if the baby is fussing, set thermometer aside on a safe surface and get the baby settled.
7. Wipe thermometer and read.
   (Be careful not ever to wash the thermometer in hot water.)

Don't be afraid you'll hurt the baby—you won't. It may cry but not from pain—possibly from wounded dignity. I want to repeat: hold your baby firmly, know you won't hurt it and your baby will respond to your confidence. Disregard its fussing and you will find this business of taking a rectal temperature a very simple procedure.

Now, what is a normal temperature? A baby's heat-regulating mechanism isn't very well established and its normal temperature ranges anywhere from about 96 degrees to 100 degrees F. A temperature taken early on a chilly morning may be as low as 95 degrees F., which simply means that the baby is cold—put on another blanket. A subnormal temperature in a baby has no serious significance. (Pay no attention to the red arrow on the thermometer scale at 98.6 degrees—this is adult normal.)

Another thing I think you couples should do before your baby is born—certainly before taking it home from the hospital—is establish contact with a clinic or doctor to whom you can take your baby for check-ups and immunization and whom you can call in case of a problem or emergency. Both clinics and doctors usually have call hours, and knowing the time and the number to call will make things go more smoothly for everyone concerned. Since there may be times when your baby will have more than just a simple cold and since there are some infections that don't start with a cold, let me make some suggestions as to when I think you should call a doctor. First, in case of infection:

1. A rectal temperature of 103 degrees or over;
2. A rectal temperature of 101 or 102 degrees that continues over a period of several days;
3. Persistent vomiting;
4. Persistent diarrhea—watery, green stools;
5. Crying as if in pain—you will very soon learn to differentiate among your baby's ways of crying.

There are other times, when infection is not involved, that I think you should call a doctor:

1. A fall or accident that may have resulted in a broken bone or a head injury;
2. Uncontrollable bleeding;
3. Burns;
4. Possible ingestion of poison (it is well also to have the number of a hospital or Poison Control Center available);
5. Red stools (before calling a doctor think back to whether you gave the baby beets the preceding day);
6. Black stools—an indication of internal bleeding.

If you are uncertain, if anything occurs that does not seem normal, it is far better to contact the doctor when it is not absolutely necessary than to run the risk of failing to make a necessary call!

Furthermore, I would suggest you find out from your doctor what medicines he would like you to have on hand and just how to use them. In addition to a rectal thermometer I always wanted the parents of my patients to have, *stored away well out of reach:*

1. Nose drops,
2. Baby aspirin (liquid),
3. A mild disinfectant in case of scratches,

and, more important, two things *which I insisted should be used only after consulting me or some doctor,* but two things that can't always be obtained quickly or easily at the time of need:

4. Syrup of ipecac,
5. A mild rectal sedative, preferably in capsule form so it can easily be inserted in the baby's rectum.

As I said earlier, a cold is the infection with which you parents will be most frequently faced. It is usually a mild affair, though occasionally it may be the forerunner of a more serious infection. However, by being as careful as you can about contacts, by being watchful for the early warning signs of infection and getting treatment started as promptly as possible, and by providing nature with the best possible environment in which to work, you parents will be carrying out your very important supporting role in the treatment of infections.

Feeding

Feeding is the second area of responsibility that falls primarily to nature, with you parents playing a supporting role. I'm sure some of you may find this statement surprising, as one usually thinks of the feeding of an infant as entirely its mother's concern. If, however, you are going to prevent feeding problems, it is very important, right from the start, to understand that a baby comes into the world with a *natural ability to determine the amount of food it needs* — in other words that nature assumes responsibility for the *amount* of food a baby eats. It is up to parents, of course, to support nature by providing the food: at first either from the breast or bottle, then by adding solids to the baby's diet until, long before the end of the first year, a baby is on three regular meals. It is up to the mother to offer well-balanced meals, to vary them, make them attractive and to keep mealtimes pleasant and relaxed. Here, however, her responsibility ends. I hope I can make it clear to you that the amount of food a baby takes is nature's responsibility! The amount will vary from meal to meal, from day to day, from baby to baby, just as with adults. But, thanks to nature, a baby or child offered food and then allowed to take as much or as little as it wants will, over a 24-hour period, eat all it needs and, moreover, will do a surprisingly good job of balancing its diet.

There is nothing new about this. Some years ago an experiment was run with a group of three children, one to one-and-a-half years of age, who were expected to have a prolonged stay in an orthopedic hospital. These children's daily meals were served to each of them on a large tray offering a wide choice of foods appropriate to the meal. The children made their own selections and were helped to eat just what and as much as they wished. They were given supplementary vitamins. Dieticians kept close tabs on what and how much was eaten, and although some of the meals were rather weird judged by ordinary standards, it was remarkable how well, over a 24- to 36-hour period, these little children balanced the fats, carbohydrates and proteins in their diets. Two of the children continued on the experiment for 6 months, till discharge, the third child for a year. On leaving the hospital all of them were gaining weight and were perfectly healthy, and their condition left no doubt in the minds of the doctors and dieticians that even very young children can be relied on to eat enough and to balance their diet if the amount and choice of food are left to them.

To clarify this point further, let me suggest you take a

look at the natural world around you. Even a quick look should be sufficient to impress you with the varied and ingenious ways by which nature provides nourishment and the means of obtaining nourishment to every living thing, from amebas to mushrooms to mollusks to man. In some species nature makes use of parents to provide food, in one way or another, but note that they merely provide it; they never assume responsibility for the amount their offspring eat. The parent robin drops the worm only into the *open* bill; the ewe leads her lamb to the tenderest pasturage and then *allows the lamb to nibble as it wants;* the barn cat shows up with her kittens at milking time but she doesn't stand around wringing her paws if her kittens fail to lap up all the milk in the saucer. Kittens, lambs and baby birds know when they've had all they want.

Now let's look at the human family. When a girl is pregnant she provides nourishment for her baby. She offers it all it wants but she has no control over the amount it takes nor does it enter her head to worry that it may not be getting enough. She has complete confidence in nature's handling of her baby's feeding over this period, and her confidence is well founded. (I might point out that during pregnancy even if a mother's diet is slightly deficient nature sees to it that her baby gets all the nourishment it needs—at the mother's expense.) Throughout pregnancy a mother provides the food and nature sees to it that her baby takes what it needs—this is nature's responsibility.

When a baby is born, thanks again to efficient planning on nature's part, the baby comes into the world complete with a sucking mechanism, an appetite and the same natural ability it had before it was born to take all the food it needs. It is still up to the mother to provide food, at this point from either the breast or a bottle. Nature still sees to it that, if plenty of food is made readily available, a normal, healthy baby will eat all it wants and then stop.

Unfortunately an understanding of the way mothers and babies and nature work together isn't generally included in a girl's education. So, for the most part, mothers aren't helped to realize that, whether their baby is inside or outside of them, it's the same baby: growing, needing to be fed and knowing naturally how much food it needs; they don't think of the feeding of their baby as a continuing responsibility they share with nature; that before and after birth if they do their part and provide food they can rest assured nature will do hers. More often than not, when babies are born and mothers hold them in their arms and watch them feeding some mothers get it into their heads that feeding is a responsibility newly and entirely theirs, that it's up to them not only to provide the food but to see to it that their baby takes the right amount. For these mothers once the cord is tied it's a brand-new ballgame. With determination they take on the whole responsibility, nature's as well as their own—and this almost always leads to trouble.

Over my years in practice, when mother after mother after mother would come into the office worried sick because their babies weren't eating enough, I used to find it difficult to help them understand that they were being needlessly upset— that they could safely leave it to their baby to eat as much or as little as it wanted. Once mothers get over on nature's side of the fence it's hard to reason them back again; and if they persist in taking over nature's responsibility for the amount their babies eat they'll almost surely end up with a feeding problem. My hope is that by helping you couples now, prenatally, to understand and to have confidence in the way nature works, I will be able to prevent your having to struggle with this unnecessary, time-wasting worry over the amount your baby eats. I hope I can help you prevent feeding problems.

Actually, as far as feeding is concerned, mothers have more than enough to do in just supporting nature. Nature can't see to it that a baby takes all it wants unless its mother not only provides plenty of food but also makes that food readily available. To do this a mother must have a thorough grasp of the technique of feeding—both breast and bottle—a subject I shall go into farther along in the book. The point I wish to make here, to you couples, is that your supporting role is both basic and demanding and you'll have your hands plenty full if you stick to your own part of the job.

I'm sure that by now you're tired of my dwelling on these same two points:

1. Nature assumes responsibility for the amount a baby eats;
2. Parents support nature by providing the food.

I have done so only because I know that it is easier for you to grasp them—to build them into your approach to feeding now, before you have your baby, than later on. Once your baby is born, so much of what you think and do will be affected by your emotions—and no doubt you've already come to realize that emotions can be kind of tricky. However, emotions inevitably and rightly creep into all aspects of the handling of your baby. I'll be pointing this out time and again as we discuss *prevention of accidents, training, discipline* and *education*.

Emotions and Feeding

Emotions can be assets or liabilities depending on how well you face up to them and channel them to advantage. Misdirected, emotions can play havoc with your support of nature in this matter of feeding. Feeding a baby is such an emotional experience! A mother derives tremendous pleasure and satisfaction from feeding her small, helpless, completely dependent infant. It is a very warm, emotional experience for a mother— it's important that it should be—and her baby is aware of, responds to and needs this emotional warmth. It is most important, however, that a mother limit her emotional satisfaction to *offering* food to her baby. If she allows her emotions to become involved in the amount of food her baby is taking, she may be headed for one of the most common mistakes a mother can make: coaxing her baby to eat.

To understand how easy it is for a mother's emotions to become misplaced in this way, let's consider the feeding of a baby over the first three or four months. First, think of the baby on the breast. The breast, thanks to nature, is a very efficient mechanism. It produces a uniformly excellent quality of milk and makes it very readily available. Moreover, as a baby grows in size and strength, and repeatedly just about empties the breasts, the breasts respond by producing larger quantities of milk. Nature sees to it that the supply is always ahead of the demand.

A baby at first gains rapidly. At about two-and-one-half to three months this rapid gain in weight slows down. It has to! The average seven-pound baby just about doubles its birth-weight in three to four months' time. If this rate of gain in weight were to continue — that is, doubling of weight every three months — at the end of a year a baby would weigh around 112 pounds — which is ridiculous! It is perfectly obvious there has to be a slowing down and this slowing down is usually accompanied by a falling off of appetite. Inasmuch as the breast-feeding mother doesn't know the exact amount her baby is taking, this drop-off in appetite takes place more or less unnoticed and feedings continue happily for mother and baby.

Now, think of the bottle-fed baby. In my experience the emotional pleasure and satisfaction experienced by the bottle-feeding mother who feeds her baby holding it in her arms is just as great as that experienced by the breast-feeding mother. This mother derives added satisfaction from seeing the bottles she prepares with care emptied by that rapidly growing, hungry baby. She finds she has constantly to increase the amount of formula in the bottles to keep the supply ahead of the demand, just as nature does for the baby on the breast. What is more, she is able to observe her baby's intake increase, ounce by ounce. But, at about two-and-one-half to three months, just like the breast-fed baby, her baby's rapid gain in weight slows down. The accompanying loss of appetite is marked, visibly, in ounces, on the bottle!

Now, as I just said, for this mother the feeding of her baby is a very satisfying, emotional experience! When this loss of appetite occurs she must have a very sound understanding of what is happening — that this drop-off in appetite is perfectly normal. If she doesn't—if she lets her emotions get mixed up in the amount her baby is taking, or rather the amount it isn't taking—she may try to get her baby to take just a little bit more. In other words, she may start coaxing.

The breast-feeding mother may run into the same emotional tangle when she starts offering her baby solids and for the first time can observe the amount of food her baby is taking. In fact, any mother, at any stage of the game, who thinks she knows how much food her baby or her child should eat and allows herself to become upset when her youngster fails to eat that amount may be led by her misplaced emotions into coaxing.

A very little coaxing can escalate rapidly into a feeding problem, and a feeding problem, I assure you, is much harder to treat than to prevent!

Coaxing

Now, just what is coaxing? So often parents aren't aware that they are coaxing and, moreover, coaxing takes on a variety of forms. But in all of them the satisfaction a mother derives from seeing her baby eat is converted by her emotional involvement into a compulsion to get her baby to eat more. When she does this, a mother climbs right over onto nature's side of the fence and sets herself up as the one who knows how much her baby should eat. For instance:

a. There is the mother who tries to get her baby to finish a bottle rather than leave an ounce or a half-ounce.

b. Or the mother who, when she starts offering solids— once she has that spoon in her hand—tries to wedge a little more cereal or fruit through her baby's closed lips.

c. There is the mother who diverts her baby's attention and tries to slip in another spoonful.

d. Or the mother of the slightly older child who urges, "Just one more bite, darling! Take just one more swallow of milk for mother!"

e. But by far the trickiest form coaxing takes and by far
the most common is the mother who shows by word
or look *delight* when her baby eats and *disappointment*
when her baby fails to eat. In other words, the mother
who acts as if her baby's appetite were her responsibility.

A mother brought her ten-month-old baby in for a check-up. The child
was in good condition, hemoglobin was normal and the gain in weight
normal. The mother was upset because she was sure her baby wasn't
eating anywhere near enough. I had known this mother, who had been
a dietician, at the Children's Hospital — she had lots of experience feeding babies and children. But now she was dealing with her own baby!
Together we went over the three reasons that a baby doesn't eat all its
mother thinks it should:
The baby may be coming down with an infection.
The mother has an exaggerated idea of the amount the baby
should eat.
By far the most common — the mother has been coaxing.
Well, this mother and I agreed her baby didn't seem sick. It looked
bloomingly healthy! I cautiously asked about meals and received a
lecture on the importance, even for a young baby, of varying the
meals, making them attractive and allowing the baby to take as much
or as little as it wanted. Very gingerly I suggested the possibility of
the baby's having been coaxed and, as I expected, the mother was
indignant — of course she knew better than to coax!
On the surface everything seemed fine, but we were still faced with
the mother's concern that her baby wasn't eating enough. So I asked
her to describe just what went on at mealtime.
"Well", said the mother, "I sit in front of the highchair, give the
bottle first and then offer solids."
"Is that all?" I asked.
"If she eats well, I'm delighted, I praise her! I clap my hands to
show her how pleased I am!"
"If she refuses?" I asked.
"If she refuses, hardly eats at all, of course I'm disappointed! I
put a lot of thought into her meals — all her meat, fruit and vegetables
are freshly prepared! I'll admit I often feel like crying. Sometimes I do."
I asked the mother if she thought her emotional response might
possibly enter into her baby's not eating. No, she really didn't believe
it could. But before she left the office she agreed *to try* to show as little
emotion as possible at meals.
Some time later she called to say she was delighted at the way
feedings were going. She frankly admitted that she just hadn't believed

that her innocent expressions of pleasure and disappointment could possibly have influenced her baby. She added, with a little laugh, "And I thought I knew all there was to know about feeding babies!"

This isn't absurd or unusual. It's difficult to believe how emotionally charged some mothers become over this matter of feeding. So often in the office a mother, when speaking about the difficulty of getting her baby to eat, would have tears in her eyes. (I'd like to add that mothers aren't the only ones who coax. Fathers and other members of the family all too often succumb to the same temptation.) Moreover, it isn't only *how much* a baby should eat, it is just as frequently *what* a baby does or does not eat that is upsetting to its mother. I'm reminded of another mother whose baby's eating had her bothered:

This mother, it turned out, was a vegetarian, and she was driven almost to distraction because her baby would eat only a little meat and a little potato—but no other vegetables. I tried to get it across to her that maybe she was getting her feelings involved in the vegetables but I felt she left the office unconvinced.

Some time later she called and said, "Now I *am* in trouble! You know, I didn't believe what you told me—that by trying to get my baby to eat vegetables I was turning him against them. So I set out to test your theory. I made a point of ignoring the vegetables and of urging my boy to eat his meat and potato. Now he's eating nothing but vegetables—just about no meat—and I suppose he should have some! What should I do now?"

I had to smile, but I assured her she wasn't in trouble. "You've learned how it works, that's all. And you've got a bright boy on your hands! From now on just offer him well-balanced meals and leave *what* and *how much* he eats up to him."

In other words, when feeding a baby a mother has to be a good poker player!

The mother who coaxes is upset—just about at her wit's end! Her baby inevitably senses this, and as the coaxing continues it becomes aware of its ability to get her stirred up. Babies are bright and they can be very perverse little tykes! They love to tease! If they sense their mother is upset, that her emotions are involved in their eating their spinach or drinking their milk, then eat spinach or finish their milk they very likely will not do! But just try to tell a mother her baby is outsmarting her! About the hardest thing I had to do when I was in practice was to convince a mother that her baby might be pulling her leg in this matter of eating. As one mother said: "But my baby wouldn't do that to me!" My dear mothers, your babies are quite capable of doing just that! It is remarkable, but babies and children who are coaxed are able to eat just enough to keep themselves going — and refuse just enough to keep their mothers going!

Now, why have I spent all this time over this matter of feeding and nature and emotions and coaxing? Simply because, over the years, I have found this to be the *A-number-one worry and the A-number-one mistake* of far too many parents!

Coaxing is a mistake!

a. Don't think that by coaxing you'll get more food into a child. Over the long run it will eat less. It will develop poor eating habits, become a fussy, "picky" eater, and more likely than not you will end up with a nervous, high-strung child on your hands.

b. Moreover, mealtimes become miserable for the whole family, parents and children alike.

c. Also let me remind you, when you coax you may miss out on one of the early signs of infection — loss of appetite.

d. But the most unfortunate consequence of coaxing is the slow breakdown of the parent-child relationship. Once your baby learns — as a result of your coaxing — to take advantage of your misplaced emotions, to manipulate them, to trifle with them, your baby begins to lose confidence in you and respect for you and (this may be hard to believe) consequently all your handling suffers! Your training, your discipline, your education, your efforts to prevent accidents — all are undermined.

The price is too high! The emotional bond between parents and child is too important to be frittered away over this matter of feeding!

Don't coax!

The aim of this book is to help you parents prevent handling and behavior problems. A feeding problem begins as a handling problem and far too frequently leads to all manner of behavior problems. I want to repeat: where feeding is concerned, your job as parents is to support nature by offering regular, sensible, attractive and well-balanced meals to your child. Leave the amount of food your child eats in nature's capable hands.

Come, let us coax our little boy
To eat his meat and peas-es,
For he can thoroughly enjoy
His dinner—when he pleases!

Promise a ride or a brand-new toy!
Promise dessert that pleases!
He only dawdles to annoy
Because he knows it teases.

LPT
(With apologies to Lewis Carroll)

Parents' Areas of Responsibility

Prevention of Accidents

I'd like now to consider one of the four areas of responsibility that fall entirely to you, as parents: the protection of your child—that is, the prevention of accidents. Here are a few sobering figures that may help you grasp the full significance of this responsibility:

Figures from the National Safety Council show that 16,500 children under the age of 15 years died in the United States during 1966 as a result of accidents. This is more deaths than from cancer, contagious diseases, heart diseases, and gastroenteritis combined. More than half (8,500) of the children who died as a result of accidents in 1966 were preschool children (birth to 4 years) . . . [Yet in the judgment of the Committee on Accident Prevention] at least 90 per cent of these accidents could have been prevented.*

It is so easy to read figures such as these and think, "Well, these are the things that happen—but to other people's babies—they'd never happen to ours." My experience in practice shows that they can happen to your baby. I've seen far too many accidents among babies and young children and most of the accidents, I felt, should have been prevented. All too often the full significance of their responsibility to prevent accidents comes to parents only after an accident or a close shave. I'd like very much to get you young couples thinking about this responsibility now—prenatally. It's not a bit too early. By the time you have your baby, thinking in terms of its safety will have become second nature. I would like to picture for you the range of accidents that can happen—even to your baby—in the course of its first year, and help prepare you to foresee and to prevent them.

In two areas of responsibility—*Treatment of Infections* and *Feeding*—nature, as we have seen, assumes the primary responsibility. Although, thanks to nature, babies come into the world knowing how much food they need and with an ability to combat infections, unfortunately they are not born knowing how to protect themselves. I wish they were! The responsibility to see to it that your baby is at all times safe will rest squarely on the shoulders of you parents. However, nature does offer you a clue as to how to safeguard your baby after it is born—note that during pregnancy nature feels free to confine the baby in close but very

---

*Accidents in Children, Committee on Accident Prevention, American Academy of Pediatrics.

safe and comfortable quarters. So, to prevent accidents, once your baby is born you too should feel free, whenever you are unable to give it your undivided attention, to confine your baby — to limit its field of activity in one way or another.

The confinement of your baby will take on a variety of forms and they will change as the baby grows and develops. They will include your learning, in the very beginning, always to keep one hand on your baby when it is out of its crib, the use of a playpen and gated areas as well as various harnesses, your holding your child's hand while crossing the street, and teaching your child obedience and responsible behavior. Just keep in mind: you *confine, restrict, restrain* (whatever you want to call it) a baby for just one reason — to prevent accidents. You must do it sensibly, intelligently, and for limited periods and in conjunction with a good schedule. And remember, no matter what form the confinement of your baby takes, it will never again be to the degree to which nature felt free to confine it before it was born. Whenever I hear unthinking, irresponsible talk about the harmful effects of restraining or confining a baby after it is born, I always expect that someone, sometime, will come up with the bright idea that the confinement of a baby before birth may have harmful effects.

When you're in the hospital, notice how comfortable the babies in the nursery are, firmly tucked into their cribs. You'll find that your baby loves to be cuddled and held closely, to be wrapped snugly in a blanket and carried about — it will respond happily to its father's strong hands. When you think of it, these are all forms of confinement and beyond question tiny babies relax with secure, firm, confident handling. For them, confinement seems to mean comfort, security and contentment.

But in this responsibility, as in all handling of a baby, emotions can so easily creep in and cause parents to lose sight of the ultimate aim of their safety measures. Parents hate to have their baby seem unhappy. Therefore, when their baby has to be left for a time and it cries on being put in its crib or playpen or settled with a harness in its highchair or stroller, rather than stick by their guns (which I'll admit can be hard) and ignore the fussing their baby makes in the hope of getting back lost attention, some parents take the easy way out—at the time. They blame the restraints, the safety measures, and kid themselves into believing what the girl next door says or what they read somewhere—that confining a baby, "taking away its freedom," will have "bad effects." Rather than stopping to weigh their distress at hearing their baby fuss against their responsibility to keep it safe, they remove the restraints and let down on the confinement, and this is so often when accidents occur. Hang on to your emotions!

Now, how do you carry out your responsibility? How can you do your best to prevent accidents?

A Tiny Baby is Completely Dependent on You For Its Safety

Always keep your baby in a safe place.

At first, except when you're holding it, most of your baby's time will be spent safely in its basket, bassinet or crib. I would suggest that you notice how nurses in the hospital settle a baby—not flat on its back or stomach but three-quarters of the way over on its stomach. Babies handle their secretions or anything they may spit up most easily in this position. Continue putting your baby down in this position, on one side or the other, until it can lift its head and move it around easily. I'll deal further with beds under *Equipment.*

Before taking a baby out of its bed for *any* procedure, *learn to think and prepare ahead.* Whether you're taking it out to change it, feed it, bathe it or for any reason whatsoever, having everything *ready and at hand in advance* becomes a most important safety measure. With practice this can become a conditioned reflex.

When you have the baby out of its bed:

1. *Always keep at least one hand on it,*
2. Or tote it with you if necessary;
3. Never leave it unsafeguarded.

If you must leave it:

1. Put it back in its bed,
2. Or on your bed, well bolstered all around with pillows;
3. Or — if you're in a tight spot — place it on the floor.

Never underestimate your baby's ability to move around!

1. Remember, there's always a *first time* it rolls over or a *first time* it wriggles itself to the edge of a bed.
2. Remember, a baby grows bigger and stronger rapidly and it can slip out from under the strap on a changing table before you know it.
3. Remember, "just a second" on the telephone so easily becomes four, five or more minutes!

An infant seat, to be safe, has to be used very carefully.

1. Used to carry a baby about, it is handy for you and comfortable for the baby — especially in the summer when it's also cooler for the baby than being carried in your arms.
2. Used as a seat, it has limitations because it is so light and tips over so easily. As a seat it is safest on the floor. Use it as a seat on a table or counter or any high place only if you are close by with one hand available — or if it is so positioned that tipping over can't possibly result in the baby's landing on the floor.

3. For the tiny baby it offers a change of scene, a change of position and the opportunity to be near you, but remember, a baby grows bigger fast and learns to lean forward, and then over it goes!

At Three to Four Months You Should Look Ahead and Prepare to Prevent Accidents that May Happen in Six to Ten Months' Time

When your baby is three to four months old, steps to prevent accidents take a new twist. Your baby is still completely helpless and dependent but the time has come to look ahead and start establishing and familiarizing your baby with the patterns of safety that will protect it at nine months to a year of age or more. At nine months your baby will still be as irresponsible and unreasoning as it is at three and four months, but it will have become increasingly *strong and active* — creeping, climbing, maybe walking — and increasingly *independent*!

The Playpen. By the time your baby is at least three or four months of age, start getting it accustomed to being in a playpen for short periods (see p. 67). At this age a baby is awake a fair amount during the day and a playpen is a safe place to leave it while you're busy with other matters. It offers your baby a chance to look at something new; the playpen can be moved about to be near you — on warm days it can be moved outside. But your baby shouldn't be left in it at any one time long enough to become bored (p. 169). I'll be taking up toys (p. 85) and learning opportunities later under *Education*.

I realize, as I know you do, that at this age your baby isn't going to go places, but by some time near eight or nine months it will be on the prowl, and that's when the playpen will become invaluable in terms of safety. If you are to successfully carry on your responsibility to prevent accidents, three to four months is the age at which to begin the process that will enable you, at nine months to a year and even later, to leave your baby in a

playpen for short periods daily, knowing that it is both safe
and happy.

The Sleeping Harness.   Again, when your baby is four
months of age, I hope you will think ahead and start to use a
sleeping harness. At four months most babies take to a sleeping
harness without batting an eye, and starting at this age, going to
sleep in one with a favorite toy very quickly becomes a conditioned reflex for a baby. The harness comes to mean sleeptime,
comfort and security. A good sleeping harness, properly used,
offers plenty of freedom for the limited time a baby should be
lying awake in its crib, either before or following sleep. I can't
overstress the importance of a good schedule in this connection
(see p. 64).

I know as well as you that at four months a baby settled
for sleep in its crib will pretty much stay put, but by nine months
to a year this will be far from true—by nine months, without a
harness, babies are moving about in their cribs in surprising
fashion. This is when the incidence of accidents begins to increase. But don't think for a minute that at nine months, with
the possibility of an accident staring you in the face, you can
easily start using a sleeping harness. Here, as in all accident
prevention, it is foresight that counts. Babies that become accustomed to a harness at four months go along very happily in
one till they're about two-and-a-half to three years of age and
ready of their own accord to give it up. For these youngsters—
as I've observed them over the years—being put to bed with
plenty of love and kisses, and with one or two special, friendly
toys, the sleeping harness that holds them safe seems merely an
added bit of reassurance and comfort. Moreover, their sleeping
harness takes on this same meaning wherever they may be. For
parents the sleeping harness offers the assurance—at night or
naptime, at home or traveling—that their baby is safe; that it is
covered; that it can't wriggle and fall off a bed; that it can't
get jammed against or caught in crib bars; and, later on, that it
can't fall or climb out of its crib.

I first encountered a sleeping harness when I was an intern at Children's Hospital Medical Center in Boston. Pediatric hospitals generally use a sleeping harness, sometimes called a jacket restraint, on all children three years old and younger and not acutely ill. Specific regulations vary from hospital to hospital, but the basic principle is the same: that small youngsters capable of climbing or falling out of cribs be restrained.

Here is a place I find myself confused. If in a hospital where a night nurse is constantly on duty it is essential to keep babies in harnesses to prevent accidents, what about safeguarding your baby alone in its room at naptime, or alone at night when you are sound asleep?

Slowly and painfully we are accepting the need to put seat belts or harnesses on both adults and children to prevent tragic, unnecessary injuries in car and plane accidents. The benefits conferred by their use are so obvious that any mental trauma associated with their use in these situations is apparently entirely overlooked. Quite rightly so—because there isn't any mental trauma. When parents have become convinced of the value of such safety devices—when their importance is driven home and the public generally accepts them—then, quite simply, the conviction of the parents is conveyed to their youngsters who in turn accept the safety devices without question. One may hope that before long the same kind of conviction will apply to the use of sleeping harnesses.

Yet this is a subject that always evokes an emotional response. I suppose this is true because emotions so often take over when experience and knowledge are lacking. A few years ago when I was giving a series of prenatal talks for couples just like you, following the talk on Prevention of Accidents, three couples stayed to speak to me.

The first couple stated vehemently that they would have no truck with a sleeping harness. As the wife said, "I can buy all your other suggestions about harnesses but not that one about the sleeping harness. We wouldn't dream of tying our baby down in bed!"

The next two couples listened, as I did, to what this first couple had to say, then turned to me and wanted to know what I considered a good harness. With friends of theirs these two couples had already learned something from experience.

One of the couples told of being at the home of friends for an evening. During supper there was a loud thump overhead. Their host's 13-month-old baby had climbed up the side of its crib and toppled out on its head. It had "never climbed up before"! The baby had a cut on its head and their doctor advised x-rays of the skull. The other couple had spent a weekend with friends. Their friends' year-and-a-half-old baby had managed to climb out of its crib in the middle of the night and had fallen down the front stairs, fracturing its collar bone. Another "first time"! Both these couples said they didn't want things like that happening to their baby.

These accidents and similar ones that I was forever running up against in practice could have been prevented. If it is important to safeguard your baby by day when you are awake and close by, how much more important to safeguard it by night!

There are three important points to bear in mind if you plan to use a sleeping harness:

1. Follow the instructions that come with the sleeping harness—fasten it tightly and securely to the bed.
2. Start using a sleeping harness by the time your baby is four months old.
3. Bear in mind that a sleeping harness is for "safety"; it is not intended to tie down a baby that's not in the least sleepy. *If you're not going to have your baby on a good schedule, don't even consider using a sleeping harness.*

Remember, I'm talking about prevention of accidents. Keep your emotions out of this.

From Six Months of Age to a Year Your Baby Will
Severely Test Your Capacity to Carry Out Your
Responsibility to Prevent Accidents

Playpen (Continued). By six, seven or eight months, babies are beginning to assert themselves. When put in their playpen, they realize they are not going to be getting your time and attention—they may put up a fuss to try you out. *This is when so many parents lose the use of a playpen.* Don't weaken when your baby fusses on being put in its pen. If you say to yourself, "You poor dear, I'll put you on the floor beside me and keep an eye on you," you're possibly headed for an accident, and almost surely for trouble.

In another short time the fussing will become much louder! In another short time your baby will become more active, more determined and more able to go places! But will you be able to persuade it to stay and play happily in its playpen? Not a chance! When this happens the playpen, for you and your baby, will have become a thing of the past. Oh, my aching head! How many times have I heard in the office:

"But, Dr. Turtle, I can't keep my baby in a playpen!"
"My baby just won't stay in a playpen! I don't know what
I'm going to do. I can't watch it all the time."

Try not to lose the use of a playpen at this early stage of the game. Try not to let your baby talk itself out of the pen. Two parents should be at least as smart as one seven-month-old baby!

But, equally, if you are to retain the use of a playpen, it is just as important not to take advantage of it. Make it work for you—and that means use it sparingly. Handled judiciously, it can be one of your best means of preventing accidents.

Above all, don't have your baby creeping around while you're doing your housework.

1. Babies are agile and at times incredibly fast.
2. This is when the number of accidents begins to build up. This is when toasters, bookends, percolators, all sorts of things come tumbling down. This is when lamps and chairs topple over; when drapes, curtains and curtain rods are pulled down; and when table-cloths and whatever is atop them are pulled off; when gas burners are turned on; when small hands get burned on hot radiators and small heads get cut on sharp corners; when drawers, cupboards and cellar doors are opened . . . I could go on.

There are two things mothers always say:

"It's the first time the baby ever —"
"I just took my eyes off the baby for a second!"

When mothers would come into the office with their babies bumped and bruised, that wasn't the time to point out that accidents such as these don't have to take place. The time to point it out is *now — to you couples — before you have your babies.* You have all sorts of ways and equipment at your disposal to prevent accidents. Take advantage of them!

For a baby, freedom is a large order. While, on the one hand, you should provide opportunity for your baby to enjoy free-dom — by setting aside periods in each day when you give your baby your undivided attention and allow it to explore, creeping — you must, on the other hand, assume full responsibility for the inherent risks.

What do I mean by *undivided attention?*

In the office I used to tell mothers it doesn't mean that you have to get down on the floor and crawl around with your baby. But it does mean that you can't really watch your baby and, at the same time, be doing anything that might divert or absorb your attention even for a second — seconds become minutes, and babies can be faster than greased lightning! If you're watching a baby, there's a risk involved if you:

1. Read anything—from a newspaper to a recipe;
2. If you sew something complicated, or knit and get lost in a dropped stitch;
3. If you cook and the sauce separates or the soup boils over;
4. Above all, if you answer the doorbell or the telephone —either can be lethal.

Additional ways and equipment are at your disposal to prevent accidents and, as always, their effectiveness depends on how well, how intelligently, you use them.

1. *A highchair (with harness)* can be used not only as the place you feed your baby but also as another safe place to put a baby for a brief time and a change of scene. It can be used in the kitchen or moved to wherever you are working—and with an interesting toy a baby can be happy in one for a time. Always use a harness— the strap from tray to seat isn't enough; babies can so easily slip under the tray and land on the floor.
2. Always use a *harness in a stroller.*
3. The use of a *harness in a car seat* is now universally accepted.
4. *A walking harness* is a wonderful piece of equipment. It permits a youngster to walk independently alongside or ahead of you. It eliminates your hand, which is sometimes an annoyance to a small child. It affords you control and the chance to offer assistance at curbs and steps.

I recently spent a summer in the hills of New Hampshire with three grandchildren, the youngest coming up two years of age. With no fences, just fields of tall grass, deep woods and streams all around,

Willy spent a good part of his time in a harness with 25 feet of clothes-line hitching him to whichever adult happened to be in charge. At the suggestion of a walk, Willy would run to fetch his harness and rope. Blueberrying, on the beach, at the swimming hole, walking or climbing over rough terrain, shopping in the supermarket, that harness permitted Willy to go right along with the rest and offered him the degree of freedom he wanted, but it also gave comfort to the one responsible for his safety. Drop your end of the harness and the minute Willy felt it trailing he would circle around, pick up the end and, with an inquiring look, place it in your hand. Then, satisfied, off he would go again.

I tell this in the hope that Willy's and my experience will broaden your understanding and evaluation of the possibilities of harnesses. Current requirements regarding the installation and use of seat belts in planes and cars should also point up the connection between harnesses and safety.

5. Properly used the *playpen* should continue as a safe spot to leave your baby for intervals until the baby can climb out of it.
6. Thereafter, a *baby-proofed room with a gate* provides safety and at the same time more scope for activity and ingenuity.
7. Out of doors an *expanded playpen* or *a yard with a gate* offer the same advantages—plenty of scope, space and safety.

I have mentioned what I consider pretty much the basic equipment needed to keep a baby safe. All sorts of other equipment is available, but before you get it be sure it answers your responsibility to prevent accidents.

Remember, as parents you must show judgment and not take undue advantage of safety devices. They are for safety and not a cover-up for poor planning or self-indulgence. You must learn to strike a balance between your need and right at times to be involved in matters other than your baby, and your baby's need at all times to be protected.

Your Responsibility to Prevent Accidents Takes on a
New Look as You Teach Your Baby Obedience and
Responsible Behavior

Playpen, harnesses and such are just the first phase of
your responsibility for your child's safety. The second, and more
difficult phase, also starts in the first year: teaching your baby
obedience and the early beginnings of responsibility for its
own safety.

Obedience is the cornerstone of the safe-conduct of a child. The
relationship between obedience and safety is basic. Take a look
at nature where survival of the young is a matter of obedience.
You don't have to live in the jungle with Mowgli to do this:

> These are the Laws of the Jungle
> and many and mighty are they.
> But the head and the hoof of the Law
> and the hump and the haunch is—OBEY.

> *The Second Jungle Book,*
> Rudyard Kipling

All you need to do is take a look around you:

> On a back country road, the peremptory "chuck" of
> the pheasant turns every scampering, downy
> chick into a motionless leaf or tuft of grass.
> The warning cluck of the hen as the shadow of a
> hawk, high in the sky, drifts slowly across the
> barnyard, sends her brood scurrying for cover.
> The cat cuffs her straying, inquiring kittens into
> obediently remaining in their basket.
> The dog nips her reckless, adventuresome pups into
> proper, discreet behavior.

But obedience must be taught, and the teaching of obedience, like so many other safety measures, must be started early

in order to anticipate the time of its greatest usefulness. Teaching a child the obedience that ensures its staying in its own yard or sticking to the sidewalk begins in the first year. I'll take this up later under *Discipline* (p. 77). The point I wish to make here is that learning to obey simple safety rules makes a child a safer child—it's impossible to overstress the importance of the relationship between safety and obedience.

> I was called one day to see a little patient who had been struck by a car. Luckily it was just a bump and the child was more frightened than hurt. The frantic mother said, "And I told her to wait on the steps while I ran back into the house for my purse!" As we cleaned up the few scrapes and scratches I thought to myself that if this little girl had stayed on the steps it would have been the first time I had ever known her to obey her mother.

Teaching your baby *responsible ways of handling itself* also begins very early. Some examples:

1. To sit rather than stand on high places.
2. How to turn around and back safely down out of a chair a baby finds it such fun and so easy to climb into.
3. How to turn around and back downstairs, one step at a time.

This second phase of your responsibility for your baby's safety is just as important as the first. If you slip up here, if you fail to transfer, gradually, responsibility for its safety over to your child, you will have only half done the job.

As your child learns obedience to carefully rationed rules; as he slowly develops and repeatedly demonstrates the ability to handle himself safely—to take care of himself—you for your part will gain confidence in your youngster's growing sense of responsibility in matters of safety. As you show your trust and confidence in him, you will stimulate the further growth of your child's sense of responsibility.

I know I have here gone into the consideration of a child well beyond a year of age, but I have done so because I want to give you a glimpse of where your early responsibility for your baby's safety is heading. What you are really doing is establishing a pattern of responsible family behavior, where safety is concerned, that proceeds somewhat according to the following:

Before birth—in the confinement of your baby;

Soon after it is born—your learning always to keep one hand on it;

In the following period—the use of cribs, playpens, harnesses and gates;

The creeping baby—stopping at a step and turning around to back down;

The small child, alone—stopping automatically at a curb to look both ways, or taking a hand to cross a busy street;

And, hopefully, to the youngster—examining the thickness of ice on a pond;

And the teenager and adult—driving a car safely and responsibly.

Your early concern properly carried forward will—I would like to think—develop into the responsibility every individual should have for his own safety and the safety of others.

Training

Training is another area of responsibility that falls entirely to you parents. It is largely a matter of giving your baby the basic equipment that will enable it to get along in this world. In part, this means getting its physical systems going in an orderly manner: its eating, sleeping, eliminating and exercising. In part, this means helping it develop a sense, first, of where it fits into the family and, later, of how it fits into the world beyond.

Before your baby is born it is nourished, it sleeps, it stirs about and occasionally it does a heap of kicking. As the time for your baby's delivery approaches you will be aware that your baby's sense of timing leaves something to be desired—it doesn't know night from day. It certainly doesn't show any consideration for your need to sleep!

Once it is born, it will continue to do all these things— eat, sleep and kick—and its timing will not have improved in the least. It still won't know night from day, it still won't worry in the least about whether either of you parents get any sleep.

Your baby's earliest training is therefore largely a matter of helping it adjust from this easy-going, irresponsible, completely self-centered way of life before birth to living happily and successfully in a world full of other human beings equally entitled to consideration.

Training over the first year consists primarily of the establishment of a series of living patterns that:

- a. Answer all your baby's needs and requirements for food, sleep, exercise, affection, social contact, play and learning time;
- b. Change constantly as your baby grows and develops and its needs and requirements change and develop;
- c. Permit others in the family to lead a reasonably normal existence (I want to make the point right here that its parents' sleep and well-being are every bit as important to a baby as its own);
- d. By the end of the first year will have brought your baby's living pattern more or less into line with that of the rest of the family.

To some, such a series of living patterns or schedules may seem a regimented way of life for a baby. But, in my experience, just as babies seem to relax and respond to the confinement and secure handling necessary to keep them safe, so they thrive and seem happiest when there is a degree of order in their existence. Moreover, as I've observed them, the mother with a schedule to hang her hat on seems to find life far easier than the mother who permits her days and nights to be determined by her baby's uncontrolled demands. Schedules need not be rigid affairs—they should be flexible and "give" as circumstances require. The world over, they can be adapted to fit the living habits and customs of the people involved.

I remember once caring for a baby whose father was a musician—his workday started in the early evening and ended around midnight to one o'clock in the morning. He wanted to be with and play with his baby in off hours, so his wife worked out a wonderful schedule for the family—one that involved dinner for the three of them at 2 A.M., that meant walking the baby at 11 o'clock on summer nights along Commonwealth Avenue in the face of the disapproving looks and occasional comments of passers-by. But it was a schedule that produced a healthy, happy baby and gave a sense of order to the family's existence and as long as the mother could translate my advice and suggestions for the baby into her hours, she had a good thing going.

There's nothing unnatural about a schedule. Nature has all living things on schedules of one sort or another. Think of the hibernation of woodchuck and chipmunk, the predictable migrations of various birds and fish, the spring run of sap, and the nightly appearance of moles and bats. A baby's schedule is merely an expression of the orderliness of the universe in one very small corner of it.

First let us see how, by training, you can get your baby's physical systems in good running order.

Feeding

Before it is born, a baby is nourished, as it were, on a demand feeding basis. After it is born, offered plenty of food and allowed to take all it wants, a baby will take *all it wants, when it wants* and put itself on a schedule of eating and sleeping completely satisfactory to itself, but one that may leave much to be desired as far as its parents are concerned. Demand feeding has a value for a limited time, as I will point out later (p. 199), but to allow your baby to continue on it indefinitely completely overlooks the fact that one of your principal responsibilities is to train your baby, to help it adjust to living in the world with other people who are also entitled to consideration.

> A young mother came into my office one day—I had never seen her before—plunked her four-month-old baby down on the examining table and asked, "Do you believe in demand feeding?"
> "Not for a baby this age," I answered.
> "Well, this baby has been on it ever since he was born, and my husband and I are just about worn out. He's turned night into day!"
> I believed her. She looked dog-tired, but her baby looked the picture of health.

All this mother needed was a little help in understanding that she and her baby could easily come to terms on a schedule that would be completely satisfactory to both of them.

Feeding to About Two-and-a-half to Three Months. Beyond question it is important that you train your baby to take its 24-hour food requirements in the 16 hours you parents are normally awake. Actually this isn't difficult. Until your baby is about three weeks old you will very likely have to face up to the 2 o'clock feeding. However, if gradually over this period you start offering your baby all it wants at four-hour intervals during the day, by about the second to third week you have been home from the hospital, your baby will be taking enough to last it through the night. This should mean the end of the "2 o'clock."

This four-hour interval business didn't just come out of somebody's hat—it's not something the hospitals dreamed up. Our old friend nature is squarely behind this. A baby that weighs six pounds or over at birth, offered the opportunity to take all the food it wants, has the strength and capacity to take enough food to keep it going three-and-one-half to 4 hours *or more*. If you offer it all it wants every four hours during the day, waking it for the feedings when necessary, by the end of five feedings it will have taken enough to carry it through — and also be ready for — a good eight-hour sleep. But, let me repeat, the two prerequisites for this eight-hour night sleep are:

    a. That the baby gets all it wants at each feeding (I'll go into this further under The Technique of Feeding);

    b. That the baby's *daytime* sleep is interrupted every 4 hours.

A good first schedule for the baby that weighs 6 pounds or more at birth is:

> 6:00 A.M. — Feed
> 9:30 A.M. — Bathe
> 10:00 A.M. — Feed
> 2:00 P.M. — Feed
> 6:00 P.M. — Feed
> 10:00 P.M. — Feed
> 2:00 A.M. — Feed?

For convenience throughout the book this is the schedule to which I'll be referring. I want to make it crystal clear, however, that:

    a. You may start feeding at any hour that fits your family routine — remember the musician's family schedule. Just keep the succeeding feedings following along at three-and-one-half- to four-hour intervals.

    b. You don't have to feed as the clock strikes — the three-and-one-half- to four-hour interval offers you a bit of leeway. What counts is working those five good feedings into your 16-hour day.

    c. Once you settle on a schedule that fits your family set-up, stick with it!

If you follow such a schedule and get the feedings going smoothly, I think you'll be both surprised and pleased at how soon your baby will come off the 2 o'clock feeding.

The smaller baby, six pounds and under at birth, will very likely not come off the "2 o'clock" quite as soon as the larger baby. It isn't as strong and its capacity is smaller. It may possibly have to be fed more frequently than every four hours, and it will have to grow bigger and stronger before it will be able to take enough during the day to carry it through an eight-hour night.

Feeding from Two-and-one-half or Three Months to About Five Months.

I mentioned earlier that over the first year you will have to establish a *series* of living patterns that will change as your baby changes. Well, just about the time you have things going smoothly—your baby and you settled happily into a good five-feeding routine—it will be time to make a change. At around two-and-one-half to three months your baby's early, rapid rate of growth will begin to slow down, *usually* with an accompanying falling off of appetite (p. 31). Your baby's appetite will now be satisfied with four feedings a day and you can drop the 10:00 P.M. feeding.

The spoon. Also, when your baby is about two-and-one-half to three months old, I suggest you start offering it a little cereal and fruit from a spoon each day. Your aim, *at this point,* is simply to teach your baby that there is such a thing as a spoon in the world; and you will accomplish this even if your baby takes as little as a quarter of a demitasse spoonful. But slowly your baby will learn to take solids in this manner and, by the time it is four, five or six months old and begins to need more than just milk in its diet, it will be quite at home eating from a spoon.

Feeding from About Four or Five Months On.

Again at around four or five months there will be another change. Your baby, bigger and stronger, will be able to satisfy its food require- ments with only three feedings a day. This brings your baby's daily feeding pattern into line with that of the other members of the family — a pattern it will follow more or less the rest of its days.

But in training, just as in prevention of accidents, it is well to keep looking ahead — to start slowly preparing your baby for changes that lie in the future. Just as you began early to accus- tom your baby to a spoon, so the time has now come to introduce it to a cup.

The cup. Dentists want babies sucking on a nipple — that is, getting their milk from either the breast or bottle — until they are about 10 months to a year of age, when they want them weaned to a cup (p. 144). But learning to drink from a cup can be a slow process for a baby. So I suggest that when your baby is ready for three meals — at around four or five months — you start offering it each day a small amount of straight fruit juice from a cup. Slowly, over the next months, it will become accus- tomed to taking liquids in this new way. At 10 months to a year of age it will be quite at home drinking from a cup and the wean- ing process will go smoothly.

Drinking from a cup and eating from a spoon are exciting new steps in your baby's first year. But — let me remind you — hang on to your enthusiasm and your emotions! You're not out to establish any records — to beat the baby next door! Your job is to train your individual baby in the art of taking liquids in this new manner, of taking solid food from this strange imple- ment. Above all, remember that the spoon isn't introduced to enable you to push food into your baby! (See p. 142.) As time goes on your baby will very likely want to take over control of the spoon and cup. Go slowly! It is your responsibility to help your baby acquire the knack of handling a cup and spoon reasonably well and, at the same time, *to train it in good eating habits.* Playing with food, slopping and messing it around, and throwing it on the floor are simply bad habits that will have to be unlearned. Don't be in a hurry to turn the cup and spoon over to your baby.

Sleeping

Now let's see what you can do to get some order into your baby's sleeping requirements.

Over the first couple of months, when babies aren't eating they're usually sleeping. They need a lot of sleep—all this feeding and growing and adjusting to a new environment is pretty strenuous business. But parents too need sleep, so while it will be up to you parents to see to it that your baby gets all the sleep he needs, it will also be up to you to train him to sleeping hours that will permit you to get a decent night's sleep. So often mothers act as if they were helplessly at the mercy of their baby's sleeping whims. Time and again in the office mothers would say:

> "But Dr. Turtle, I just can't get my baby to sleep through the night!"

> "My baby will sleep only in the morning—I can't get her to take an afternoon nap!"

> "I know my baby needs two naps! I can hardly waken him after an hour and a half of sleep in the morning and another couple of hours in the afternoon. Yet when we settle him at night, sometimes he's still awake when we're ready to go to bed!"

This sort of thing is both unnecessary and unthinking. Just as you can satisfy your baby's feeding requirements in an orderly fashion, so you can let your baby have all the sleep it wants—but on a reasonable basis. Granted, over the first weeks, your night's sleep will almost surely be interrupted and you must be prepared to snatch naps as you can. However, as you keep breaking into your baby's day sleep with a feeding every four hours and then, by not waking it for the 2 o'clock feeding, you give it the opportunity to have a prolonged stretch of sleep, you will find that shortly the prolonged sleep will lengthen into close to an eight-hour sleep. By the time your baby is three weeks old it should be satisfying its sleeping requirements on a schedule that will offer you parents a respectable night's sleep.

6 A.M.—Feed
    Sleep
9:30 A.M.—Bathe
    Sleep
10 A.M.—Feed
    Sleep
2 P.M.—Feed
    Sleep
6 P.M.—Feed
    Sleep
10 P.M.—Feed
    Prolonged
    sleep

Sleeping to About Two and One-Half or Three Months.
As it gets bigger and stronger your baby's sleeping requirements
will naturally begin to drop off. So, at some point over the first
two months, in order to keep your baby sleeping all night, you
will have to break further into its day sleep:

a. By moving bath time to around 8 A.M.—further cutting into the sleep time between the 6 A.M. and 10 A.M.
   feedings;

b. By waking your baby for a half hour to an hour of
   play and exercise time around 4 P.M.—thus breaking
   into its sleep between the 2 P.M. and 6 P.M. feedings.

6 A.M.—Feed
    Sleep
8 A.M.—Bathe
    Sleep
10 A.M.—Feed
    Sleep
2 P.M.—Feed
    Sleep
4 P.M.—Play
    Sleep
6 P.M.—Feed
    Sleep
10 P.M.—Feed
    Sleep

No one but your baby can tell you when these breaks into day sleep should be started—their timing and duration should be determined 100 per cent by the way your baby sleeps through the night.

Sleeping from About Two and One-Half or Three Months to About Five Months. When your baby drops the 10 P.M. feeding and is on only four feedings, you have several possible schedules:

6 A.M.—Feed	7 A.M.—Feed
Sleep	Sleep
8 A.M.—Bathe	9 A.M.—Bathe
Sleep	Sleep
10 A.M.—Feed	11 A.M.—Feed
Sleep	Sleep
2 P.M.—Feed	3 P.M.—Feed
Sleep	Sleep
4 P.M.—Play	5 P.M.—Play
Sleep	Sleep
6 P.M.—Feed	7 P.M.—Feed
Sleep	Sleep

Here is one that is just as good, that offers you a bit of a break, and that many mothers used to prefer:

7 A.M.—Feed
  Sleep
8:30 A.M.—Bathe
  Sleep
10:30 A.M.—Feed
  Sleep
2:15 P.M.—Feed
  Sleep
4 P.M.—Play
  Sleep
6 P.M.—Feed
  Sleep

I remember another mother who came into the office and asked what the dickens she was to do. She said that their baby—granted it was over a year of age—was waking up each morning about 4 o'clock, getting out of its crib and climbing cheerfully into their bed, complete with toys.

"And Dr. Turtle, the worst of it is, he always brings his beloved musical bear—the one we put him down with—and he wants it wound over and over again! My husband says that at 4:30 in the morning, after twenty windings, the Brahms Lullaby completely loses its lull. What are we going to do?"

But with all that, it wasn't easy to get that mother to see the connection between her boy's long afternoon nap—"he must need it; it's awfully hard to waken him!"—and those jolly early morning visits.

Don't let your baby's fussing on being wakened either after its morning or afternoon nap weaken you into allowing it to go on sleeping—*if it is staying awake half the night.* Just, gently, give it a little time to "come to"—don't hurry it. And remember the night!

I hope I've given you a general idea of the way this sleeping business works. Here, as in all aspects of training, you have to use common sense and good judgment, and you have to have your ultimate objective in mind at all times:

    a. Having your baby sleep all night;
    b. Having your baby's afternoon nap the longer one.

Mothers are understandably reluctant to drop the morning nap, or any nap. Baby's naps are often among the few times in a day a mother can call her soul her own. But the one nap—the afternoon nap—leads smoothly into the time when your child, maybe two and one-half to three years of age, will be having no nap at all—only a rest period: a quiet time, by itself, on a bed or in its room with a few chosen toys; a time when a small child after an especially busy morning can curl down and take a sleep—and maybe its mother can too.

The intelligent organization of sleeptime is, however,

far more important than appears on the surface. A baby put down to sleep, if the schedule is handled properly, should be sound asleep within 15 minutes to a half hour—and should be gotten up within 15 minutes to a half hour upon wakening. The child lying awake, bored, not sleepy may find comfort in sucking on a thumb or fingers (p. 169), may start masturbating (p. 175), things a good schedule discourages. The child lying awake, bored, not sleepy may get notions about exploring:

> I remember an 18-month-old boy who was returned, dripping, to his startled parents by a neighbor who had scooped him out of her fishpond at 5:30 in the morning. A shallow pond—but plenty deep for a little one.

> And another small youngster, going on two years old, who wakened early one fine spring morning, slipped unheard out of the house and took off. Picture the parents who, hearing no sound from their child's room, had prolonged their own sleep and then awoke to discover the empty bed. They were frantically searching the house and yard when the policeman who patrolled the neighborhood appeared, carrying their pajama-clad child. That youngster had crossed two main thoroughfares on his little early morning expedition.

In *Prevention of Accidents* I stated that a baby in a sleeping harness should be lying awake for only a limited time before and after sleep, that a sleeping harness should be used only in conjunction with a good schedule. Its sole purpose is to prevent accidents; you shouldn't take advantage of it to restrain a baby *who isn't anywhere near ready to go to sleep or one whose sleep is long since over and who is all primed to get up.* You have it in your power to control your baby's sleeping schedule.

You don't have to follow the schedules I've suggested, but they can serve as guidelines. Just be sure to maintain a reasonable balance between your baby's sleeping and waking hours and, especially for the baby under a year of age, a fair degree of regularity from day to day. In my experience the eight- and nine-month-old babies who have come along on a fairly smooth routine are blessed with nervous systems less jangled than the babies whose days and nights are hit or miss and never the same.

Bowel Training

The baby leading a fairly regular existence may be ready, before the end of the first year, to slowly have its bowels trained. When a baby is anywhere from eight months to a year of age, occasionally it seems to settle down to having a bowel movement at about the same time each day. Frequently a mother watching her baby seems to sense, seems to have a general idea, when her baby might be going to have a bowel movement.

When this happens, take advantage of it—it just may work. Put your baby on a training seat that is securely fastened on the regular toilet seat. Give your baby a particularly satisfying toy to play with—if you can rig up a table in front of the baby to put the toy on, so much the better. Stay in the bathroom, so your baby sees you close by and you know it's safe, *but busy yourself* about something other than the baby. Don't leave it on the training seat longer than about 3 to 5 minutes.

This is quite a step forward in your baby's progress—but play it cool! Don t let your baby think you attach any great significance to this event. If the baby has a bowel movement, very mild praise is sufficient. If the baby doesn't have a bowel movement, show no sign of disappointment.

If after three or four days of this you have no results, give your baby an infant glycerine suppository just before putting it on the training seat. Your aim is to have your baby associate the training seat with the sensation of having a bowel movement. If after two weeks or so the process isn't working, put the whole thing off for several weeks or a month or so and then try again. You may have to repeat this putting off and trying again process several times. You don't want your baby to become either bored or annoyed by the procedure. Some babies train more slowly than others, but sooner or later you and your baby will work this out.

Above all, watch your emotions. Let me warn you—if your baby senses you want it to have a bowel movement on the training seat, it's almost sure not to! As you'll find out, this is just the way babies work.

I've suggested using the kind of training seat that fastens on the regular toilet seat. Actually this is another bit of training. As time goes on, the shift from the training seat to the regular seat poses no problem. With babies you always want to be thinking today of the changes that will take place tomorrow.

In this discussion I'm referring only to bowel training. Most children are not ready to be bladder-trained until they are about three years of age.

Exercise

The time will come when it will be your responsibility to see to it that your child has the opportunity to get plenty of exercise. In their first year, however, babies do a good job of exercising themselves. The exertions a baby normally expends kicking in its crib, in its bath, as you change it, and occasionally crying—all these are early forms of exercise. As you play with it in periods of undivided attention and as it plays by itself in its playpen—rolling, reaching, hauling itself around, struggling to pull itself to its feet—all these things will be exercise for your baby. When it starts creeping and walking it will be exercise for you as well—plenty of it. You'll be hard put to keep up with your baby at this point.

* * * * * * * *

There's a lot to this aspect of *Training*. Answering a baby's physical needs and requirements in a satisfying but orderly manner—its feeding, sleeping, eliminating and exercising—is much like getting a new, delicate and very complicated motor broken in and running smoothly. If you parents carry on a program of careful, responsible maintenance, you may in time pass on to your growing child an understanding of the importance of respecting and properly maintaining his own physical systems.

However, *Training* over the first year isn t just a matter of providing a healthy, regular, satisfying existence for your baby. It also means starting early to provide it with the tools needed to cope with its social environment, at home and abroad.

At Home

The Playpen. As you regulate your baby's sleep — cutting down on the amount it sleeps by day in order to keep it sleeping through the night — you will bump up against the problem of how to handle its ever-increasing waking hours. You first break into its day sleep when it's somewhere around six to eight weeks old, and you shift the bath to 8 o'clock and start a play and exercise time in the afternoon. These will be fun times for you and your baby, times when you will be giving it your un-divided attention. But these times awake will gradually have to be increased and you won't always be able to give your baby your undivided attention, so, when your baby is around two and one-half to three months of age, I suggest you start using a playpen to get your baby accustomed to being on its own for short periods. Your baby will enjoy the change of scene and, with soft toys around it and bright ones dangling above it, a playpen is a grand place to stretch and observe things. (Don't use the crib for these times awake — cribs are for sleeping.)

Over the next months your baby will have to be kept awake for additional and longer periods in the daytime, and the playpen will become increasingly useful as a place to put it when you have other matters to attend to. You must be careful always to balance its use against the times you set aside just to be with your baby. Until your baby is five or six months old, the amount of time it spends in the playpen will necessarily be short.

In *Prevention of Accidents* I pointed out how important it is to be able to use the playpen when your baby, around seven to nine months of age, starts getting about—starts creeping. It's a very safe place to leave an inquisitive baby when you are unable to give it your undivided attention. But the playpen is just as invaluable, just as important, when it comes to *Training*. As you settle your baby in the playpen and leave it for a bit, you're not only making use of the playpen to prevent accidents but are also making use of it to train your baby in awareness that there are times when you must attend to other than baby matters— that it can't always have your undivided attention. And, more than this, when you leave it to amuse itself for a little time you are also giving it the opportunity to learn to be on its own—to be resourceful and independent. These are big things to teach a little baby, but little babies "catch on ' earlier and faster than you'd think possible.

What you most certainly don't want your baby to do is "catch on" to the possibility that if it fusses on being left in the playpen you'll take it out. Don't join the big group of mothers who give in to their emotions and lose the use of the playpen before the first year is half over. The playpen has too much to offer you in all your areas of responsibility to lose the use of it prematurely. (I'll go into this further under *Discipline* and *Education*). In training it is your responsibility over this first year and beyond to give your baby the opportunity to learn to interest and amuse itself for short periods, with its toys, in its playpen *but with you right there,* coming and going about your housework, talking to it from the kitchen, pausing to admire what it's doing and to give it a kiss and a pat. Don't do as did one mother who told me:

> "I *do* put her in her playpen and I *do* leave her—even though she
> cries! But whenever she sees me or even hears me she starts crying
> again, so I go around in my stocking feet and whenever I go by the

door of the room where the pen is I get down on my hands and knees
so she won't see me. I just can't bear to hear her cry!"

This mother had momentarily lost sight of where she was heading, and her baby had caught sight of her weak spot. The playpen offers you the opportunity to begin the early cultivation of
two useful and helpful qualities in your child: resourcefulness
and thoughtfulness of others — exceedingly handy "tools."

Undivided Attention. If all this about the playpen
sounds like grim and serious business, just remember that the
other side of the scales are heavily weighted. The times when
you will be giving your baby your undivided attention will fill
up the greater part of its waking hours — and should. A baby's
days are a constant round of feedings, changings, going-downs,
getting-ups, baths and clean-ups — all of these times filled with
tender, loving care, with delights and surprises for everyone.
Babies need unending affection and it flows naturally from
parents. Never be afraid to express it — never fail to respond
to and encourage your baby's earliest expressions of love and
warmth.

Added to these times of caring for your baby will be the
playtimes. At first these will be times when you have your
baby on a big bed or on a blanket on the floor: admiring it,
amusing and animating it, giving it all your attention. Later on,
the play will become more boisterous and strenuous — these will
be exciting, letting-off-steam times.

Overpossessiveness. But life won t always be just you and
your baby. Training, even as early as the first year, involves
helping your baby become accustomed to other people. You
can help greatly by getting it used early to going to others, to
being held and tended by others. Start from the very beginning
to encourage it to accept and enjoy members of your families
and close friends.

Some parents find it difficult to enjoy, seem even to resent seeing their baby happy with others. An occasional mother carries this so far she seems even to resent seeing her baby want to go to its father. Watch that you don't allow your emotions to trip you up in this way. Overpossessiveness on the part of parents can make growing up very difficult and unhappy for a child.

In time you will want to go out of an afternoon or evening, leaving your baby in the care of someone — a relative, friend or baby-sitter. If your baby isn't used to being handled by anyone but you, your time off won't be exactly a success from anyone's point of view. Furthermore, the baby that for some unforeseen reason has to be turned over to others — it has to be hospitalized, both parents are sick, an emergency of any sort — that baby, if it's wholly unaccustomed to being cared for by others, will, for a time, be a very unhappy baby.

The Big World

I would like to get you thinking just a little about an aspect of training that points up rather forcibly a responsibility to which many parents seem to give very little thought. It will be up to you to help your baby relate to people around it — to the workaday world in which it lives. Your own approach to people — to your own families, the neighbors, the mailman, salespeople, doctors and other repairmen — will inevitably rub off on your baby. Even before the end of the first year you can do much to encourage your baby to be outgoing and friendly: to smile, to wave a hand.

Good habits, good manners vary depending on where you happen to live in the world — from culture to culture — but the principles that underlie them are pretty much the same. Possession of a few can help smooth a little child's path. For example:

> I sat in a living room one day with a young couple and their little youngster — he was close to two years of age. It was the first time I had met the family. The child was playing on the floor at our feet with

blocks and cars, making little arrangements that pleased him, completely absorbed in what he was doing. From time to time one of us would hand him a block or help him with a problem of balancing. Each time he would murmur, "Thank you," without looking up, going right on with his play. I congratulated his parents on having taught him to be so naturally polite. They grinned at each other and the father said, sheepishly: "Well, I'll admit we've made a point of it. Actually, my wife and I have never been so polite to each other as we have been since *he* came along!"

Years ago I took care of two small boys whose father was a cheerful young man who, when he talked, swore just about as naturally as he breathed. The family rule was: *No one can talk like Daddy till they're 21 years old.* As time went by, however, and the boys came in to the office for check-ups and booster shots, it was quite obvious that the rule wasn't being too well observed. Here was a nice little problem, not only for the boys and their parents but for the parents of their playmates as well.

Good habits, good manners and good language are not all-important, but I tend to think of them as among the useful tools you can give your child to take with him wherever he goes. Looking ahead to see where this aspect of training leads, bear in mind that intentionally or unintentionally, like it or not, as parents, your behavior and your outlook on life — good and bad — will inevitably make up much of the equipment your youngster will be carrying with him the rest of his days.

Discipline

Now that I've covered two of the areas of responsibility that fall to you parents I hope I'm beginning to get it across that there will be plenty for you to think about and do over the first year in order to get your baby off to a good start. Indeed there will be so much for you to do that you simply won't be able to afford to waste time worrying over whether or not your baby eats squash or some such thing. You'll be only too glad to leave such things to nature.

I'd like now to consider *Discipline*—another responsibility that falls entirely to you parents—another one to keep you busy. Discipline has much in common with training—it too is a matter of giving your youngster some of the equipment it will need to get along in this world. Training, as I've suggested, in part involves getting your new baby's physical systems in good working order—getting its little motors running smoothly. In a similar vein, discipline means equipping your youngster with controls—with a good braking system. At first it will be up to you parents to apply the brakes, but as time goes on you will want to help your child learn *how* and *when* to put them on—to help your child understand *where* and *how far* it can go—to help it develop some self-control. Home is far and away the kindest place for a child to begin to learn such things.

Most parents are surprised at how early the need for discipline arises—at how soon the brakes should be applied. But if you are on the lookout and get your discipline started early, long before problems begin to crop up, it will be so much easier for your baby and for you. Early in practice I received some helpful insight into this question of discipline that has stuck with me and has been constantly reinforced over the years as I've tried to help parents.

A mother came to the office one day with a little youngster, well over a year of age. This was a new patient, the family had recently moved to Boston. I gave the child a thorough going-over—and I wish right here to make the point that a doctor takes distinct pleasure and satisfaction in examining a youngster who has been well handled: the examination is complete and the entire affair is a simple and happy one for the child and the mother.

When I had finished this particular examination I complimented the mother on what was obviously the result of good handling on her part. She thanked me but added hastily that she had had help. She said they had previously lived in a small town in Maine, and the family doctor— the one and only, who took care of the entire community— had right from the beginning been at great pains to make it clear to her how important and helpful her early discipline would be for her baby.

"He was forever referring to my early chances to discipline as 'opportunities' — opportunities that would make life easier for my child later on. I've gradually come to see what he meant, and I've tried to make good use of his suggestion. I've tried to take advantage of my 'opportunities.' "

Well, I too have taken advantage of that doctor's suggestion, and I'd like now to show you *how* and *when* these early "opportunities" to discipline — to anticipate and to prevent handling problems — will turn up in the course of your baby's first year.

Discipline Over the First Six Months

Unnecessary Fussing. Somewhere between the time he reaches six to eight weeks of age, that bright baby of yours, the minute you put it down in its bed, may start fussing. I suggest you pick it up. If it stops crying at once you might be *suspicious,* but check carefully for a pin or anything that might be making it uncomfortable. If you find nothing wrong, put it down. Should it start fussing again, give it the benefit of the doubt and a second check. If it stops fussing again, immediately upon being picked up, you should be *very suspicious!* If all systems are "go" — put it down and let it fuss. This will be your first "opportunity" to teach your baby you will not respond to unnecessary fussing — to its attempts to get its own way. You will have many more such "opportunities." This is when discipline starts and it is most important for your baby and for you that you get in on the ground floor, when such a little discipline will accomplish so much.

Your baby won't learn overnight. It will keep right on trying you out. Never question its ability to persist. Also, never question how easily your emotions can draw you off the beam. At a bare eight weeks of age your baby will be quite capable of observing any signs of weakening on your part, and if it does, in a remarkably short time it will more than likely start taking advantage of them. So if you manage to ignore its unnecessary fussing for three days running, don't, on the fourth day—just because your baby seems so tiny and helpless—give in and rock it to sleep. If you do, you'll just be playing into its hands. Furthermore, if you keep on giving in and make excuses for yourself—say, on the grounds that your baby has inherited the stubborn streak that runs through your husband's family—you're simply missing out on this early opportunity, this relatively mild bit of discipline, that can make things so much easier for your baby as time goes on. Somehow, you are going to have to convince not just your baby but also yourself that you are going to be consistent in this matter of not responding to unnecessary fussing.

As time goes on you will have other opportunities to ignore fussing as you do things needed for your baby's daily care—things your baby seems to consider a waste of time or indignities: changing its diapers, changing its clothes, washing its face, occasionally taking its temperature or giving it nose drops. You can't imagine how many times mothers would call about a sick baby and when I would suggest taking its temperature or giving it nose drops the mother would say: "But he won't let me take his temperature!" or "She struggles so! I'm not able to give her nose drops!" This is ridiculous! Right from the start, when your baby squirms and wriggles and fusses as you carry out necessary procedures:

> Hold it with a gentle but firm hand;
> Explain what you are doing in a quiet "it's got to be done so let's get it over with" tone of voice;
> And do both these things consistently.

I can't possibly overstress the importance both for your baby and for you of getting your discipline started early—when it is relatively easy all round. So many parents aren't aware of and miss these early opportunities. Having to change the diapers of a struggling, fighting year-old baby in stiff-soled shoes or trying to ignore the unnecessary fussing of a one-year-old whose yells can be heard down the block are things that aren't done easily. Early discipline is your real opportunity to prevent what can so easily become behavior problems.

Discipline Around Six to Nine Months

At about five to seven months of age, your baby may again confront you with this matter of unnecessary fussing. As you leave it in its playpen to attend to other things, it may give the old fussing routine another try, and at this point your baby, older, stronger, more determined and most definitely louder, can pose something of a problem with its fussing—certainly one hard to ignore. If you've been maintaining fairly good, consistent discipline right along, it should take just a little added firmness on your part—a little added pressure on the brakes—to convince your baby that fussing isn't going to work. This burst of fussing over being left in the playpen will be just one of a series of repeated challenges to your discipline—just one of the many opportunities that mother from Maine learned to take advantage of. (In all fairness, however, you will do well to reassess your day schedule to make sure you are keeping a proper balance of playpen and undivided attention time. *Discipline*, like *Prevention of Accidents*, can be satisfactorily carried out only in conjunction with a good schedule.)

As I pointed out under *Training*, this is the time when so many mothers give up the use of the playpen. Here is where discipline can serve to back up training, but if a mother hasn't been aware of and has missed out on getting discipline started early, it's awfully hard to begin it at this stage of the game.

I would like to pause here and consider once again what intelligent use of the playpen can mean to your baby and you:

1. *You can use it to prevent accidents*—and its greatest value in this area comes when your baby at nine months to a year starts to creep.
2. *You can use it to train* your baby in awareness that it can't always have your undivided attention—to train it in consideration of others and in resourcefulness.

3. *You can also use it to discipline* your baby—to teach it that it can't always have its own way.

If you show judgment you can make the playpen work for you both. Try not to give it up any sooner than you have to—not until your baby can climb out of it.

Let me make a suggestion about how you can get out of what I'll admit is a difficult situation, especially if you live in an apartment and your baby has good lungs. If your baby has taken to protesting on being left for a time in its playpen, after it has fussed all you think you and the neighbors can stand:

> *Without any emotion* whatsoever take it out of the playpen and
>
> *DO something to it—anything routine:* give it a drink, change its diapers, anything at all. And take your time to do it if things have been particularly rough.
>
> *You know perfectly well* you're taking it out because it is making such a ruckus;
>
> *Your baby will think:* "The old girl took me out, not because I was fussing but because she was ready to —"

Then, if your baby should be put back in the playpen, or the next time you put it there, try to get your own conviction of the reasonableness of your course of action in your manner and voice. In time your baby will accept it and, just as it got over fussing on being put to bed, so it will get over fussing on being left for short periods in its playpen. Some mothers find this very difficult to believe!

As I see it, discipline over the first year is primarily a matter of:

1. Not responding to your baby's unnecessary fussing— in its bed, playpen, anywhere at all.
2. A loving hand holding your baby down firmly whenever you have to do something needed for its care.

3. A reassuring, explaining voice as you do these things.
4. All three of them done consistently.

If you stick with it, if you keep your ultimate aim in mind at all times, you'll be astonished at how quickly your baby catches on — at how very reasonable a small baby can be.

Discipline from About Nine Months On

"No's" and "Don't's." Toward the end of the first year you will bump up against a new phase of discipline — a different way to help your baby. When your baby starts to creep and you allow it to explore, giving it your undivided attention:

1. You can't have your crawling baby pulling books out of the bookcase;
2. You can't have your crawling baby yanking things off tables, tipping lamps over on its head and so forth;
3. Equally, you shouldn't have to baby-proof the entire house.

When your baby is able to get around under its own steam it is also ready to learn that there are things it may do and things it may not do. Increased freedom brings restrictions. Reasonable limits have to be set. Remember, it's a big world for a little baby! This is when your baby should learn the meaning of the words *No* and *Don't.* If you say them meaningfully and firmly, if you back them up with disciplinary action — which at this stage of the game means limiting your baby's freedom and depriving it for a time of your undivided attention — your baby will be getting its first lessons in obedience. Don't ever underestimate your baby's ability to learn this lesson — sooner or later — if *you* hang on.

(There's a great deal of talk about the proper words to use, but, as a year-old baby primarily understands only the tone of your voice — you've been talking to it for a long time — the actual words don't matter.) Say them firmly — once or twice.

Back them up with discipline. Do this consistently so your baby will know where it stands. Above all, don't keep on saying *No* and *Don't* meaninglessly all day long!

To show you how this works:

> Your baby, on the prowl, starts pulling books out of the bookcase. You say, "No! Don't do that!"
>
> Your baby doesn't pay any attention.
>
> In all fairness you want to be sure it has heard you. You go over to it, indicate the books and again, more firmly, say, "NO! DON'T TOUCH!"
>
> If your baby still fails to take the hint, I suggest you pick it up and move it to the other side of the room. It may forget the whole thing — but there'll be plenty more opportunities. However, it may crawl right back to the bookcase again. If so, repeat the warning a couple of times. If it sticks to its guns, pick it up and *without any show of emotion,* put it in its playpen or highchair — some place *where it is safe, but where it will have lost its freedom and your undivided attention.* As you do so you should quietly explain what this is all about.

This procedure repeated time and again will eventually pay off. Don't forget to praise your baby when, as time goes on, it passes the bookcase without touching it — when it shows some self-control. After all, this is what you're aiming for!

Discipline, to be successful, should be a two-man job. Parents should share in it and should back each other up in administering it. It does no good for Mummy to ignore fussing all day long if the minute Daddy comes home he goes and picks up the baby at the first fuss! It's tough enough to give out punishments, and tougher still to follow through on them. It's next to impossible to do either one alone, without any cooperation or support. To make a success of a *small* child's discipline, parents should present a united front. There should be discussion, there should be good communication between them — *behind the scenes!*

Don't think for a moment that I think discipline is easy — you may well find it the hardest of all your responsibilities. But I'm very anxious to get you thinking about it now, before you have your baby. After all, I've worked at this job of being a parent too, and I know how tricky discipline can be. It's hard, I think, principally for two reasons:

1. Because those old emotions of ours can interfere in any number of ways;
2. Because it's not always easy either to see the results of our discipline or to keep the end picture in mind at all times.

A look ahead at a few examples of each of these reasons may help to point up some of the difficulties.

I stopped one evening on my way home from the office to give a youngster a shot. There were four children in the family, and the mother hadn't been able to get in to the office. This was a family I'd been taking care of for a number of years. As I went into the house I heard sounds from upstairs suggesting that somebody was in a little trouble and was being spanked.

By the time I had my coat off—and I didn't hurry—all four kids were clustered around me, jabbering away. I felt sure that one in the group had a red bottom, but I couldn't tell which one. "Where's Mummy?" I asked.

Shrugs all around—nobody seemed particularly interested.

Pretty soon Mummy came down and it was obvious she'd been crying. That spanking had hurt the mother so much more than the child with the red bottom—whichever one it was!

Disciplining children is no fun! It hurts parents. That is why parents try in the most remarkable ways to get out of punishing. Their minds are incredibly agile when it comes to thinking up excuses—any excuse rather than punish or carry through on a punishment.

Try not to duck out on disciplining because it's hard.

Don't make excuses—to yourself, to your child, to your husband/wife, to anyone!

Try hard not to kid yourself.

A mother brought her three-year-old boy into the office for a check-up. It was the first time I'd seen them. My physical examination was completely unsatisfactory—the child was so out-of-hand. I told the mother that, from appearances and from what little I had been able to do, there seemed to be nothing wrong with the boy physically. I did suggest, however, that maybe we should go into the matter of her discipline.

"Well, you see," she said, "I have quite a problem here. I can't handle this child the way other children are handled. You see, his father is very bright—he graduated from college at eighteen and had his Ph.D. at twenty-two!"

I scratched my head at that one, but I told her I thought she was just finding discipline difficult—that she was kidding herself! I rather expected she'd get mad, and walk out of the office.

She did get red, but then she thanked me and said, "I know I've been running away from it. To be honest, I just don't know how to go about it. I'd very much appreciate a little help."

There are other ways in which emotions get in the way. You have to learn to hang on to them and, especially when tired, neither give in to your child, nor take it out on your child. I'm not pretending that this is easy—it's terribly hard to be taking care of kids all day and not, at times, as evening comes and there are baths to give and suppers to get, feel pushed to the wall. I've often been asked:

"Isn't a mother entitled to let off steam now and then?"

"Shouldn't children be made to realize that parents have feelings too?"

I can only say: right you are, but remember, if you're forever teeing off, in time your children may be left completely unimpressed, or they may needle you a bit—just for the fun of seeing you blow your top. If you can't control your temper, you might just as well not bother to discipline. Emotions, out of control, may cancel the effectiveness of your discipline.

A mother brought her four-year-old boy in to the office for a check-up. "I don't know what I'm going to do!" she said. "I'm forever spanking— and it does no good. He's right back at it!"

I knew this mother had a real temper. I'd seen her lose it on the golf course a few times, and I had seen red marks on her boy's bottom occasionally. I said, "When you spank, how do you go about it?"

"Oh," she replied, "I'm so mad! I grab the . . . little fellow, and I have a paddle; I really let him have it!"

I tried to point out that, sure those spankings hurt, but maybe their effectiveness was in part canceled out by the fun her boy had seeing her so hopping mad! I advised her to spank half as hard, and *only* when she could control her temper. But I felt she left the office questioning my advice.

I saw her a couple of months later, and she said, "Glory be! Believe it or not I think I've finally caught on! Anyhow, I'm trying to hang on to my temper and I'm not having to spank anywhere near as often. Things are going a lot better!"

Emotions have their place, but not in discipline.

But good discipline, started early, has so much to offer! I want again to make the point that a doctor finds it very satisfactory to examine a child — either in the home or in the office — in the presence of parents who are maintaining good discipline.

I had a call one day from a mother asking me to speak to her husband. She said he was cruel to their little three-year-old girl — "he spanks her!" I knew the husband and I found it hard to believe he would be cruel to his youngster. Had she discussed the problem with her husband? Well, no — she would rather I talked with him. I suggested she have a talk with him and then, if they wanted, they could both come in and we'd go over it. Nothing further came of that.

Sometime later the mother called one morning — first thing. Their little girl had a temperature of over 105 degrees, would I please stop in. She added, rather surprisingly, "Don't come till after ten o'clock."

In the course of calls, I arrived at the house at about a quarter of ten. I started to examine the child and she raised the dickens! I couldn't get near her. The mother was no help.

About ten o'clock the "cruel" father showed up. "My goodness! What's the matter, Sugar?" he asked. She held his hand, and I had no further trouble examining her. She had pneumonia and I thought she would do better in the hospital.

In the hospital, each morning when I saw her, she would ask, "Where's Daddy?" The day came when I thought she might be ready to go home. I saw her first thing in the morning. She was a cute little thing! The nurses had fixed her up with a bow in her hair. As I came in the room she looked up at me with a wicked twinkle in her eye. "Where's Mummy?" she asked. There was a world of meaning in her voice.

Mummy she could twist around her little finger! Mummy was her best plaything! She was feeling better and she was ready for fun.

Sick or well, a child, in the presence of parents who discipline, seems secure. It has confidence in those parents — it is easy, relaxed and happy. In practice, I always used to feel sorry for the undisciplined youngsters. They seemed so alone. They seemed to have no one to lean on.

I suggested earlier, in *Prevention of Accidents*, that an obedient child is a safer child. It is also my experience that the disciplined child, the child who is slowly learning to apply his own brakes, gets better treatment from his playfellows. Other children can be very rough on the youngster who expects and insists on getting his own way. So often this is the child at the bottom of the pig-pile; this is the child in the sandbox who gets hit over the head with a shovel, the child whose mittens get thrown over the fence, who walks home from school alone. This too, more frequently than not, may be the child whose first days and weeks in school are difficult — "whose teacher doesn't understand him!" It's hard to discipline over the first year, but it's harder still to see your child unhappy — getting his first tastes of discipline out of the home.

Education

A fourth area of responsibility that falls to you parents over the first year is the education of your baby. Here's an area that is such a mixed bag of fun, excitement and responsibility that it's a real challenge. As we have seen in the other five areas of responsibility, babies come into the world equipped in a variety of ways by nature, completely irresponsible and self-centered, but exceedingly adaptable and responsive. In *Training* and *Discipline* we saw how unbelievably early they learn to assert themselves — and the discrepancy between their physical helplessness and dependence and their mental alertness and capacity often proves unsettling and confusing to parents. So, right from the start, it's well to realize and accept the fact that babies are bright! Parents who underestimate their baby's intelligence run the risk of ending up the first year right in the palm of their baby's tiny hand.

Among the various pieces of equipment with which nature endows your baby is a mind like a fresh, new blotter — everything that happens, everything your baby hears, sees and feels is taken up. You will have endless opportunity to encourage and stimulate this budding comprehension in all your handling of your baby — which means the greater part of each day; when you're feeding it, bathing it, changing it, playing with it, getting it up and putting it down. The happier, the broader, the more varied and the more oft-repeated the exposure to all manner of stimuli, the better!

From the time you first start handling your baby, converse with it. In time it will prick up its ears, first to the sound of your coming, then to the sound of your voices: explaining, reassuring, encouraging, cautioning, restraining. In time your baby's ears will be tuned to every shade of meaning in your voices. Throughout the first year you will find yourselves talking sense and nonsense to it; repeating nursery rhymes over and over again — babies love beat and rhythm; singing to it — some children pick up a musical interval or a melody surprisingly early; playing music: records, the radio, the piano, any instrument you have the hang of. You parents will discover hidden talents and resources in yourselves and in each other. By all means, let yourselves go — your baby will be a most uncritical and appreciative audience.

Slowly your baby will begin to observe things round about it: your smiling faces bent over it, the bright toy you place at the head of its bed, all the things you produce to attract, interest and amuse it. As time goes on, string up colorful and moving objects over its crib, its playpen and its changing table—having clothes or diapers changed is a tiresome procedure and something to look at or hang onto helps considerably. Pictures and mobiles in strategic places to observe and reflect upon seem to offer food for a baby's thoughts.

> I remember a mother bringing in her three-month-old baby for a check-up. Things were going well—the family had settled into a smooth-running schedule. "The baby is just wonderful! So good! We're having such fun with him! And do you know what, Dr. Turtle? Last night I had a long-distance call—my husband's away on a business trip and he almost never calls when he's away. I was scared! He called, and he was so excited! He's found just the right picture to hang over the baby's crib!"

Well, here's where a lot of the fun lies. You'll find you can put so much of yourselves into the handling of your baby. You'll come up with endless ideas of your own, and your baby will ask for and respond to everything your education, your experience and your ingenuity can come up with.

As the year goes along, the periods of undivided attention that provide breaks in a good schedule afford opportunities to encourage your baby's developing dexterity—its ability to:

> Reach for things, grasp and hang on to them, manipulate them;
> Put things into a cup and take them out again;
> Put tops on and take them off;
> Take things apart and put them together again;
> Pile things up and knock them down;
> Screw and unscrew things;
> Roll, push and drop things.

As you observe and encourage your baby's ever-increasing alertness and enterprise with all manner of inducements and incentives, you'll be delighted and constantly impressed with how quickly it responds to your teaching and how unlimited is its capacity to learn.

Toys. Mothers were forever asking, "What kind of toys should I get my baby?" or, "What's a good educational toy?" At this stage of the game you can't miss! — you don't have to buy a lot of expensive toys. *Everything and anything your baby is exposed to is educational!* To my way of thinking, some of the toys that are the most fun and every bit as instructive as the so-called educational toys you have right around your home, especially in your kitchen equipment.

Mothers, in the office, would apologize for the battered old pie tin or beat-up measuring cup their baby would hang on to and wave about all the time I'd be examining it. "She has some beautiful toys at home but for some reason she seems to just love this thing!"

It isn't the *kind* of toys you get your baby; it's the use you make of them, the *way you handle them*, that counts. Where toys are concerned, the first thing to think of is — *is it safe?* For example:

1. Remember that from four months to over a year of age everything a baby gets hold of goes into its mouth, so watch out for toys that are too small, that a baby may choke on or swallow. Watch out for toys that are long and thin, that a baby may poke down its throat and gag on or fall on, injuring its mouth or throat.
2. Remember that babies can be rough on toys — watch out for toys that might break easily or splinter.
3. A teething baby can bite the eyes or ears off toy dolls or animals.
4. Watch out for hard objects with sharp edges or corners that a baby in a pen might fall on.

The second thing to think of is the *way you use the toys.*

1. *Don't expose your baby to too many toys at a time.* I used to visit in homes after Christmas or a birthday and there would be so many toys in the crib or playpen that it was all I could do to find the baby. This kind of clutter is confusing to a baby and encourages destructiveness. *Learn to stockpile gifts* and bring them out a few at a time. Put away toys that are too old for a baby—let the baby grow up to them. If you show judgment in the handling of your child's toys, bit by bit you'll be teaching your child appreciation and proper care of his possessions.

2. *Set aside a particular toy or two for going to bed:* something safe, soft and cuddly. In time the toy plus bed will produce a conditioned reflex and going to sleep will become a happy, friendly affair. Don't use a bottle or a pacifier!

3. Have a few new or "special occasion" toys tucked away for the "sick time" or the rainy day. Well-loved, well-worn but mended toys put away and produced at a trying moment can be a great help and comfort.

4. Have an extra-special toy for your baby on the training seat.

5. Just as you do a little advance planning to make the playpen "work" for you and your baby, so, learn to think ahead and be prepared for the time your baby may be bored. Learn to have something tucked away in your pocket or handbag for:
   a. The shopping trip—these can be very tough and tedious for little folk;
   b. The visit to relatives or friends—the ones who can't be counted on to produce play material of their own;
   c. The boring drive—don't expect a baby or child to "go for" scenery or grown-up chatter for very long! Have something in your pocket!

In other words, learn to make toys "work" for your baby and you.

As your baby slowly begins to acquire proficiency in handling *itself* and in handling its toys, its attention span will grow. This is when it will begin to be content and happy on its own for short periods—when it will begin to develop the resourcefulness and independence I referred to in *Training*.

Toward the end of the first year—though the time varies greatly from baby to baby—will come the creeping and exploring times: more experiences to be soaked up by your baby's thirsty brain, more fun and exciting times for all of you, more frosting on the cake! And ahead lie the times for looking at pictures, learning colors, recognizing objects, repeating sounds, making associations. There seems to be no end to what you can do to increase your baby's comprehension and alertness!

There also seems to be no end to the books and the talk that goes on suggesting ways to sharpen your baby's wits and how important this is. Because this is so easy and such fun, and because babies are so amazingly bright and receptive, parents are often persuaded, sometimes persuade themselves, that *this is what constitutes their baby's education* and spend a disproportionate amount of time cudgeling their baby's brain, pressing for bright responses so their baby will grow up to be the brightest child in the neighborhood.

Mothers sometimes get so excited about this that they let their schedules and housework go to pot, and husbands come home to find themselves getting supper and doing the washing. Fathers sometimes do the same thing. They offer to baby-sit on a Saturday or Sunday, and mother gets everything lined up; then mother comes home to find the schedule knocked galley west and the baby tired, fussy and overstimulated.

Complete Education

Sure, this stimulation of your bright baby is important—and it's fun too! But this isn't all there is to a baby's education—

not by a long shot! Your baby's complete education is far more inclusive—it takes in its training, its discipline, the measures you take to keep it safe, as well as all you have to offer to direct and stimulate its mental capacities and energy. To push any one of these aspects of its education at the expense of another is most unfortunate because, properly balanced and coordinated, they merge, overlap and support each other.

1. When you start early to accustom your baby to patterns of safety and it learns to accept occasional restraints; when, as time goes on, you teach it to handle itself in safe ways and to obey simple rules of safe-conduct—this is part of its complete education.

2. When you keep your baby's physical systems running smoothly and routinely; when you teach it to be outgoing and friendly, and help it acquire, little by little, some good habits, some good manners—this is part of its complete education.

3. When you take advantage of your early opportunities to help your baby understand that fussing won't get it its own way; when slowly you teach it that there are necessary limits to what it can do, to how it can behave—this is part of its complete education.

4. When you expose your baby to sounds, shapes, textures, colors—quickening its perceptions; when you teach it to play peek-a-boo, to pull a cord and make a music-box play, to remove a cover and find out what's inside, to set one block on top of another; when you encourage and stimulate its curiosity and adventuresomeness in every way you can think of—this is part of its complete education, a very important part!

All these and more are things you can begin to teach your baby over the first year or two—things your bright baby will be so quick to learn. But because the first three areas can be difficult and demanding, and aren't, generally speaking, thought of as education—because there's so much talk about what can be done to build up your baby's intelligence, from the word go, and because this is fascinating and a whale of a lot of fun—it's very easy to be thrown off and put all your time and effort into the last area. May I suggest, however, that as time goes on, you will find that you will be able to offer your youngster so much more in this last area if the other three are under control—and not only you, but before long, your child's teachers as well.

A mother brought her three-year-old boy in for a routine check-up, and except for a bruised shoulder—the result, his mother said, of having been pushed off the porch by the neighbor kids—there was nothing wrong with him. But I had a difficult time examining him—I always had had! His mother had an even more difficult time getting him dressed—trying to catch him. He was all over the office, into everything. His mother said "Don't" any number of times, but he paid absolutely no attention.

I offered him a lollipop and he grabbed it. His mother said, "What do you say to Dr. Turtle?" He said nothing. To cover her embarrassment his mother said, "But he's so bright! We've been able to teach him so much! He can count almost to twenty! And he can spell—Jimmy, spell cat for Dr. Turtle."

"D-O-G."

Well, we all have our off days—and as far as I was concerned it didn't matter how Jimmy spelled "cat." He was plenty bright—he would have no trouble with that part of his learning. I did think, however, that as time went on he just might continue to have a little trouble getting along with his playmates, and maybe with his teachers as well. This is the sort of thing that can happen —and it makes it so much harder for the child—when one aspect of his education is stressed at the expense of the others.

Now, if you'll bear with me—to get back for just a minute to your baby in its first year:

When your baby, close to a year of age, learns to become absorbed and intent in his own small playpen world, examining things and working them over, quite oblivious for a spell about what goes on around him—this will be the early beginnings of his learning: to accept restraints, to be considerate and self-controlled, to be independent, resourceful and imaginative. All your responsibilities will be working together and your baby's complete education will be under way.

As parents this will be your big challenge: To understand and appreciate the importance of and maintain a sensible balance among the four responsibilities that rest squarely on your shoulders: the protection, the training, the discipline, and the, as it were, formal education of your baby.

The Fence

I have now taken up all six of the areas of responsibility in the care and handling of babies which, as I suggested in the *Introduction*, will be delivered to you along with your baby. As you shoulder the primary responsibility in each of the four areas we have just covered, it may give you comfort to think back to the first two areas we considered, *Treatment of Infections* and *Feeding*, and to the big assist nature gives you in both of them. I can't possibly overemphasize the importance of leaving the primary responsibility in those two areas to nature. In practice, I used to try to make this separation of responsibilities clear by picturing a fence:

> *On one side:* Nature's Responsibilities
> Treatment of Infections
> Feeding

> *On the other side:* Parents' Responsibilities
> Prevention of Accidents
> Training
> Discipline
> Education

When a question or problem of handling arises—as they're bound to—stop to think on which side of the fence it lies:

You're worried because your one-year-old won't eat vegetables.

> Don't worry—feeding is nature's responsibility. Offer well-balanced, small meals and—stick on your own side of the fence.

You're upset because your one-year-old wakes and fusses or cries every morning from about five o'clock on.

> Training—your side of the fence. Have you reviewed your schedule lately? How about naps—too many or too long?

Maybe this image of the fence will help give you a clearer picture of where your jobs as parents primarily lie, so you won't waste time and energy over nature's part of the job and slip up on your own.

Maternal Caress by Mary Cassatt. (Courtesy of the Honolulu
Academy of Arts, Honolulu, Hawaii.)

Chapter Two

The Technique of Feeding

2 — The Technique of Feeding

The "Gray Zone"

Now that we have gone over the six areas of responsibility — the general theory and philosophy in the care and handling of your baby over the first year — let's get down to specifics. The feeding of your baby will be the first job you'll tackle. As we have seen (p. 26), nature assumes primary responsibility in this area — sees to it that your baby comes into this world with a sucking apparatus and reflex, an appetite, and the ability to decide how much food it wants. It will be up to you to support nature by providing the food, either from the breast or bottle, and by learning the techniques of making it very readily available to your baby.

The importance of helping you acquire, prenatally, an understanding of these techniques was brought home to me one day as I played golf with an obstetrician friend of mine, who said, "Now that you're retired from practice, what are you going to do with yourself? You can't play golf and curl all the time!" I told him a little about my plans to organize prenatal discussion groups with the hope of helping mothers prevent the development of unnecessary problems in the handling of their babies. His reaction was, "Good! Then you can do something about the 'gray zone'!" As I didn't know what he was talking about, he went on to explain:

Some years ago, in an address to the American Obstetrical Society, a retiring president spoke with considerable feeling about the number of mothers who came for their six weeks' post-partum check-up looking dog-tired, pale, worn out from loss of sleep, discouraged because their babies were not going smoothly. This finding was so routine, it was such a specific entity — especially among mothers of first babies — that he referred to the first six weeks following delivery as the "gray zone."

My friend added, "And that 'gray zone' is for real! You know how happy and blooming most girls look during pregnancy? Well, it's most upsetting to us obstetricians to see some of them six weeks after delivery! Why haven't you pediatricians been doing something about this?"

My only answer is: All right, if, after reading this book, you girls experience the "gray zone," I'll feel I haven't done a very good job!

A Few General Remarks About Feeding

1. First I want to make it perfectly clear—*babies are not in the least fussy about where their food comes from—they just want plenty of it.* As far as feeding is concerned your primary aim should be to see to it that your baby has the opportunity to get all the food it wants.

> "To a baby that's wholly intent on its dinner,
> A breast or a bottle—either's a winner!"
>
> LPT

2. *The decision to breast-feed or bottle-feed is a personal matter and should be left entirely to the mother.* No one should tell her that something awful may happen. Her baby will do equally well on the breast or bottle—and in my experience this is what counts with mothers. Sometimes a mother may not be able to breast-feed—she may have to get back to work; she may have inverted nipples; she just plain may not want to breast-feed. This is her business, and her decision should be respected. In practice, when a mother was undecided and asked my advice, I always suggested that she try breast-feeding—my experience indicates that most girls get a great deal of satisfaction out of breast-feeding. If it doesn't work, at least the mother has the satisfaction of having tried. *But, however she decides to feed her baby, a mother should be given all the encouragement and help possible.*

3. *A baby these days should do equally well on the breast or bottle.*

This has not always been so. In the relatively short time I've been in practice there have been tremendous changes in the make-up and production of formulas—mother's milk substitutes. Formulas used to be incredibly complicated affairs, their preparation time-consuming and entirely the mother's task. Moreover, cow's milk as a substitute for mother's milk was widely suspect: it was felt that "prematures" and sickly babies could survive only on mother's milk. In my days as intern, mothers with an overabundance of milk could sell it and make a good thing out of it. The Boston Lying-In Hospital had a "Mother's Milk Directory" where mother's milk was bought, frozen, and stored to be shipped all over the country.

For one short period, every morning my path used to cross that of a father delivering his wife's surplus breast milk to the hospital. We would greet each other and pass the time of day. One morning I missed him and the next day asked where he'd been. He grinned and replied, "We had a little mix-up at our house night before last. We were having friends in for dinner. My wife tends to get flustered when we have company. It wasn't until just before dinner—when it was almost finished baking—that she 'came to' that she'd put that day's breast milk into the bread pudding. It was too late then! All my wife could say was: 'Well, it's never done the baby any harm!' It worked out fine! My friend had two helpings and he said it was 'the best damned bread pudding' he'd ever eaten."

(Not exactly a Julia Child recipe—but a suggestion if you're in a pinch.)

Well, in any case, the bottom has dropped out of that market! Formulas are now easy to prepare, safe, sterile, inexpensive, and babies thrive on them. Today it is even felt that "prematures" do better on a cow's milk formula than on mother's milk. As far as I am concerned, it's not possible, on examining a two- or 3-month-old baby, to tell whether it has been breast- or bottle-fed. But the old days of low standards in the quality of milk production and of complicated formulas have left a legacy of misinformation and misguided attitudes toward both breast- and bottle-feeding that have still to be lived down.

4. One hears it said, now and again, that *any mother—if she really wants to—can breast-feed. If a mother isn't able to breast-feed, it's her fault—she hasn't really tried hard enough.* Well, first, let me say that there is no truth in these statements; second, that they are most unkind; and third, that they are quite beside the point.

For some reason or other, some mothers just don't produce enough milk to feed their baby. As far as I know, no one knows why this is so—this is one place nature seems to have let us down. However, it *is* so, and it *has always been* so—there is nothing *new* or *different* about girls today. There are just great variations in the amount of milk mothers' breasts secrete—sometimes even for the same mother with a different baby. This variation in the amount of milk mothers produce has accounted for the thriving business of wet-nurses down through the ages.

It accounted for the good price the "Mother's Milk Directory" used to pay for mother's milk—30¢ an ounce!—and that was before inflation!

It has contributed to high infant mortality in times past when mother's milk substitutes were either unavailable, inadequate or unsafe. It contributes to high infant mortality in some of the less developed areas of the world today.

However, *there is nothing in the least "different" or "wrong" about the mother who doesn't have enough milk to breast-feed her baby!* Most certainly she should not be made to feel guilty if she "takes to the nursing-bottle." After all, let me repeat, her primary aim—*the whole point of feeding*—is to see to it that her baby has the opportunity to get all the food it wants.

Without doubt it is possible to stumble along and do all manner of things to try to stimulate the secretion of breast milk: keep a hungry baby sucking at frequent intervals, feed it whenever it cries, give oneself up wholly and completely to the business of breast-feeding—there are girls who want to do this above all else. To me, there is far more to good mothering than just satisfying a desire to breast-feed.

As I see it, "mothering," from a tiny, new baby's point of

view, means being held in its mother's arms, drinking all the warm, sweet milk it can hold, falling asleep, waking up some place warm and comfortable, and asking for and getting more mother and more milk. From a mother's point of view, "mothering" over the first weeks and months means holding her baby in her arms and offering it, from either the breast or bottle, all the food it wants until, completely satisfied, it closes its eyes and falls asleep; tucking it into its bed, full and content, and going about her household chores or being with and caring for the other members of the family, or taking a needed rest; peeking occasionally to see if her baby is all right; getting it up at fairly regular intervals throughout the day to repeat this same happy, refueling process.

These are the mothers who used to bring their babies into the office for a six weeks' check-up, the mothers well-rested, their babies healthy and *relaxed*, and say, "This baby is so good! And such fun! Mostly just eats and sleeps — but when it's awake so good-natured you'd hardly know there's a baby in the house!" No "gray zone" here! No undue worry over breast- or bottle-feeding! Just satisfied mothers and babies off to an easy start.

It should be an easy start! And since our primary concern here is to prevent the development of problems such as the "gray zone," it is essential, whether you plan to breast- or bottle-feed, that you understand how both work.

If you breast-feed, you will inevitably be offering your baby sterile water and dilute fruit juice from a bottle; and you may, in addition, find it necessary, while your breast-milk supply is being established, to offer occasional supplemental feedings of formula. Moreover, since the dental profession wants all babies sucking on a nipple, either breast or bottle, until they are 10 or 11 months of age, you may, before that time, wish to shift your baby to whole milk from a bottle. An understanding of the mechanics of bottle-feeding will, therefore, prove helpful.

The technique of bottle-feeding, on the other hand, is

based on the way a baby on the breast gets its milk—an efficiently designed system which the bottle-feeder should understand and imitate as closely as possible.

Hospital Stay (Breast- and Bottle-Feeding Mothers)

I'm not going to say much about your stay in the hospital—hospital routines vary and the doctors and nurses will give you all the help necessary. I do, however, want to make a few points—first, with an eye to your going home and second, to contribute to your peace of mind by explaining a few things that mothers in the hospital sometimes worry about unnecessarily.

About Rest

a. *Your stay in the hospital is very short—use it to get all the rest you possibly can!* Don't spend time and energy going all over the hospital, socializing. Every bit of rest you get will pay off once you get home.

b. If your room happens to be near the nursery and around two in the morning you hear a baby crying, don't lie awake and worry. Remember, there's more than one baby in the nursery—the crying baby isn't necessarily yours! Nurses take exceedingly good care of all babies. The important thing for you is to get your rest!

c. As far as "rooming in" is concerned—this is up to you and the hospital regulations. I've always been lukewarm about it—and, especially in these days when hospital stays are short, I feel that "rooming in" doesn't give you mothers the chance to get the rest you need. Bear in mind that this baby is going to be with you a long time. As I see it, from your baby's point of view, it's more important to have you begin its home care in the best possible shape than to experience these few added days of togetherness.

About Breast-Feeding

a. It is well to know that breast milk doesn't "come in" at once—not till the third, fourth, possibly the fifth day. Nature sees to it that a baby comes into the world well supplied with nourishment and fluids to last over this period. Your baby's first need, like yours, is for rest.

b. Don't be upset, therefore, if your baby doesn't want to suck the first few times it's put on the breast. Give it a little time; as soon as it's hungry and thirsty it will suck.

c. In the first few days you may notice a milklike substance, colostrum, a small amount of which is secreted as the forerunner of milk. Relatively little is known about its function. It is fairly high in nourishment, but, because there is so little of it, its importance as far as the human infant is concerned would seem to be negligible.

d. Before your milk comes in, your breasts will swell, feel tight, possibly be painful. This discomfort is very temporary and no reason at all to become discouraged about breast-feeding—certainly no reason to give it up. The nurses will help to keep you comfortable.

e. *Start nursing very, very slowly.* Your baby isn't hungry and the important thing as you start nursing is to *respect your nipples.* Let your baby toughen them *slowly.* If they are sore the first few times you nurse, one or two minutes on each breast is quite sufficient. If you try to be spartan about this, you may lose out. By the third day, if your nipples are still a bit sore, don't try to nurse more than four or five minutes on each breast. This slow nursing will cut down on the possibility of your nipples cracking; cracked nipples could mean the end of breast-feeding. Breast shields are available, but in my experience they aren't much help. *Slow and easy does it.*

About Bottle-Feeding

Don't be surprised or bothered if, on the second day, when you offer your baby a bit of formula or sweetened water, it seems completely uninterested. Don't try to press your baby to take it. Remember, for the breast-fed baby at this point, there's just about *no* food available! A little more rest, and your baby's appetite will be right there!

Your baby, in the hospital, will lose weight—and not because you're not feeding it. This loss of weight is actually the result of a loss of fluids. Your baby has been lying inside you soaked in fluid—inevitably it is going to dry out a bit and lose weight—nothing to worry about.

You may notice a puffiness around your baby's eyes, again due to this excess of fluids. This is nothing to worry about, and will disappear as soon as your baby dries out.

The Technique of Breast-Feeding

"However she decides to feed her baby, a mother should be given all the encouragement and help possible"—that's what I would like now to offer those of you who want to breast-feed.

Generally speaking, when it comes to maintaining the human race, nature has worked out a good system in breast-feeding; however, from the viewpoint of individual mothers, the system, at times, tends to be rather haphazard. As I've already pointed out, the amount of milk breasts secrete varies tremendously from mother to mother—it varies over a 24-hour period anywhere from 4 ounces for one mother to 50 ounces for another mother.* You've no way of knowing in advance what your particular breasts are going to produce. Should you have an ample supply, breast-feeding will be easy. As one mother with plenty of milk once said in my office, "I don't understand why some of my friends have *so much* trouble breast-feeding! It's so simple! Just duck soup!"

Well, so it is—for the mother with a good milk supply. But, it isn't all that easy for the mother whose supply may be

*Waller, Harold: British Medical Bulletin, Vol. 5, 1947–48, p. 1110.

limited. There are things this mother can do that may *improve* her chances of breast-feeding—there are also things she may do that will *cut down* on her chances. Probably the most helpful thing she can do, the most helpful approach to breast-feeding for any girl, is, first, to keep in mind that her primary aim is to see to it that her baby gets all it wants to eat; and, second, to be willing to face up to the possibility that her milk may be in short supply. The mother who can do this can relax and settle down to doing the simple, common-sense, often effective things that will enable nature to build up her milk supply to *her* maximum.

All too often, however, it is the "facing up to the possibility" of a shortage of milk that comes hard to mothers—principally, it seems to me, for two reasons:

1. *Because of emotions.* We've already seen that there are times when emotions complicate the handling of a baby. This can be such a time. Some mothers, because of their emotions, flatly refuse even to *entertain the possibility* that they may not have enough breast milk. They seem to feel that sheer determination will provide what nature hasn't. They get their priorities so mixed up that they don't know which comes first—their breasts or their baby—and, struggling desperately to prove to themselves and the world-at-large that they have plenty of milk, they further undermine their chances of breast-feeding and risk heading into the "gray zone."
2. *Because they try to follow all the bits and pieces of information that come their way:*
   a. From well-meaning family and friends. (It's my impression that no other field has so many *authorities*.)
   b. From magazine and newspaper articles—some good, some middling, some not so good—but most of them, more often than not, contradictory and confusing.

These mothers fail to consider that, as individual mothers dealing with their individual baby, much of what they hear and read just plain doesn't apply to them or their baby—mothers and babies are all so different!

Oh no, breast-feeding isn't always "duck soup," by any means! The fact of the matter is that girls differ in innumerable ways—height, weight, complexion, taste, temperament and so on. When it comes to having a baby there are just as many differences. For some—having a baby is as easy as rolling off a log. Others have difficulty carrying a baby full-term—or even conceiving in the first place. For some, labor is short; for others, more prolonged. Most of their babies come head first; but some come feet first. Usually their babies come singly, but sometimes they come in twos or threes or more. Some mothers want to breast-feed; some prefer to bottle-feed.

In view of these and other generally accepted but innumerable and unpredictable differences and variations, it beats me why anyone should expect all mothers always to be able to come up with enough breast milk to satisfy their babies!

There *is* one thing, however, that all mothers *can* count on—their baby will develop an appetite; and, as I see it, the only way to satisfy that appetite, the only way to have feedings go smoothly, the only way to stay clear of the "gray zone," is to be sure to offer their baby the opportunity to take all the food it wants.

Now let's consider how *you*, wanting to make a success of breast-feeding, should proceed—and by "success" I mean:

1. Seeing to it that your baby gets all it wants to eat;
2. Satisfying to the fullest possible extent your desire to breast-feed;
3. Maintaining a sense of proportion as far as your baby's needs and those of the other members of the family are concerned.

The period I shall cover here will be the first days and weeks at home—the period when you are getting feedings ironed out.

How Breasts Work

Basic to breast-feeding is an understanding of the way breasts seem to work. Breasts are remarkably constructed:

1. Like girls, breasts come in all shapes and sizes. However, the shape and size have absolutely nothing to do with *what* or *how much* they produce.

2. *The breast produces a uniformly excellent quality of milk.* When you see your milk for the first time you may not feel complimented. It looks very dilute—like watered-down cow's milk. But it's good! There's nothing wrong with its quality—it's only the quantity that sometimes lets you down.

3. The well-stocked breast supplies milk in response to demand with a surprising degree of efficiency.
   a. We've already seen that milk doesn't "come in" till the third, usually the fourth, day—about the time the baby begins to build up an appetite. Then, for some mothers, their milk supply is established almost with a rush. For other mothers, it's a slower process—a matter of anywhere from a few days to a week or ten days or possibly, let's face it, not at all.
   b. It sometimes takes a little time for the supply-demand mechanism to become adjusted. Your baby may not at first be able to take all the milk your breasts produce. You may have to "express by hand" or use a breast pump for a time to draw off enough of the surplus milk to keep your breasts comfortable. Gradually, however, your breasts will adjust the supply down to meet the demand.
   c. *It is the emptying or near emptying of breasts that stimulates them to produce.* As your baby grows and wants more and repeatedly just about empties your breasts, your breasts respond by producing more—always keeping the supply ahead of the demand.
   d. To me it makes sense, as things settle down, to balance the time your baby nurses on each breast. In this way you keep them equally emptied, equally stimulated and equally comfortable.

 e. When it comes time to wean, the entire process is reversed (p. 114). As you cut down the demand, *very slowly,* by dropping one feeding at a time, over a period of a week to ten days, or so, your breasts respond by cutting down the supply and finally stopping it altogether.

 f. If nature only weren't quite so casual about the amount of milk different mothers' breasts secrete, this supply-demand mechanism would be near perfect.

4. The breast is shaped and textured to close around a baby's mouth as it sucks. A baby doesn't usually close its lips tightly when it sucks as you do—it sometimes leaves little openings around the edge and at the corners of its mouth. The breast closes over these openings pretty effectively so that the baby on the breast swallows relatively little air and bubbling is hardly a problem.

5. The nipple has multiple tiny holes, 15 or more, plus a valve control of some sort that:

 a. *Opens as a baby sucks* to permit milk to flow very freely— it positively spurts in response to the suction established by vigorous sucking, and

 b. *Closes as a baby stops sucking,* and very effectively, from your baby's point of view, cutting off the flow of milk so the baby doesn't choke. It is not always so effective from your point of view. You may at times be bothered by leakage.

What You Should Know Before You Breast-Feed

 Now for some of the things you should know and understand about yourself, your breasts and your baby; and also some of the procedures you should be prepared to follow in order to have breast-feeding go as smoothly as possible.

1. *A place to feed*
Before you go to the hospital it is well to set up a place to feed your baby when you come home.

a. A comfortable chair (a rocking-chair works well), *low* enough so that both your feet can rest on the floor — preferably *with arms* so that your arm, holding the baby, will be supported.
b. In a *quiet place* — out of the main line of traffic.
c. A *subdued light nearby* for night feeding — don't have the place lit up like a ball park the night of a game.

The chances of feedings going smoothly are much better if you and your baby are comfortable, quiet and relaxed.

2. *Your approach to feeding*
   Feeding, to a baby, is an important matter and it will respond happily to your wholehearted involvement. This is a wonderful time to talk quietly to your baby. It's a very poor time to chatter with a girl friend about a shoe sale or have a disagreement with your husband.

3. By getting *plenty of rest* and being as *free from worry* as possible, a mother improves her chances a having a good milk supply.

4. It's equally important that a baby get plenty of rest. *Babies tire very easily!* Just being handled — even nursing — can be a tiring procedure for a baby.

5. *How long should a baby nurse? The ten-minute maximum*
   Because breast milk flows so readily and your baby gets it so easily, ten minutes on each breast is the maximum time your baby should be allowed to nurse. Actually your baby may not need as much as ten minutes on each breast to get all it wants. It may get all it wants in five, six or seven minutes on each breast and fall asleep. Don't take the ten minute rule too seriously and try to keep your baby awake and sucking by flicking its cheeks or its feet. *If there's milk available,* ten minutes on each breast is as much time as a baby needs to get all it wants and be satisfied.

Adequate Milk Supply

6. *How can you tell whether or not you have plenty of milk?*

   Your baby can be counted on to provide you with three very convincing clues as to the state of your breast-milk supply. I think of them as the three requirements which must be satisfied to show you conclusively that you have plenty of milk.

The Three Requirements of Breast-Feeding

The First Requirement
While feeding, your baby becomes drowsy, very likely falls asleep in your arms—obviously completely satisfied. Even bubbling won't rouse it.

The Second Requirement
Most of the time, following feedings, your baby sleeps three and one-half to four hours—often has to be wakened for the next feeding. As I pointed out in *Training* the average 6-pound baby has the strength and capacity to take enough food at a feeding—provided plenty of food is easily available—to carry it for about three and one-half to four hours or more.

   These first two Requirements serve as indicators of the establishment of and the adequacy of your breast-milk supply. They pave the way for the establishment of a schedule (see below) which, in turn, leads to:

The Third Requirement
As soon as you establish a regular routine of five daytime feedings, the length of time your baby sleeps at night following the 10 o'clock feeding gradually extends till, by the end of the third week home (on the average), the 2 o'clock feeding becomes a thing of the past.

When all three Requirements are being regularly fulfilled — when your baby provides you with all three clues:

You can be sure you have plenty of milk, and your baby is getting all it wants to eat.

I shall refer frequently to these *Three Requirements* — they're such helpful guidelines. Here they are again in capsule form:

First Requirement — Your baby falls asleep, nursing.
Second Requirement — Your baby sleeps 3½ to 4 hours following feedings. And, as soon as you have the day schedule established,
Third Requirement — Your baby's night's sleep slowly expands.

(Let me warn you not to be thrown off and think you have loads of breast milk just because your breasts leak or because milk dribbles down your baby's chin when it nurses. These things may happen whether or not you have an adequate supply of breast milk. They are not, in themselves, an indication of a good supply.)

7. *A good schedule — important alike for baby and parents*
To fully appreciate the importance of a schedule, I suggest you turn back to the section on *Training* (p. 51 and following).

As you can see, a good schedule is closely tied in with the *Three Requirements* and the two points to grasp here are:
a. As the first Two Requirements are met it becomes possible to start waking and feeding your baby at four-hour intervals for five daytime feedings.
b. By interrupting your baby's daytime sleep every four hours during the 16 hours you are awake, and by giving it all it wants to eat at five feedings, you achieve the Third

Requirement and any need to feed it during the night gradually comes to an end.

The average first schedule is:

```
    6:00 A.M. — Feed
         Sleep
    9:00 A.M. — Bathe
   10:00 A.M. — Feed
         Sleep
    2:00 P.M. — Feed
         Sleep
    6:00 P.M. — Feed
         Sleep
   10:00 P.M. — Feed
         Sleep
? ? 2:00 A.M. — Feed ? ?
```

See *Training* for possible variations in time and so on (p. 53).

8. Breast milk flows so easily that ten minutes on each breast enables a baby to get all it wants—if the milk is available.

   But suppose, after ten minutes on each breast, your baby doesn't become drowsy, doesn't seem satisfied, wants to go on sucking?

   I know you'll hear (on all sides) that sucking stimulates the breasts to produce. The fact is—as we have seen—that it's the *emptying* or *near-emptying* of breasts that does this. *Sucking* has nothing to do with it.

   Actually, *it is important that a baby should not be allowed to suck away on an empty breast* because:

   a. *The baby tires*—becomes too tired to take a supplemental feeding if offered.

   b. The baby will very likely *swallow a lot of air and may develop colic.*

   c. Prolonged sucking may *cause your nipples to crack.*

   So—stick to the ten-minute *maximum!* Don't let the baby go on sucking!

9. *Listen to the greatest living authority on your milk supply—your baby!*

Sooner or later you will catch on to the fact that, right from the start, your baby is talking to you — telling you things important to both of you — in the only way it can: by its behavior. Your baby will know more than anyone else, you included, about your supply of breast milk. If you have plenty, it will tell you so by meeting the first *Two Requirements* and enabling you slowly to work it onto a good schedule. If your supply is limited, again it will tell you so.

a. It may lose interest and stop nursing — short of ten minutes on each breast.

b. It may, if allowed, go on and on hopefully sucking long after ten minutes on each breast.

In either case, it won't begin to meet the second *Requirement,* and any sort of schedule to put an end to the "2:00 o'clock" is completely out of the question. Your baby will be saying to you as plainly as it possibly can: *"Mummy, you've run out of milk! And I'm still hungry!"*

10. *Don't hesitate to offer formula — you don't want your baby hungry!* Rest assured, your baby won't take formula if it doesn't want it. But it's important if the baby doesn't seem satisfied to offer it the opportunity to refuse or to take some formula, and to take all it wants, *after the breast-feeding.* Your baby won't overeat. (I understand horses sometimes eat till they almost burst — well, babies don't. When they've had all they want, they stop. You'll catch on to this in a hurry!)

I'm sure you'll be told that if you offer formula you'll cut down your chances of breast-feeding. In my experience the results can be just the opposite.

At this point what you need to build up your milk supply is:

a. To have your baby empty your breasts — to stimulate them to produce more.

b. To have your baby's hunger satisfied with breast milk plus formula, if necessary. Then it can have a good sleep.

c. To have the quiet and peace of mind that will enable you

to rest. How on earth can you possibly get the rest needed to build up a good milk supply if your baby is crying and you're upset! There's a lot of truth in what's said about "contented cows"!

By offering formula, whenever necessary, to satisfy your baby's hunger and by getting yourself rested you enable nature to build up your milk supply to its fullest extent—in other words, you greatly improve your chances of being able to breast-feed.

11. *Keep track of how much formula your baby takes*
    a. *It may take ½ oz., 1 oz. or nothing* after its breast-feedings. *Slowly it may stop taking any* and you'll know that it's getting all it wants from you—that it's satisfied—and that your milk supply has at last become established and you're off to a good breast-feeding start.
    b. *It may continue to take 1 oz. or ½ oz.* after each feeding. If so, I'd suggest giving a 6:00 P.M. bottle (see below). You may very well find that you have enough for four but not five good breast-feedings.
    c. *It may continue to take 2 oz. or 3 oz. after each feeding.* If so, once you are satisfied that you have given your breasts a fair chance to declare themselves, I suggest you think seriously of weaning. Half breast and half bottle isn't particularly satisfactory for mother or baby.

12. *The 6:00 P.M. bottle-feeding*
    I mention this because I have found it has a great deal to offer many breast-feeding mothers at different stages and for different reasons.
    If one could graph the average mother's milk supply, it would be found to be highest in the morning, after a good night's sleep. Over the course of the day it drops off to reach a low point in the evening—as a busy mother tires.
    A 6:00 P.M. bottle-feeding can help to kill an awful lot of birds:

a. It gives your baby a chance to take all it wants to eat at 6:00 o'clock and go to sleep, satisfied.

b. It means that you parents will have a quiet evening.

c. It gives your breasts a chance to fill up and provide your baby with a good big feeding at 10:00 P.M. — helping to ensure a night's sleep all around.

d. If you are questioning your milk supply, the amount your baby takes at this bottle-feeding offers an additional way of evaluating how much your baby is getting at its other feedings.

e. It gives you experience in giving a bottle.

f. It gives your baby experience in taking formula from a bottle.

g. It can give a father experience in giving a bottle and a dandy opportunity to get into the baby picture.

h. Finally, and by no means least important, it gives a mother a chance to call in a relative, friend or babysitter and talk her husband into taking her out for supper and the evening.

A 6:00 P.M. bottle-feeding has enabled many a mother to continue breast-feeding who might otherwise have had to give it up.

13. *Bubbling*
Because of the shape and texture of the breast, a baby on the breast, as long as there's plenty of milk available, swallows very little air, but it needs opportunities at each feeding to get rid of even that little bit. However,

a. When you give water in between feedings;

b. If you offer a supplemental bit of formula;

c. If you give a 6:00 P.M. bottle;

your baby, like all bottle-fed babies, will need more bubbling. (See 7. *The Technique of Bubbling*, under *Bottle-feeding*, p. 127.)

14. *Weaning*

The decision to wean, like the decision to breast-feed or bottle-feed, is an entirely personal matter. It should be left up to you mothers. If you have ample breast milk but wish, for any reason at all, to wean at two weeks, six weeks, or three, seven or ten months—anytime—you should feel free to do so. Your baby will do well in any case, and you can go on being just as good a mother whether you breast- or bottle-feed. If your supply of breast milk is limited but you want to continue to breast-feed and offer supplemental formula, this again is up to you. Just be sure your baby is given the opportunity to get all the food it wants.

When you consider weaning, however, two points should be borne in mind:

a. On the advice of the dental profession you should wean, at the latest, at around 10 months to a year (p. 144). *If you plan to wean much before this, be sure to wean to a bottle, not to a cup.*

b. It isn't so much *when* you wean as *how* you go about it that matters. *Go slowly*—weaning isn't like turning off a faucet! The length of time it takes to wean depends on your milk supply. Since this is not a definitely known entity, when you decide to wean be sure you're allowing yourself plenty of time. It's better to figure in terms of two weeks or ten days, and then find it takes only one week, than to allow yourself five days to wean—before going on a trip, or back to work—and then discover you should have allowed a week or ten days. You can't get into trouble going slowly, but if you go too fast you can develop a breast abscess—which could mean hospitalization.

Drop one breast-feeding at a time—the speed at which you proceed depends on the fullness of your breasts and on your comfort.

c. If you are giving five or six feedings a day, I suggest you drop the 6:00 P.M. feeding first (p. 112). Then, possibly, after a couple of days, depending on your comfort, the 10:00 A.M. feeding can be skipped. Thereafter proceed slowly, letting your breasts tell you *how soon* and *which* feedings to drop.

d. If you are giving four feedings a day, I'd suggest starting with one of the two middle feedings, in either order.

e. If you are giving three feedings a day, I'd suggest dropping the noon feeding first.

Just remember, don't try to hurry this procedure. If at any time your breasts are full and uncomfortable, be sure to nurse!

I've tried to fill you in on all the information fundamental to beginning breast-feeding that I can think of. There's a lot of it, I know, but as we apply it to the wide variety of breast-feeding experiences that mothers in general face over the first three or four weeks, I think you will find it begins to take shape and seems logical and reasonable.

Let's glance quickly at your first days and weeks at home so that you can see how some of the material we've covered applies, right from the start, and so that you can get a feel as to where it is heading. I'll be going over this again, in greater detail, in the first *Postnatal* chapter.

Your First Days and Weeks at Home

On the average, you mothers go home from the hospital on the fourth or fifth day. Your baby is just beginning to get hungry. Your breast milk is just beginning to be established — though for some this is a longer process than for others.

The first important thing is for you to get rested. Therefore, for the first three, four, or five days at home I suggest you *feed your baby on demand.*

> When it cries, feed it.
> When it sleeps, you get some rest.
> When it cries shortly after being fed, offer it sterile water
>   with a little sugar in it (p. 188).

This is a time when you fathers should, whenever you are able, get into the act. Offer help in any way you can and get accustomed to handling your baby. The point is that by getting as much rest as possible a mother *improves her chances of a good milk supply.*

The second important thing is to see to it that your baby gets all it wants to eat. If repeated breast-feedings and repeated offerings of sterile water seem not to satisfy your baby, don't hesitate to offer formula, after the breast-feeding.
Let me repeat—this does not cut down your chances of breast-feeding. In my experience, by giving you a chance to get rested (p. 111) it improves your chances.

The third important thing is to work your baby onto a schedule. Either by breast-feeding or by breast-feeding supplemented with formula,

> Your baby's appetite will be satisfied;
> You will be meeting the first two *Requirements;*
> You will be getting rested.

As soon as possible, therefore, start waking your baby at four-hour intervals for five daytime feedings.
Your aim over these first days and weeks at home— actually, the *"simple and single aim of all baby feeding"*—is to offer your baby all it wants to eat, and, following this, *to get your days*

ironed out—get feedings going smoothly just as soon as you possibly can.

Don't forget—while *you* may not always know how much breast milk you have, *your baby will know* and will tell you:

1. By the way it meets the first two *Requirements,*
2. By the way it settles onto a schedule and gradually meets the third *Requirement.*

At the same time, because it does happen, I should add that it is quite possible:

1. To *close your ears* to what your baby is telling you;
2. To *close your mind* to the *"simple and single aim of all baby feeding";*
3. To *submit to your emotions* and make a fetish out of breast-feeding.

As you can readily see, your breast-feeding experience over the first days and weeks can proceed in any one of a number of ways:

1. You may find that for you breast-feeding will be just "duck soup."
2. You may find that, with a 6:00 P.M. bottle-feeding assist, breast-feeding will go along very satisfactorily for your baby and for you.
3. You may find that breast-feeding is not for you and discover the equal pleasure and satisfaction of bottle-feeding.

However, by the end of three weeks, more or less, with the help of your baby, you should achieve the three *Requirements* and your baby will be contentedly settled onto a schedule that fits in with that of the rest of the family. (In the first *Postnatal* chapter I'll take up how to work your baby off the "2:00 o'clock.")

In any case you'll be giving your baby all he wants to eat and not dragging him, yourself and the rest of your family through that twilight of confusion, anxiety and sleeplessness that can develop if a mother insists on trying to continue feeding her baby from a meager supply of breast milk.

I'm always mindful of the challenge my obstetrician friend threw at me about the "gray zone." The surest way I know to stay clear of that is for the *two of you* to have *in advance* as much information about the mechanics of breast-feeding plus as clear an understanding as possible about the way nature, mothers and babies work. Then, when the time comes, you can help each other—back each other up—and, together, with some rather pointed suggestions from your baby, work things out.

Misinformation

Bits of *misinformation about breast-feeding* keep cropping up and I'd like to comment on some of them.

1. It's often said that the trouble with breast-feeding is that once you start you have to keep it up. It should be obvious by now that you can start weaning whenever you wish—it must just be done slowly (p. 114).
2. One sometimes hears that if a mother breast-feeds she won't become pregnant. This just isn't true. Even the mother with a full complement of breast milk runs at least a 10 per cent chance of becoming pregnant while breast-feeding. I assure you, there are other more reliable ways of preventing pregnancy.
3. One sometimes hears that the mother who breast-feeds is less likely to develop breast cancer than the mother who bottle-feeds. A recent international study by the World Health Organization (1970) does not bear this out. I quote from a summary of the study:

In the light of this and other recent evidence, it is unlikely that lactation has any protective effect against breast cancer in women, and other explanations must be sought for the remarkable international differences in the frequency of the disease.*

4. It's sometimes said that if a baby's sucking reflex isn't satisfied all sorts of dire things may happen. Well, let those who thought that one up walk the floor with their hungry, colicky babies! Just let me once again draw your attention to the fact that the babies of mothers who have plenty of milk suck for a comparatively short time before falling asleep, completely satisfied. These babies couldn't possibly be wakened for more sucking. Over a 24-hour period the amount these babies suck is minimal — yet nobody worries about these babies growing up to be monsters.

   As far as I can see, sucking is a practical method designed by nature to enable a baby to get its food until such time as it learns to use its hands and teeth for the purpose — thereafter, sucking can be limited to sodas, shakes and frappés.

5. You may hear a lot of talk about what you should or should not eat while breast-feeding. My advice is that you eat a perfectly normal diet. If you eat much in the way of *greens* or *chocolate* or *any one particular food* and the following day or days your baby has diarrhea, common sense will tell you to omit that particular food while breast-feeding. As usual, *your baby* gives you the message.

   Don't take a friend's advice about diet — all babies are different. Follow your obstetrician's instructions and remember to drink plenty of milk.

---

*MacMahon, B., et al.: Lactation and Cancer of the Breast. Bulletin WHO, *42*:185, 1970.

The Technique of Bottle-Feeding

I've spent a lot ot time over the technique of breast-feeding and, if it has seemed complicated, it may come as a surprise to learn that more often than not an expectant mother is told by her friends to "be sure to breast-feed—it's so much easier than bottle-feeding"—that "if you bottle-feed, you'll have a lot more trouble with your baby."

Well, as far as I can see, it doesn't make a bit of difference how you feed your baby—breast or bottle, it will do well. Either way, to make sure your feedings go smoothly, you should have, in advance, some knowledge of the mechanics of feeding, *breast and bottle,* plus an understanding of the way nature, mothers and babies work. In breast-feeding there may be uncertainty about the size of the milk supply but, on the other hand, the equipment—the human breast and nipple—is, mechanically, most efficient. In bottle-feeding it's quite the reverse: the milk supply is well within your control, but the equipment—the bottle and artificial nipple—leaves much to be desired. This makes the *mechanics* of bottle-feeding more of a challenge and increases the need for effective bubbling.

Those of you who plan to bottle-feed should appreciate that breast-feeding is an extremely efficient and felicitous system evolved by nature over countless centuries. Nature was anything but casual when among other things, she developed the multiple tiny nipple holes, to permit a free flow of milk, and a valve control to check the flow so that a baby, nursing, can pause to swallow or breathe without choking; when she positioned the breasts so that a baby, nursing, is held in its mother's arms; when she shaped and textured the breast to close over a baby's lips, cutting down on the amount of air swallowed. *To approximate such a system raises the technique of bottle-feeding to something approaching a fine art.*

The point I wish to drive home is that to bottle-feed properly *you mothers can't afford to be casual either.* You can't just jam a bottle of formula into a baby's mouth, call it bottle-feeding and expect things to go smoothly.

The "gray zone" is right there in the offing for the bottle-feeding mother — possibly even closer at hand than for the breast-feeding mother. Both mothers *may* fetch up there — but by different routes: the breast-feeding mother because she either *can't or won't believe her milk supply is inadequate*; the bottle-feeding mother because, while she has an unlimited milk supply, *her delivery system is faulty.*

What You Should Know Before You Bottle-Feed

Now let's consider how *you*, wanting to make a success of bottle-feeding, should proceed. By "success" I mean: mastering the technique of feeding from a bottle so that your baby, *easily*, gets all it wants to eat and settles comfortably into a schedule that takes all members of the family into consideration.

First, let's go into some of the things you should know about yourself, nature and your baby, and also some of the procedures you should be prepared to carry out in order to have bottle-feeding go as smoothly as possible.

1. *A place to feed*
   Before you go to the hospital set up a place to feed your baby when you come home. Feedings are of prime importance to a baby — don't treat them casually and just perch anywhere. Here are some suggestions:
   a. A comfortable chair (see *Breast-Feeding*, p. 107) — not necessarily your husband's favorite armchair.
   b. A quiet place — where your baby's feeding can be the focus of your attention.
   c. A subdued light for night feeding.
   d. A shelf or table beside the chair for a pan of hot water or a bottle warmer and for a jar containing a supply of sterile nipples.

If a mother is quiet, comfortable and relaxed, her baby will be relaxed and the chances of feedings going well are much better.

2. *Your approach to feeding*
   a. Keep your motions slow and unhurried. Babies don't like to be rushed. The mother who by nature is quick — moves rapidly — should make a point of trying to slow down. A baby wants to be held securely and confidently — to be moved slowly. I want to repeat what I said under *Breast-Feeding*:
   b. A baby responds to your wholehearted involvement in this matter of its mealtime. Feeding to a baby is an important business. This is a wonderful opportunity to talk quietly to your baby. It's a very poor time to discuss bargains with a girl friend, or to have a disagreement with your husband.
   c. After all I've said about nature I suppose it's unnecessary to make the point that being held in its mother's arms is, for a baby, an essential part of feeding. Also, I know that babies will drink cold milk, but it's well to reflect — nature provides milk at body temperature, not chilled.

3. I can't repeat too often: *by getting plenty of rest and being as free from worry as possible* a mother will be relaxed — this, in turn, means a relaxed baby and increases the likelihood of feedings going smoothly.

4. It is equally important to see to it that *the baby gets plenty of rest.* Babies tire easily — being handled, even nursing, tires a baby.

5. *How much should you offer your baby?*
   Offer your baby all it wants to eat — just as nature does a

baby on the breast. The baby on the breast nurses till it's satisfied — its mother has no idea how much it is taking. The amount a baby on the bottle takes can likewise be left entirely to nature and the baby.

If the baby takes all there is in the bottle at one feeding, be sure to put in more at the next feeding. Ideally speaking a baby should *always refuse a* little: then you can be sure it's had all it wants — in other words, then you know you're keeping the supply ahead of the demand.

6. *How best can you deliver food to your baby so it gets all it wants easily?*

    When you bottle-feed you should constantly bear in mind how a baby on the breast gets its milk — you'll be hard put to improve on nature's arrangements.

    a. *The holes in the nipple*

       The human nipple has 15 to 18 or more holes in it plus a valvelike control that opens as a baby sucks, so the baby on the breast gets its milk *very freely* and *easily* (p. 106). The artificial nipple comes with one, maybe two or three, tiny little holes in it — a baby really has to work to get anything through it.

       (1) Sucking milk through it is much like trying to suck a thick, ice cream milk shake through one very small straw. If you have two straws, or better yet one good big one, it's much easier.

       (2) Hold a new nipple up to the light and try to see through it. If light barely gets through the hole, how on earth do you expect milk to!

       So the first thing you should do is to enlarge a hole in the artificial nipple so the milk flows through it as freely as from the breast nipple — then your baby can get its milk without a struggle. (Remember — babies tire quickly!)

(3) To do this you will have to *burn* one or more additional holes in the artificial nipple with a red-hot needle. Just poking a needle through the nipple won't work—the hole has to be burned.

(4) Take a cork and stick the eye end of a needle in it. Use a small sewing needle, a #3 to #5.

(5) Next, have a source of heat—a gas burner or a candle. Most important: have the heat source, the cork-with-needle and the nipple close together.

(You can't have the heat source on one side of the kitchen and the nipple on a counter on the other side of the kitchen and expect the needle to stay red-hot while you go from one to the other.)

(6) Holding the cork-with-needle in one hand and the nipple in the other, heat the needle till it's red-hot and stick it quickly through the tip of the nipple. You should hear a pss't and smell burning rubber! No pss't + no smell = no hole burned! Do it again. Now hold up the nipple and look through it—you should easily see light! (If not—repeat the process.) (A little black collects on the needle as you heat it and may come off on the nipple—it's harmless and will eventually wash and wear off.)

Well and good! You're now beginning to approximate nature—you've got a nipple through which the milk flows freely. But the valve control in the breast nipple not only opens to permit milk to flow very freely as the baby sucks—just as importantly, as the baby stops sucking it closes to cut off the flow. The baby can then pause to swallow or breathe.

A baby, *lying* in its mother's arms, sucking through the freely flowing, artificial nipple you've just produced, won't be able to take time out to swallow, let alone breathe. The milk will flow so continuously the baby will almost surely choke! What can you do about this?

b. *The position of the baby when feeding*

Well, if you were lying down in bed or even if you were reclining and I offered you a glass of water — what would you do? You wouldn't attempt to drink from the glass lying down — or half-lying! You would reflexly sit up to drink it! And *sitting up* is the position your baby should be in to take a freely flowing nipple. You should position your baby on your lap, almost upright, tucked snugly against you in the crook of your arm.

(1) Then, holding the bottle almost horizontal, tilting it slightly, being sure always to keep the nipple full of milk, you'll find your baby will be able to suck its milk easily, without tiring, and you will with a bit of practice be able pretty effectively to control the flow. In this upright position a baby can swallow as easily as you do drinking from a glass. In this upright position a baby can handle a fairly fast nipple without choking.

(2) It takes a bit of experimenting to get the holes in nipples just right for your particular baby. Some babies can handle a faster nipple than others. As a rule, mothers tend to underestimate how fast a nipple their baby can take — better a little too fast than too slow. Remember, *the baby's position has as much to do with the speed of the flow as does the size of the hole in the nipple.*

(3) If you really think you've made the hole, or holes, in the nipple too big, don't throw the nipple away — set it aside. As your baby grows it will be able to take a faster nipple. Boiling tends to soften a nipple and to change the flow of milk through it. Your job is to keep the nipple flowing so that your baby continues to get its food easily.

Whenever a mother who was new at it would worry about the holes in the nipple being too big, I would recall with amusement a mother who came in to the office one afternoon, bringing her three-month-old baby—her fifth. After we'd gone over the baby, she had several little problems involving the older youngsters she wanted to discuss, and she asked if I'd mind her feeding the baby while we talked.

She took a nursing bottle of milk out of a bag, and a little jar containing a sterile nipple which she put on the bottle. Then, holding her baby upright on her lap, supporting it with one capable hand, she began feeding it and—oldtimer though I was—I was completely taken aback to see that she had snipped the end right off that nipple. It was just one big hole! I was about to utter a warning; then I said to myself, "Turtle, this girl knows more about feeding babies than you'll ever know," so I kept quiet and watched. Her baby sat there happy and relaxed as she slowly and methodically more or less poured the milk into it: gulp —— gulp, the mother allowed a pause for a breath, gulp —— gulp ——. The feeding was over in no time—no need to bubble.

I don't recommend this—I know the dentists wouldn't (p. 143). But it does serve to show that there's no need to worry too much about getting the holes in the nipples too big.

c. So, the holes in the nipple and the position of the baby when feeding are important in bottle-feeding. But nature, for the baby on the breast, has another bit of refinement which is very effective but not easy to copy.

A mother's breast, as I've pointed out, is shaped and textured to cover over the openings a baby may leave around and at the corners of its mouth as it sucks. The artificial nipple + nursing bottle has nothing comparable to offer, so, as a rule, the bottle-fed baby swallows much more air than the baby on the breast and has, therefore, to be bubbled far more frequently.

There are several reasons why it is important to get up the bubbles, to get up as much of the air a baby swallows as possible:
(1) To prevent colic. (I'll be taking this up after *Bubbling*.)
(2) Because, sometimes, when a baby brings up a big bubble, it brings up a good bit of its meal with it. Not only is this messy but it may leave the baby hungry.

(3) Because satisfaction of hunger is partly a matter of distention of the stomach. A baby nursing, especially a baby on the bottle, swallows milk and some air along with it. In due course, if the air isn't gotten up, the baby will have the sensation of a comfortably full stomach, be satisfied, stop nursing and fall asleep. Its stomach, however, is distended partly with milk and partly with air; and the air will either pass on out of the stomach into the intestinal tract or come up. In either case, the baby will almost surely wake up feeling short-changed and hungry long before time for the next feeding—and there goes your schedule!

Bubbling

The technique of bubbling—for breast- and bottle-feeding mothers
Bubbling is often referred to as "burping." I use the term "bubbling" simply because I feel it gives a better picture of what is going on.

a. All mothers have to learn how much their individual baby has to be bubbled. Babies feed in such different ways: some babies are neat feeders, some are sloppy, some are deliberate and some always seem to be ravenous. As a result, the amount of air swallowed and the amount of bubbling needed vary greatly.

b. *Position.* A baby, particularly a first baby, should be held up against its mother's chest to be bubbled. "Old hands," nurses in the hospital and others with long experience can sit the baby on a knee and bubble it; but a baby bubbles best when it is relaxed, and when you hold it firmly against your chest it feels safe and secure and, consequently, relaxes. Just as important, this position ensures a more or less straight passage from stomach to mouth, making it easier for air to come up.

Gentle patting on the baby's back may help dislodge the bubble and get it moving, but there's no need to pound the baby.

I should like to put in a kind word here for the

"bubble-cloth." It is impossible to predict *when* or *how* a bubble may come up. Establishing a routine habit of having a bubble-cloth over the shoulder helps preserve one's sweetness and cuts down on cleaner's bills.

c. *When to bubble.* A hungry baby, feeding vigorously at the beginning of a feeding, is apt to swallow a surprising amount of air—breast or bottle. So you should bubble *frequently, early* in the feeding.

(1) The *bottle-feeder* may find she has to bubble after the first ounce—maybe even the first half ounce. Again, after the second and possibly after the third ounce. Then, as the baby settles down to quiet feeding, she may be able to go on to the end of the feeding before bubbling again.

(2) The *breast-feeder* may find she has to bubble halfway through the first breast, then again as she shifts to the second breast, and not again till the end of the feeding.

(3) The baby, especially the hungry baby, may resent early bubbling—may protest at being taken from the nipple. You'll just have to gently but firmly carry out a procedure you know to be necessary. Your baby will catch on in time and learn to respect your firmness.

But each baby is different and each mother has to catch on to her baby's curves.

d. *The Trapped Bubble.* It isn't *how often* or *how long* you bubble that matters—it's *when* you bubble that counts. Mothers used to call and say, "I'm having a lot of trouble getting up the air—I seem to spend half the day bubbling!" This isn't necessary! If you're having trouble getting up the bubbles, either there isn't a bubble—which is a rare bird—or the bubble has been trapped.

What seems to happen is this: A hungry baby, at the beginning of a feeding, really goes at it, gobbles down the milk and inevitably some air along with it. If the baby is allowed to nurse too long before bringing up that air—

say the baby takes two ounces or so — the air may become trapped under a lot of milk. No amount of bubbling will get it up. Therefore, when a bubble fails to come up after a minute or two of bubbling:

e. *Try a Shift in Position.* Holding the baby gently but firmly, *slowly* lower it and lay it — on its back — across your lap. Let it lie there for one or two minutes. This shift in position apparently (more or less in accordance with the laws of physics) serves to dislodge the trapped bubbles of air, to bring them up on top of the milk, so that, as you again slowly raise your baby to a position against your chest, up comes the air!

I've done this with success too often myself and had too many mothers say "Thanks a lot for that 'shift in position' suggestion" not to believe there's merit in the method. Sometimes you may have to repeat the "shift in position" once, maybe twice, but, by and large, it works remarkably well. If, however, you have to resort to this frequently, for goodness' sakes, profit by it! Bubble earlier — don't let so much milk go down and trap the bubble!

f. One more suggestion: when the feeding and the bubbling is over, lay the baby on its stomach on a pad somewhere where it will be safe — your bed or the floor — while you get the crib ready. Then, before putting it down, give it a final bubbling. This often gets up that one last bit of air and saves soiling a nice clean crib.

g. *You'll know you're doing a good job of bubbling:*
   (1) If you're meeting the first two *Requirements* and slowly working your baby onto a good daytime schedule.
   (2) If your baby isn't spitting up much.
   (3) If your baby doesn't pass a lot of air by rectum. Some mothers refer to their baby as being "gassy." Air passed by rectum is primarily air you failed to get up.
   (4) If you have no problem with colic.

Colic

Here's a controversial subject and—turtle that I am—I'm going to stick my neck out and make a few pronouncements on the subject, based entirely on my experience in practice.

a. It's my belief that a baby has colic simply because that individual baby is not being fed properly and/or bubbled correctly.
b. I believe colic can be treated.
c. I believe colic can be prevented.
d. It is my belief that colic is the result of air a baby has swallowed during feeding which has not been gotten up. The air passes through the lower end of the stomach, through the pyloric valve and into the intestinal tract. At this point there is only one way it can get out. It has slowly to wind its way through the baby's 20 odd feet of intestine, stretching the intestine and causing pain and discomfort on the way, finally passing out the rectum. That this is what happens seems amply borne out, in my experience, both by the *symptoms* and *occurrence* of colic -and by the *treatment* and *prevention*.

Symptoms
a. A baby with colic rarely seems comfortable and relaxed. Even in sleep it squirms and is restless.
b. When awake the baby is constantly fretting or crying as if in pain.
c. It may draw up its knees as if experiencing sharp cramps.
d. When picked up, the baby usually doesn't stop crying for long.
e. It usually passes an excessive amount of air by rectum.

Occurrence

In my experience colic occurs:

a. Usually in first babies, far less frequently in second or third babies, and I don't think I've ever seen it in a fourth. Experience in handling and feeding seems to make a difference — to enter in here.

b. Much more commonly in bottle-fed than in breast-fed babies — a baby on the bottle as a rule swallows more air than a baby on the breast.

c. When it does occur in a breast-fed baby, usually the mother is found to have a rather limited supply of milk.

Treatment

Treatment for colic is to provide proper handling for the baby; that is: *get the mechanics of feeding going smoothly and the mother rested.*

a. This isn't easy for the mother. So often, when the colicky baby is brought to a doctor's attention, the mother is dog-tired and tense and, as a result, the baby is also. A vicious circle develops in which the feedings degenerate. With a little mild sedative to quiet and ease the baby, plus some help with the technique of feeding to educate the mother, the situation, *over a period of time,* can be corrected.

b. It's far quicker, however, to get in an "old hand," a grandmother, a nurse or an experienced friend who can get the feedings going smoothly and give the mother a chance to get rested.

c. In the past, when hospital rates weren't prohibitive, three or four days in the hospital, in experienced hands, got the baby back on the track and gave the mother a good chance to get rested at home.

Once rested, a mother can be helped to understand and get the mechanics of feeding her baby going smoothly. This brings us right back to what should have happened in the first place — to what is far better and easier than treatment — namely:

Prevention

a. Prevention of colic, as far as feeding is concerned, means *cutting down on the amount of air a baby swallows.*
   If you breast-feed — remember:
   (1) A baby tugging and sucking away on empty breasts swallows a lot of air.
   (2) So, be sure you have plenty of milk. How can you be sure?
   (3) If you have the first two Requirements you know you have enough breast milk.
   If you bottle-feed — remember:
   (1) A baby struggling to suck milk through too small holes swallows a lot of air in the process.
   (2) Have the nipple holes large enough so the baby gets its food easily.
   (3) Have the baby in an upright position so it can take a fast nipple.

b. Prevention of colic, as far as bubbling is concerned, means *getting up as much of the air your baby swallows as possible.*
   (1) Bubble early in the feeding — the hungry baby, feeding vigorously, swallows the most air.
   (2) Bubble your baby while holding it securely against your chest — then it will feel safe and be relaxed and the bubbles will come up more easily.
   (3) This position also provides a fairly straight passage from the stomach to the mouth, making it easier for the air to come up.
   (4) If you allow too much milk to go down and trap the bubble, try the "shift in position."

c. *Just as important as anything else to successful feeding—breast or bottle—and consequently to the prevention of colic:*
   (1) Feed in a quiet place where you can be comfortable and relaxed—then your baby will be relaxed and both feeding and bubbling will go better.
   (2) Keep as rested as you possibly can.

To my way of thinking, there is no necessity for a couple and their baby to have to go through the throes of colic.

Is Your Bottle-Fed Baby Getting All It Needs?

How can you be sure you have the mechanics of bottle-feeding going properly? How can you be sure your baby is getting all it wants to eat?

In breast-feeding, as we have seen, the three Requirements serve to show:
a. Whether or not you have plenty of breast milk, and as a result,
b. Whether or not your baby is getting all it wants to eat.

In bottle-feeding the three Requirements serve to show:
a. Whether or not you have the mechanics of feeding going properly, and as a result,
b. Whether or not your baby is getting all it wants to eat.

We've seen how the three Requirements clue you in in breast-feeding; now let's examine *how you can make use of them in bottle-feeding—how they can help.*

The Three Requirements of Bottle-Feeding

The First Requirement

While feeding, your baby becomes drowsy, very likely falls asleep in your arms, obviously completely satisfied. Even bubbling won't rouse it!

a. A baby sucking on a nipple with too small holes may become tired, worn out from sucking, refuse any more milk and fall asleep in your arms—exhausted, too tired to be roused even by bubbling!

b. A baby on the bottle, especially a baby sucking on a nipple with too small holes, swallows a fair amount of air. If you fail to get up that air, the baby may feel satisfied—temporarily—because of a stomach distended by a combination of milk and air. It also will become drowsy and refuse any more milk—its stomach feels full —and it may fall asleep in your arms. Bubbling won't rouse it, very likely.

c. A baby, sitting just about upright in your arms, sucking on a nipple with holes that permit the milk to flow freely, bubbled frequently early in the feeding and again at the end, will become drowsy, refuse more milk because it's had all it wants and fall asleep in your arms. Bubbling won't rouse it.

All three babies would seem, on the surface, to satisfy the first *Requirement.*

The Second Requirement

Most of the time, following feedings, your baby sleeps three and one-half to four hours — often has to be wakened for the next feeding.

a. The baby that falls asleep in your arms — tired from sucking against odds,

The baby that falls asleep in your arms — half full of air,

The baby that falls asleep in your arms — maybe from a combination of the two —

None of these babies get all they want at a feeding!

None of these babies will sleep three and one-half to four hours. They'll be awake and hungry after two hours, more or less. None of these babies can possibly satisfy the second *Requirement*.

b. Only the baby in example *c* above — only the baby that easily gets all it wants to eat at a feeding — will satisfy the second *Requirement*.

The Third Requirement

As soon as you establish a regular routine of five daytime feedings, the length of time your baby sleeps at night following the 10 o'clock gradually extends till, by the end of the third week home (on the average), the "2 o'clock" becomes a thing of the past.

Only when you have the mechanics of feeding going properly, only when your baby is getting all it wants at its feedings, will it satisfy the first two *Requirements*, and only then can you hope to achieve the third.

Schedule

A good schedule is important alike for baby and parents. To fully appreciate the importance of a schedule, I suggest you turn back to the section on *Training* (pp. 52–55).

As you can see, a good schedule is closely tied in with the three *Requirements* and the two points to grasp here are:

a. As the first two *Requirements* are met it becomes possible to start waking and feeding your baby at four-hour intervals for five daytime feedings.

b. By interrupting your baby's daytime sleep every four hours during the 16 hours you're awake, and by giving it all it wants to eat at five feedings, you achieve the third *Requirement* and any need to feed during the night comes to an end.

The average first schedule is:

<pre>
 6:00 A.M. — Feed
      Sleep
 9:00 A.M. — Bathe
10:00 A.M. — Feed
      Sleep
 2:00 P.M. — Feed
      Sleep
 6:00 P.M. — Feed
      Sleep
10:00 P.M. — Feed
      Sleep
? ? 2:00 A.M. — Feed ? ?
</pre>

See *Training* for possible variations in time and so on (p. 55).

Weaning

Weaning from a bottle presents very little in the way of a problem. Some mothers do it by simply dropping all bottle-feedings at once and offering milk from a cup. I used to suggest going at it a little more gradually — I think it's easier for the baby.

You can start anytime from around *ten months to a year of age,* as recommended by the dentists (p. 144). Plan to take maybe ten days to two weeks to do it. Skip one bottle at a time.

As a rule a baby doesn't, at first, take as much milk from a cup as from a bottle, and by discontinuing one bottle at a time a baby has a little more chance to adjust slowly to this new way of drinking its milk. In this way the drop-off in its milk intake will not be so abrupt.

Drop the noon bottle first, then, after several days, the morning bottle and again, after a few more days, the evening bottle. The speed at which you go ahead depends entirely upon how readily your baby settles into taking its milk from a cup. Just be sure to have your baby off the bottle at pretty close to a year of age.

If, after your baby is weaned, its milk intake drops below a pint of milk a day, there are other ways of introducing milk into its diet (pp. 254–255).

Just as in breast-feeding I've tried to fill you in on all the information fundamental to bottle-feeding that I can think of. Again, there's a lot of it, I know, but once you grasp the underlying principle—the importance of following as closely as possible the way nature feeds a baby on the breast and makes sure it easily gets all it wants—it narrows down to four very simple points:

1. The size of the holes in the nipple;
2. The position of the baby when feeding;
3. The importance of getting up all the bubbles;
4. Your slow and relaxed handling.

Let's now take a quick look at your first days and weeks at home so that I may give you an idea of how this information will shake down and become practically applicable. I'll be going into this in more detail in the first *Postnatal* chapter—this just serves as a quickie preview.

The Formula. The doctor in the hospital or your own doctor will give you a formula. These days formulas—mother's milk substitutes—are very satisfactory and easy to prepare. If feedings don't go smoothly at once, don't start by blaming the formula. Your problems will almost surely have more to do with something outside the bottle—your mechanics of feeding—than with what's inside the bottle.

Your First Days and Weeks at Home

When you go home from the hospital make a point of getting all the rest you possibly can. Your baby will likely go home on a schedule of sorts, but your first days may be a bit shaky as you get things set up and organized. Getting the mechanics of feeding going properly takes some catching on—the holes in the nipples, the position of the baby, the speed of the flow of milk, the bubbling, your handling in general.

For the first few days, therefore, feel free to feed on demand.
> When your baby cries—feed it.
> When your baby sleeps—you rest.

This is a good time for a father to help out in any way he can: with the housework, by all means; but over and beyond this, to involve himself in the care and handling of his baby. Fathers are very good at burning holes in nipples, at changing a baby; moreover, they do surprisingly well at feeding a baby—babies respond very happily to their father's firm grasp and larger, stronger hands.

Your baby will be telling you:
> 1. How your mechanics of feeding are progressing,
> 2. How completely its appetite is being satisfied,
> 3. How comfortable it is,

by the way it begins to meet the first two *Requirements.*

After a few days, as soon as you're beginning to feel

rested, start waking the baby at four-hour intervals for its five daytime feedings. I predict you'll be surprised at how soon you will have feedings going smoothly and on schedule, at how soon your baby will be ready to have you start getting it off the "2 o'clock." (I'll be taking this up in the first *Postnatal* chapter.)

This all may sound relatively simple and straightforward. It should be and it will be if I have managed to get across to you — here, *well in advance* — the importance of having those holes in the nipples large enough and of having your baby positioned sufficiently upright to enable him to get his milk easily.

If I seem to have labored these points unduly, it's because it wasn't always that simple and obvious when I was in practice. In those days I sometimes wouldn't be called to see a new mother and baby until they were home from the hospital. Even if I did see the mother in the hospital the visit was of necessity short, too short to be very helpful. Once a mother has gone home with her baby and become emotionally involved in its care and feedings don't go at all smoothly, things take on a different, an almost threatening, aspect. At this point it's not easy for a mother to accept new ideas about bottle-feeding, let alone the theory behind them. I would go over the same points with a mother, morning after morning at "call hour" and finally, if things weren't straightening out, I'd drop by her home or ask her to come into the office at feeding time — baby, bottle of formula and all. Almost invariably the upshot was: miserable holes in the nipple! I'd have to give the bottle a good shake to get anything out of it. And I can still hear the mother protesting, "But, I've tried it! If the holes are any bigger my baby chokes!"

So, then and there we'd have a practice session in how to position a baby so it can take a fast nipple — we might even go so far as to burn an adequate hole or two. I can still see the pleased look of surprise and relief on the mother's face, when, tucked up close against her, in the proper position, her baby, with no trouble at all, without choking, would take big, satisfying swallows of formula.

To top things off, we might practice a good bubbling position plus the "change in position" should a bubble prove stubborn.

The obvious point I wish to make is that the two of you — taking all this in *together* and *ahead of time* — should be able to do better. When the time comes, you can assist and appraise each other's feeding technique — and your baby will be right there adding its comments. To bottle-feed properly you have to understand and appreciate what nature has been at pains to work out to make breast-feeding go smoothly — and then endeavor to imitate her as well as you can — doing your level best to see to it that your baby has the opportunity to *easily* get all it wants.

I think you can see how inevitably the mother who fails to understand the significance of these points — and who fails to put them into operation — can end up with a hungry, unhappy baby in spite of having a limitless supply of formula right at hand. I think you can see how a bottle-feeding mother can find her way into my obstetrician friend's "gray zone."

Misinformation

Most of the comments and advice against bottle-feeding that may come your way I believe I've already dealt with:

1. A baby on the bottle should do just as well as a baby on the breast.
2. The mother who decides to bottle-feed is just as good a mother as the mother who breast-feeds.
3. Colic should not be more of a problem for the bottle-feeding than for the breast-feeding mother.

You may hear that breast-feeding provides a baby with more immunity than bottle-feeding. I can only say that it hasn't been my experience that bottle-fed babies have any more infections than breast-fed babies.

You'll more than likely be told that you'll have trouble finding a formula that will agree with your baby. I've already pointed out that your early feeding problems will have more to do with your mechanics of feeding than with what's inside the bottle. However, the question of sensitivity, while extremely rare, should always be in the back of your mind, and if your difficulties continue, you should consult your clinic or doctor.

As I bring this lengthy section on *Feeding* to a close, there are two or three things upon which I'd like to comment.

Feeding in General over the First Year

Let's look briefly ahead so that I can give you an idea of where feeding over the first year is heading once you have mastered the early techniques.

First, you should know that *milk, either from the breast or bottle, is the backbone of a baby's diet.* Breast milk or "cow's milk with a sugar additive" provides all the protein, calcium and carbohydrates a baby needs for the first several months. I used to find that mothers as a rule failed to think of milk as food. To them it was something to drink as an accompaniment to a meal. But for a baby, breast milk or breast milk substitute is a *complete food.* (I'll be taking up vitamins, fluoride and iron as we go along.) I know perfectly well there are other approaches to feeding — to satisfying a baby's appetite — than the ones I offer in this book. I know that when a baby on the breast isn't sleeping well following feedings, cries a lot, has to be fed frequently there are those who suggest starting the baby on soft solids: cereals, soups, fruits. To me this is a possible but very questionable solution. When your baby doesn't seem to be satisfied by the amount of breast milk you have to offer, don't make the mistake of offering soft solids at two or three weeks of age. *Don't kid yourselves that this isn't supplementing!* Face up to the fact that your breast milk may be in short supply and supplement with *milk* from another source—cow's milk modified to approximate mother's milk—thus sticking as closely as possible to the kind of food nature has seen fit to provide for babies: *milk*.

Sometimes, when a baby on the bottle isn't taking enough formula to satisfy its hunger, again there are those who suggest, as early as two or three weeks, starting the baby on soft-solid food: cereals, soups, fruits. Once more, to me this is a questionable way of feeding a baby. It completely overlooks the fact that milk is a baby's primary food. So before you resort to supplementing with soft solids, check out your milk delivery system: open up the holes in the nipples, position your baby so that it can easily get all the milk it wants, bubble it—and stick as closely as possible to nature's way of feeding a baby. In other words, see to it that over the first few months your baby gets all the milk it wants—breast or bottle.

However, the time will come when, to satisfy adequately its growing needs and consequently its appetite, your baby will need more than just milk in its diet. If, past five or six months of age, a baby is allowed to continue to satisfy its appetite with milk alone—which occasionally a baby is quite content to do, sometimes pushing up its milk consumption to a quart-and-a-half or two quarts a day—that baby could develop a "milk anemia." For a baby past five or six months, milk no longer supplies all the nourishment needed—iron, for instance.

Therefore, as I pointed out in *Training* (p. 56), at about two and one-half to three months you should start offering your baby a little cereal and fruit. But don't be in a rush about this! You will be doing this *purely for educational reasons*—just to get your baby used to a spoon and to the knack of handling a different kind of food in a different manner. Start this educational process slowly so that at around 4, 5 or 6 months, when your baby begins to need more than just milk in its diet, it will be all ready for this new step.

In the same spirit, at whatever time your baby is ready for three meals — at, say, about four to five months — I suggest that you start offering a little straight fruit juice from a cup. Again, don't push this. *This is for educational reasons* — simply to begin to accustom your baby to taking its liquids in this new manner. Then, when the time comes to start weaning your baby from the breast or bottle, at around ten months of age, as recommended by the dentists, your baby will be all set to start drinking its milk from a cup.

The Sucking Mechanism

This recommendation by the dentists is based on the fact that *nature has specifically designed an infant to get its food by sucking on a nipple. "The mechanism for suckle at this age, however, is distinctly an infantile characteristic* distinguished from a related learned act of sucking in the older child."* The mouth — the oral cavity — of an infant is narrowed by pads of fat in its cheeks, the tongue is comparatively large and positioned so that its tip can effectively indent the nipple against the hard palate above, and suction is established by related action of the body of the tongue and the jaw. This oversimplified description only begins to hint at the varied complexities of the infantile sucking mechanism. The point is that the mechanism is there, and it is intended to be used to obtain nourishment. Babies in early infancy are carefully structured by nature to obtain their food by sucking on a nipple. Moreover, dentists see this structure of the mouth and its proper use as basic to the development of jaws and teeth.

---

*Lis, Edward F., in Biologic Basis of Pediatric Practice, edited by R. E. Coke. McGraw-Hill Book Company, New York, 1968.

However, babies grow and change. The infantile sucking mechanism is slowly modified, physiologic controls develop, working teeth erupt, one by one. In other words, nature gradually *re*structures babies to enable them to obtain their nourishment, no longer by sucking on a nipple but by the integrated action of lips, tongue, cheeks, teeth and jaws which enables them to deal with increasingly coarser foods and to drink their milk from a cup.

Once again dentists see this restructuring of the mouth and its proper use as basic to the continued development of jaws and teeth. In their view babies should be sucking on a nipple — breast or bottle — while the infantile sucking mechanism is in working order, that is, till around ten months of age. Babies should then, over the next few months, be weaned so that by the time they are around a year of age and the new eating mechanism is in operation they will be completely off all nipples.

It is the considered judgment of dentists working in the dental clinic of Children's Hospital Medical Center in Boston that a program of infant feeding that follows the obvious dictates of nature best promotes normal dentition. This, in their view, is good preventive dental medicine.

What all this boils down to is that nature has been at this baby feeding business since long before pediatricians or the medical profession in general were even thought of. To me it seems reasonable to respect and make use of her long experience.

I suggest, therefore, that over the better part of the first year you see to it that plenty of breast milk or breast milk substitute is readily available to your baby. That you feed your baby as nature intended it to be fed — held in your arms, sucking its milk through a nipple, breast or bottle. That you take your time about pushing your baby's acquaintance with spoon and cup. Introduce them gradually to your baby so as to make the transition to dealing with solid food, to taking liquids other than by sucking, as easy as possible.

Variations in the Three Requirements

The three *Requirements* are immensely valuable to you whether you are breast- or bottle-feeding. They are too useful not to take the time to point out that, like any other guide to human behavior, they are subject to variations.

The First Requirement holds remarkably true for most babies for about the first six weeks.

The Second Requirement is subject to more variations.
1. There are times when a baby may be uncomfortable — too hot or too cold — have a bowel movement that may waken it, be startled, wakened by a loud noise, have a leftover bubble and so on. Usually, as soon as the problem is corrected, the baby goes back to sleep.
2. Until they are around six weeks old, very few babies lie awake — with their eyes open — without crying. Most babies are apt to have an unexplained crying spell at some point in the day. When this happens check out any possible cause, offer sterile water, comfort and reassurance. If the crying continues, don't hesitate to get organized and push the next feeding up a bit.

The fact remains that until they are around six to eight weeks of age, as long as they are getting all they want to eat, most of the time babies sleep contentedly for three and one-half to four hours between feedings.

The Third Requirement. The baby that is getting all it wants to eat, once the schedule is going smoothly, proceeds pretty routinely. It should be off the "2 o'clock" anywhere from the end of the second to the end of the fourth week home.

"Gray Zone" (Concluded)

By way of final reply to my obstetrician friend I would like to suggest that the "gray zone" is nothing more than trying to live in the same house with a new baby who's always a little, sometimes more than a little, on the hungry side.

I've made the point, again and again, that when a mother goes home from the hospital two things are of utmost importance:

1. That she gets rested;
2. That her baby gets all it wants to eat.

These two things are completely dependent, one on the other; but they can and should be worked out over the first week or so. However, if they aren't worked out, this is so often when the "gray zone" begins to close in.

For instance:

Here's a mother who wants to breast-feed. She "knows" she has plenty of milk, but for some reason her baby sleeps only fitfully, wakens frequently and cries. She nurses it repeatedly, knowing this will help to further build up her milk supply. But, in spite of giving it all it seems to want (and there is no need questioning her milk supply—she knows she has plenty), her baby cries an awful lot of the time.

Now, here's a mother who wants to bottle-feed. She offers her baby a good bottle at every feeding. But it takes just a little and goes to sleep only to waken after an hour or two, obviously hungry. She feeds it again. Again it takes only a little before losing interest and dozing off. It spits up frequently—sometimes almost as much as it's taken. It's awake and crying the better part of the day.

Both these mothers are doing their level best—continually, as they think, offering their babies all they want to eat. They're forever feeding them! Still their babies are awake and crying most of the day. These mothers are anxious and upset. They have little chance for a decent rest. They're becoming more and more tired. They are slowly drifting into the "gray zone."

Their husbands come home at night to find them discouraged and pretty near bushed. There's been *no* time to do housework—the washing is piling up, the kitchen is full of dirty dishes, the whole place is cluttered. They've spent the greater part of the day feeding and tending the baby.

The fathers help out as best they can, but meals are sketchy and the baby has one or the other or both of them up half the night. The fathers leave for work in the morning, a bit the worse for wear, often unfed—glad to get out but a little guilty at feeling so. They are puzzled at why their wives are having so much trouble and hoping that this day things will go better.

But the days and nights go on pretty much the same, hectically, exhaustingly, sometimes right up to the time the mothers go for their post-delivery check-up, and my obstetrician friend sees them: worn out, pale, discouraged. This sort of thing can keep up quite a time—babies are remarkably tough; mothers are young and durable. *But the fabric of the home undergoes considerable strain. This is the gray zone.*

The duration of and the degree of involvement in the "gray zone" vary. Slowly, in one way or another, things work out. Mothers, babies, fathers survive. Mothers work their way through it and plough ahead with scarce a backward glance. Only an occasional mother would say, "I've had it! Here's my family! I'll never go through that again!"

But it leaves its mark. It's surprising the number of grandmothers and grandfathers who say, "Oh, those dreadful first weeks! Those awful nights with our first baby! I'll never forget them." One seasoned grandmother remarked grimly, "A girl hasn't lived till she's gone through those first weeks."

Tommyrot!

What an utter waste of time, energy and brains! There's no need to have your family life turned topsy-turvy in this way! So many other, more important responsibilities are lined up, ready to bear down on you parents that you can't afford to spend all this time over early feeding!

I don't mean for one minute to suggest that all or most mothers go through the "gray zone." There are any number of mothers and grandmothers who wouldn't know what I am talking about here: the mothers who from the start work out a good bottle-feeding technique; the mothers who have plenty of breast milk or who, if they don't, make sure their babies have all they want to eat; these mothers don't become befogged. But an unfortunate number of mothers do, as my obstetrician friend has pointed out.

I refuse, however, to believe that the "gray zone" is necessary for any mother—that it "has to be lived through." In this chapter on *The Technique of Feeding* I've explained the importance of and how to go about getting rested and giving your baby all it wants to eat. I've offered you workable guidelines:

1. The *first two Requirements*—to enable you to tell whether or not your baby is getting all it wants to eat.
2. The *schedule*—to make your days go smoothly.
3. The third *Requirement*—putting an end to the "2 o'clock" so that, before long, nights will be a time of sleep for the entire family.

I've suggested you listen to and respect what your baby has to tell you about your supply of breast milk and the progress of your mechanics of bottle-feeding and bubbling.

I've stressed the importance for the whole family, baby included, of getting your household back to normal as soon as possible. I'll be going over more or less this same ground in the first *Postnatal* chapter.

I've done what I can to meet my obstetrician friend's challenge—"Why haven't you pediatricians been doing something about this?"

I've done my best to show you that the "gray zone" should and can be prevented.

Baby's crying?
Baby's talking.
Daddy, stop your floor walking.
Mummy, dry your eyes and listen.
Baby's stating his position:
"Gee, I'm hungry! I've got bubbles!
Small-holed nipple's causing troubles!
Do you have to be so breezy?
Mummy, dear, please take it easy!
If you'd keep my schedule right
By day—I'd sleep all through the night."

LPT

Mother and Child by Mary Cassatt. (Courtesy of The Brooklyn Museum. Carl H. De Silver Fund.)

Chapter Three

Specific
Problems
in
Care
and
Handling

3 — Specific Problems in Care and Handling

Fluoride and Vitamins

Babies need vitamins and fluoride in addition to food and sleep. Let me point out, however, that in this matter there are so many variables that here is a place you parents are going to have to assume a good deal of responsibility. Let's consider fluoride first.

Fluoride

Research and controlled experimentation over 25 years and more have convinced the dental profession in this country and abroad of the effectiveness of fluoride, administered from infancy through childhood, in reducing the incidence of dental caries — that is, cavities — in children's teeth by anywhere from 50 to 70 per cent or more.

Dentists and nutritionists at the Harvard Dental School recommend that all babies and children receive fluoride from some source from the time they are around three weeks of age until they are at least 12 to 14 years of age. They further recommend that, whether or not fluoride is present in the drinking water supply, babies receive *supplemental fluoride from about three weeks to age one-and-a-half years* ". . . since the most important effect of fluoridation appears to be upon the formation of tooth structure before teeth erupt into the mouth. . . ."*
Fluoridation is a relatively new and controversial subject. However, it is my advice that you accept the judgment of the dental profession and see to it to the best of your ability that your child's teeth get this protection.

***

*Dunning, James M.: Current Status of Fluoridation. New Eng. J. Med., January 7 and 14, 1965.

Even though fluoride is present in the drinking water supplies,

1. Breast milk does not contain fluoride in anything approaching the necessary concentration to benefit a baby.*
2. Babies, up to around a year-and-a-half of age, drink very little water—nowhere near enough to protect their developing teeth.
3. The amount of water used in formula preparation is insufficient to offer adequate protection.

Therefore, from three weeks to one-and-a-half years, all babies should receive supplemental fluoride. This can be achieved by giving fluoride drops or by giving fluoride in combination with an infant vitamin preparation. Your doctor or clinic will advise you on what preparation to use and the dosage.

Now let's consider vitamins over this same period—that is, till your baby is about one-and-a-half years old.

Vitamins

Fortunately the importance of vitamins is now generally accepted. But because here the variables begin to pile up, several points should be made clear so there will be no chance of your slipping up in this matter of your baby's vitamins.

The variables lie in the fact that:

1. Some formulas contain vitamins—some do not.
2. Breast milk contains vitamins, though its vitamin C content may be very low.
3. Whole milk contains no vitamins, unless vitamin D has been added—which only throws in another unnecessary variable.

---

*Adler, P., et al.: Fluorides and Health, pp. 104, 145, 214. World Health Organization, Geneva, 1970.

Now, how to make this as easy for you as possible?

The simplest, safest, surest way to see to it that your baby gets what it needs in the way of vitamins and fluoride is to start at three weeks to give your baby daily an infant preparation of vitamins A, C and D with fluoride and to continue this practice up to around one-and-a-half years. I say this so emphatically because I have found that:

1. The mother who accustoms herself *early* to giving vitamins with fluoride at a *routine time* is less apt to forget, less apt to be casual — and *this is important!*
2. *The baby who becomes accustomed at about three weeks to taking a vitamin-fluoride preparation continues taking it without any fuss as long as it is given.* Some babies who first start taking it at three or four months or older don't like the taste and refuse to take it — a mother may have to try several preparations before finding one her baby will take.

Now — What to Give?

1. *If you breast-feed,* you obviously don't have to give supplemental vitamins but you should give fluoride drops daily starting at about age three weeks.
   a. You should take care either to *maintain your own vitamin C intake* by daily drinking fruit or vegetable juice containing vitamin C or you should daily give your baby dilute fruit juice, either orange juice (a citrus fruit) or a fruit juice you know to be fortified with vitamin C. Start at three weeks to give it 1 oz. fruit juice mixed with 1 oz. cool sterile water and slowly build up to 2 oz. fruit juice mixed with 1 oz. cool sterile water by around age six weeks.
   b. If you wean to a formula which *contains vitamins, continue to give fluoride drops daily.*
      If you wean to a formula which *does not contain vitamins* (which makes a lot more sense), *stop the fluoride drops and give daily an infant preparation of vitamins with fluoride.*
   c. *When you wean to whole milk be sure to give an infant prepara-*

tion of vitamins with fluoride and continue to age one-and-a-half years.

I used to find that many mothers felt that as long as they had to give fluoride drops every day, plus maybe fruit juice, it was a lot easier to start at three weeks giving an infant preparation of vitamins with fluoride and to keep it up to age one-and-a-half years. In this case the baby, over the first few months, gets a little more vitamins than absolutely necessary, but this will do the baby no harm. It does, however, add a little to the expense.

2. *If you bottle-feed:*
   a. I advise that you ask your doctor in the hospital to put your baby on a formula *without* vitamins. *Then you can start at three weeks giving daily an infant preparation of vitamins with fluoride and continue to around age one-and-a-half.*
   b. If your baby is put on a *formula containing vitamins, be sure to start fluoride drops at around three weeks of age.* When you shift your baby to whole milk be sure also to shift to an infant preparation of vitamins with fluoride and continue to give daily to around age one-and-a-half.
   c. In either case *a* or *b*, above, should you at any time change formula be sure you know *whether or not* it contains vitamins and act accordingly.

When to Give

I suggest you get in the habit of giving the infant preparation of vitamins with fluoride or the fluoride drops at a routine time every day — say, before the bath. You mothers are busy and unless you establish this as a daily habit it is so easy to forget! Mothers used to come into the office and say, "I forgot all about the vitamins for two whole weeks! Will it do any harm?" Well, it won't do any harm for short periods, but, let's face it, the easiest and safest way to reduce this possibility is to set up a routine time — then it becomes second nature.

How Much to Give

1. *Vitamins with fluoride* come in a little bottle with a dropper and two marks on the dropper.

   At three weeks give up to the first mark (equivalent of 5 drops), daily.

   At a month give up to the second mark (equivalent of 10 drops), daily.

2. *Fluoride drops* should be given as directed by your doctor or clinic.

How to Give

1. *Vitamins with fluoride.* Sit your baby up straight on your lap and squirt the liquid from the dropper directly into the side of the baby's mouth.

   a. *Sitting up,* there is no chance your baby will choke and get the drops into his lungs.

   b. *By squirting directly into his mouth, you're sure the baby gets the proper amount.* If you put the drops in a bottle of formula or juice, some may adhere to the sides of the bottle and the baby won't get it all. Also, it so frequently happens that that will be the one bottle in the day the baby doesn't finish!

2. *Fluoride drops* should be given as directed by your doctor or clinic.

Fluoride and Vitamins from Age One-and-a-half On

1. *If the drinking water supply contains fluoride* (in proportions anywhere from 0.6 to 1.0 part per million), the dentists think that a child will receive the necessary amount from drinking the water and having food cooked in it, so there is no further necessity to give supplemental fluoride.

   Your child will, however, continue to need vitamins until at least three or four years of age. You may now, at a year-and-a-half, find it easier to shift to a chewable vitamin—though it's perfectly all right to continue giving vitamin drops without the fluoride if you prefer.

2. *If the drinking water supply contains no fluoride* (or contains fluoride in proportions less than 0.6 part per million), the dentists think that a child should continue to receive it in some form:

   a. As long as you continue to give vitamins, the easiest way to give the fluoride is in combination with the vitamins — either in chewable or in drop form.

   b. Whenever after age three or four years you discontinue vitamins, you should, on the basis of what the dentists tell us, continue to give supplemental fluoride until the child is at least 12 years old.

> There is no question about the effectiveness of supplemental fluorides. If they are not available in the community water supplies, then one of the many approved compounds commercially available should be prescribed. There is no convincing evidence that approved sources of these compounds have unacceptable effects on *any* child. They should be prescribed by the pediatrician in the first six months of life and continued through the years of dental development until at least age 12. Fluoride compounds in dentifrices, topical application by the dentist and supplemental dietary intake are all useful, and all three may be received simultaneously by the child.*

Of these, at present the most effective is supplemental dietary intake of fluoride drops, solutions or tablets. However, I've been dealing with couples just like you over the years and I realize that seeing to it that your child continues up to 12 years of age to get fluoride in his diet takes time, energy and determined effort on your part.

I only hope that your generation will do far better about backing fluoridation of public water supplies than my generation has done — that if you live in an area where fluoridation of the community water supplies is not possible, you

---

*Losch, Paul K., and Swanson, Lennard T., in Cooke, Robert E. (Ed.): The Biologic Basis of Pediatric Practice. Vol. I. New York, McGraw-Hill Book Company, 1968.

will press you local Board of Health or the United States Health Service for programs of school water fluoridation or the development of a reliable home water fluoridating device. Some practical way should be worked out to make the dental benefits of fluoride available to all youngsters.

Odds and Ends

In this section I shall attempt to answer, in advance, questions that will inevitably arise in the course of your baby's first year. I say this with assurance because these are the questions I have been asked repeatedly by parents, over the years. These are questions relating primarily to the physical care of a baby, and, as usual, the best treatment for the various problems results from foreknowledge — from anticipating the problem and preventing it.

In thinking back, I am struck by the fact that for every question of this nature that arose in the course of an afternoon of office appointments, there would be six to ten questions involving behavior or feeding — questions harder to answer and more difficult for parents to deal with.

Circumcision

Almost the first question you will be asked when you go to the hospital to have your baby will be: "Do you plan to breast- or bottle-feed?" The second question will be: "If it's a boy, do you wish it to be circumcised or not?" Some of the points to bear in mind are:

1. If the baby is to be circumcised, the *easiest time for the baby* is to have it done before the baby leaves the hospital.
2. If the baby has an *abnormally long foreskin*, the doctors

will advise you to have it done then and there, and I think it should be.

3. If either parent has any feeling whatsoever in the matter, that feeling should be respected.
4. In my judgment, for the average baby with the average foreskin, it really makes no difference.

The important thing, whether or not the baby is circumcised, is that parents understand that the baby's penis requires a certain amount of care.

Circumcised

When you first see the baby's penis you may be upset at how red and sore it appears. Don't worry about this! The baby is bothered very little.

You can promote healing by having a supply of 3-inch squares of soft cotton material, torn from an old sheet or pillow case, on which you can put a little Vaseline, and which you can then put over the end of the penis to protect it from the rougher material of the diaper. Do this for about a week to ten days or until the condition clears up.

Something to watch for, when the boy is about five or six months of age, is an ulceration, a sore, at the opening of the penis. Up to this time the baby's diet is primarily fluid but as solid food is added the baby's fluid intake begins to drop off, and the baby's urine becomes more concentrated. The high ammonia content of the urine plus constant rubbing on the diaper can be highly irritating.

Over the opening of the penis a scab may form which is broken every time the baby voids. On voiding, the baby may cry out. Voiding may be painful and you may see a few drops of blood at the end of the penis or on the diaper.

The end of the world hasn't come—this is just something to be on your toes about. To treat it, go back to the little squares of soft cotton material with Vaseline and again protect the end of the penis from harsh treatment.

You may have to repeat this procedure, off and on, until the boy is trained.

Uncircumcised

As you tend your baby boy you will notice that the opening at the end of the foreskin is small.

At the time of your boy's routine check-ups, the doctor will slowly push back and stretch the foreskin. When a boy is born the foreskin is lightly attached to the end, the glans of the penis. Each time the doctor pushes back the foreskin, he will break some of this attachment, some of these normal adhesions. He will show you how to put Vaseline under the foreskin to prevent these adhesions from re-forming.

By the time the boy is six months old, the foreskin should be completely stretched and all the adhesions broken, so you will be able to wash under the foreskin at every bathtime as easily as you wash every other part of the baby's body. Done early in this way, the stretching of the foreskin and breaking of the adhesions bothers the baby very little.

Remember, doctors are busy, so at each check-up be sure to ask if the foreskin is all right.

Rashes

Mothers take great pride in keeping their babies' skin clear! By and large, rashes bother mothers far more than they bother the babies!

Rashes vary greatly from child to child, depending on how sensitive the skin is.

Dry Skin. Of course a tendency to dry skin may be inherited. Remember, however, before a baby is born it lies inside its mother, soaked in fluid. As the baby dries out, it is reasonable to expect its skin to dry out also.

When you get home from the hospital, until the cord drops off and the navel is dry (see p. 214), give your baby a soap-and-water sponge bath, and thereafter a regular soap-and-water tub bath each day—nothing is as cleansing as soap and water. *After* the baths, if the baby's skin is dry, put on baby oil.

If the condition continues, you may have to use a super-fatted soap as well as the oil, for a time.

If the condition persists, ask your doctor about it at check-up time.

Cheek Rash. *Babies really insult their cheeks!* They spit up and may sleep in the mess. They suck their fists or fingers and draw saliva across their cheeks. When they feel their teeth, they drool and often sleep in a puddle of saliva. Two things help:

1. Have a folded piece of cloth—a diaper or a piece of torn sheeting—stretched tightly across the bed, directly under the baby's head. This may be *shifted, refolded* or *changed* frequently, to provide a clean, *dry* place for the baby's head to rest upon, without the need to change the entire bed. As I suggest in *Equipment* (p. 184), you will find such a "headpiece" extremely useful.

2. Keep your baby's cheeks *clean* with soap and water. You may be told not to do this, but in my experience by using soap and water you'll be pleased at how free from rash your baby's cheeks will be.

Diaper Rash. Babies are rough on their skin! A diaper rash that has been allowed to go on, unchecked, is a red, raw, sore-looking affair! Your aim should be to *prevent* diaper rash.

Don't buy a lot of ointments and then blame the ointments because the diaper rash doesn't clear up!

Use soap and water to wash off the offending matter, *then* put on a protective coating of some kind of ointment. Putting on the ointment without a soap-and-water wash simply seals in the urine or feces that you may *wipe* but not *wash* off, and may make matters worse.

At around three months of age, when your baby no longer has a 10:00 P.M. feeding, and goes unchanged from the 6:00 P.M. to the 6:00 A.M. feeding, your baby's bottom may not be able to stand such prolonged contact with the ammonia in the urine. At 10:00 P.M. or whenever you go to bed, wash your baby's bottom and change its diapers. If you're reasonably quiet and don't turn on a bright light, your baby will more than likely sleep through the change. Most babies wet soon after being put down and may not void again till shortly before being gotten up in the morning. A change and a wash-off at 10:00 P.M. can do much to keep their bottom clear. After washing put on some kind of ointment — it will act as a protective coating when the baby voids in the morning. Obviously if your baby's bottom is not presenting a problem there will be no need for this nightly wash-off.

Rubber pants have to be watched as heat serves to aggravate the effect of concentrated ammonia on the skin.

It all depends on the particular baby's skin: some babies can take a whole night in rubber pants. Some babies' bottoms have to be washed off with soap and water after every voiding as well as after every bowel movement.

I remember a mother who used to set her alarm for 2 o'clock every morning and wash and change her baby — her baby's skin *was* very sensitive. When I suggested that that was going pretty far, she pointed out — rather tartly — that it was her night's sleep and, to keep her baby's skin clear, it was worth it.

Heat Rash. Here's a rash that worries a mother more than it upsets a baby. Babies are hot little tykes and develop heat rash very easily. They need surprisingly little in the way of blankets. As a rule, when you need two blankets, your baby may need only one.

Babies that sleep on their stomachs and are too hot will have a very fine red rash on their stomachs. If they sleep on their backs, that's where the rash will be. Just keep the baby cooler. In summer a little powder may help.

Rash Behind the Ears. Actually, this is a crusting or crack that develops behind a baby's ears. This may persist, possibly itch, and cause the baby to rub or dig behind its ears. This condition develops easily because of moisture. A mother so often dries her baby carefully after a bath but just rubs the towel back, across the ears, not thinking of making a point of drying carefully behind the ears as well.

Cradle Cap.   It's always nice to come up with something that isn't in any way a mother's fault. Cradle cap is such a thing. It is a dirty-looking crust that sometimes forms on a baby's scalp. It comes because babies usually haven't enough hair to take up the oil produced by the oil glands in their scalp. Dust and lint gather in this oil to form a crust, and it doesn't mean that you are not taking meticulous care of your baby.

I would advise against trying to scratch it off with a comb. At night put a little baby oil or olive oil on the scalp — in the morning be sure to wash it off with soap and water. Some or all of the crust will wash off at the same time, but, if necessary, repeat the following night. Thereafter, keep watch, and if the cradle cap starts to re-form, repeat the treatment. Always be careful to wash off the oil in the morning. Left on, the oil itself might cause a rash.

Bowel Movements

Number.   Babies sometimes do a rather mean thing. They may spread out a single bowel movement over several changes of diapers, and if at the end of the day you count the soiled diapers, you may worry that your baby has had too many movements. However, it's not the *number* of bowel movements that need primarily concern you; it's the following:

Color and Consistency.   The stools of a breast-fed baby are brown, sometimes slightly greenish (breast milk acts as a mild laxative). The stools of a baby on the bottle are lighter, almost yellow. In either case the stools should be *soft* — they're sometimes curdy in appearance, but they should not be formed.

Constipation.   If stools become formed or hard or if

your baby fails to have a bowel movement over a 24-hour period, this is early constipation. Don't allow it to continue; keep ahead of the situation. Don't turn to artificial laxatives — a baby's food properly used provides plenty of natural laxatives:

> *Fruit juices* — apple and especially prune are usually the most effective;
>
> *Fruit pulps* — again, apple and prune are most effective;
>
> *Cereals* — their effectiveness usually depends on their bran content. Graham crackers broken up with milk on them is a mildly laxative cereal, and, of course, bran flakes or various mixtures that include all-bran.

The effectiveness of all of these varies greatly from baby to baby. Don't worry that you will give too much — if you do, your baby will tell you so by having some loose movements and you'll naturally slow up. Each mother has to learn *what* works best for her particular baby and *how much* and *how often*. In any case, the best treatment for constipation is *prevention*.

You don't want a baby to be constipated. Babies develop internal hemorrhoids easily. If stools are firm and streaked with red, get in touch with your doctor.

Special Precautions. In *Treatment of Infections* I referred to the "later signs of infection," one of them being *diarrhea — frequent, watery, definitely green stools* (p. 22). There I discussed the simple, preliminary treatment and the importance of calling a doctor if the diarrhea persists (p. 25).

In the same section I list reasons, other than infection, to call a doctor. If a baby has a *black* or a *definitely red stool*, this indicates bleeding somewhere along the digestive tract, and a doctor should be consulted at once.

Hiccups

Babies up to six weeks to two months of age frequently have unexplainable bouts of hiccups. Once again, here is something perfectly normal, something you don't have to worry about, and something that is definitely not your fault. You may be told the hiccups occur because you fed "too slowly," "too fast," "too much" or "not enough." Pay no attention. No one knows just why tiny babies are prone to hiccups—they seem to do the baby no harm.

You can usually stop them with a drink of water but, more than likely, before you get around to giving it, the hiccups will have stopped of their own accord.

In the rare event that the hiccups persist for the better part of a day or night, consult your doctor.

Teething and Eruption of Teeth

Babies start feeling their teeth at a surprisingly young age. The *early signs*—a little excess saliva, moist lips, a bit of drool, blowing bubbles—begin anywhere from six weeks to two months of age and aren't usually thought of as teething. The time for the eruption of teeth seems still such a long way off! However, slowly but surely these early signs increase and intensify and finally become definitely recognizable as teething.

There are great variations in the time a first tooth appears. An occasional baby is born with a tooth or teeth—this is rare. A first tooth usually erupts anywhere from as early as four months to as late as eight or nine months. In my experience, and from what the dentists tell me, by and large, there is no need for concern as to the quality of teeth which erupt within these normal time limits.

Any number of things are erroneously and conveniently blamed on teething: for example, high temperature, poor appetite and convulsions. As I see it, however, the advanced signs of teething are in themselves trying enough without dragging in a lot of unrelated symptoms. The sensation from and the discomfort of teeth slowly working their way through the gums cause increased salivation, and babies handle this excess saliva in a variety of ways. Each mother thinks her baby's way is the worst.

Advanced Signs — by Day

1. Some babies get rid of a large part of the saliva by simply allowing it to run out of their mouths. *They drool and dribble from morning to night.* It's hard, even with drool bibs, to keep the baby dry and presentable. It's difficult to keep these babies' cheeks and chins clear of rash.

2. Some babies manage fairly neatly to swallow most of the excess saliva but, as it piles up in their stomachs, their stomachs reject it. *These babies spit up small, slimy, sour-smelling messes at intervals throughout the day.* The spitting up is usually worst at the end of the day — just when you've changed clothes and guests arrive for dinner.

3. Some babies' stomachs apparently manage to cope with the saliva and pass it along. These babies may have slimy bowel movements, often in increased numbers. They have to be changed frequently and they often present a bottom rash problem.

Advanced Signs — by Night

1. The baby that sleeps on its back may develop a *night cough* from the dripping of saliva down its throat. Elevating the head of the bed — putting blocks of wood or old phone books under the casters — may facilitate drainage and ease the cough.

2. The baby that sleeps on its front drips and drools and soaks its headpiece. Frequent shifts or changes of the headpiece plus frequent washings with soap and water will help keep this baby's face clear of rash.

3. The baby that swallows the saliva all night may spit up most of its breakfast in an attempt to get rid of the stuff. Giving this baby a drink of juice or water *first thing* in the morning may enable it to spit up the slimy accumulation and then eat and retain its breakfast.

4. As a tooth is working its way along inside the gum it may hit a nerve and cause pain. A baby may cry out suddenly in the middle of the night and by the time you get to it be sound asleep again. However, it may not go to sleep again at once. Rubbing its gums with a clean finger is soothing. Some parents think a little paregoric on the finger helps, but I'm inclined to think it's the *rubbing* that does it.

Any of these day and night manifestations of teething may occur — singly or in combination. All babies are different — a second baby rarely teethes in the same way as a first. The degree of discomfort experienced by babies varies but rarely seems to amount to very much — the nuisance experienced by mothers is another matter! It's the early teeth that seem to give the most trouble. I don't remember teething posing much of a problem after the first year or year-and-a-half.

One thing that just about all babies do when they're teething is chew, bite or gnaw on anything and everything that's handy: fists, fingers, playpens, toys, bedding, clothing — anything they can get into their mouths. A good chew — pressure on those uncomfortable gums — eases the discomfort!

Which brings us to the subject of . . .

Thumb-Sucking

This may include *thumbs, fingers, knuckles or fists* — I'll use the term "thumb-sucking" to cover the lot of them. Whichever one a baby sucks on, here's a subject that's packed with emotion!

Thumb-chewing or thumb-sucking most often starts as an indication that a baby is feeling its teeth.

A thumb is a friendly thing to chew on. It's of good consistency, pleasantly firm and very handy!

Don't try to stop a baby from chewing on its thumb. Recognize the thumb for what it is — a teething implement — and show no undue concern.

1. Keep the baby busy with its play in the daytime and have plenty of good, safe, chewable toys readily available.
2. Watch the day schedule to be sure there aren't long, unbroken periods when the baby may chew and suck its thumb because there's nothing better to do.
3. At bedtimes be sure the baby has something satisfying to chew on within easy reach.
4. See to it the schedule is organized so the baby won't be lying awake for long stretches, either before going to sleep or on waking, and as a result seek comfort in thumb-sucking.

In my experience most babies on a well-organized, well-balanced schedule, as the discomfort of teeth subsides, stop thumb-chewing or sucking. However, two things can counter this normal tendency to abandon the practice.

1. As I've pointed out earlier—*babies can be perverse.* If you make a point of trying to stop their chewing or sucking on their thumbs over this teething period— *physically*, by the use of elbow splints or aluminum mitts or application of bad-tasting stuff to the thumbs, or *emotionally*, by showing unhappiness, disapproval or exasperation—chances are *the baby will continue the habit out of frustration or obstinacy.* Some babies go right on sucking a thumb, at first to catch or hold your attention and then, as time goes on, to pester you.
2. Besides seeking the comfort to sore gums obtained by chewing on a thumb, babies may slowly develop a need, in times of weariness, stress or boredom, for the consolation or reassurance that comes from sucking on a thumb. Many babies and small children receive such needed comfort from a blanket, a pillow, a particular toy, a lock of hair or from hanging on to an ear. But some youngsters receive it only from *con-*

tinuing to suck on a thumb long after its original usefulness as a teether has passed.

Thumb-sucking, however, will usually taper off and come
to an end at around one-and-a-half to two years of age if you
do the following:

Accept early thumb-chewing for what it is and *keep your
emotions out of the picture.*
Maintain a good day schedule. Keep a sensible balance
between periods when you give lots of undivided attention and
periods when your baby is left on its own with a reasonable
assortment of things to chew on and objects to interest it close
at hand — *ever watchful that these periods aren't allowed to stretch
out into periods of weariness or boredom.*
Keep your home running smoothly and happily so that
your baby isn't *continually* and *constantly* subjected to an atmosphere of undue stress and strain.
Watch the sleeping schedule.

However, I'd like to be realistic and do my level best to
take a little of the heat and sting out of this business of thumb-
sucking. You can't imagine how many mothers used to come
into the office worried sick over it:

"I've tried *everything* and I just can't get this child to stop sucking its
thumb!"
When I'd ask, "Why are you so upset about it?" the answer, after
a pause, might run something like this:
"I thought it was very bad — it looks so dirty — I hate to see it. He
appears so stupid when he does it. Won't it do something or other to
his teeth?"

Well, let's take up this business of the teeth — the last
point — first. According to the dentists, the most common reason
for having to straighten a child's teeth is that the child's jaws
just don't match — it has, say, its mother's upper and its father's
lower jaw.

The next three most common reasons — and they're just about on a par — are:

1. *Prematurely stopping a baby's sucking on a nipple* — breast or bottle — that is, before about ten months of age.
2. *Prolonged sucking on a nipple* — breast or bottle (or pacifier) much past a year of age.
3. *Thumb-sucking persisting past the time the permanent incisors erupt*, at about six years of age.*

Those other points seem to me indications of a fairly widespread, emotional reaction of parents, grandparents and others to thumb-sucking. Sure — we all like to see our youngsters present a bright and attractive appearance, and the thumb creeping into the mouth doesn't improve matters.

But if you can just keep *yourselves* and *your feelings* out of the picture — see to it that the thumb, from five or six months to a year or a year-and-a-half of age or so, is only one of the pieces of teething equipment readily available to your baby; carry out the suggestions I've made about keeping your baby's days and nights going smoothly; follow through on the dentist's advice as far as sucking on a nipple is concerned — I think you will find that thumb-sucking won't present much in the way of problems for your youngster, your youngster's teeth or for you two parents.

Pacifiers

I'm probably going out on a limb here! Many mothers use pacifiers — many doctors recommend them — but I'm not in favor of them. I think they're *quite unnecessary.*

1. *Early in the game, at two or three weeks of age when a baby is fussing or cyring, it's trying to tell you something — it's saying something is wrong with the feeding, the schedule,*

---

*Losch, Paul K., and Swanson, Lennard T., in Cooke, Robert E. (Ed.): The Biologic Basis of Pediatric Practice. Vol. I. New York, McGraw-Hill Book Company, 1968.

the way it feels. Don't take the lazy way out and, instead of trying to dope out what is wrong and correct it, stuff a pacifier in the baby's mouth and stop up its lines of communication.

> Pacifier! Pacifier!
> You ingenious little liar!
> You plug up all baby's sayin',
> Thereby washing mommy's brain!
>   LPT

2. *Sucking Reflex*

I know perfectly well what is said about the use of a pacifier — about its importance in satisfying the sucking reflex. But I find myself unimpressed about this sucking reflex business.

Beyond a doubt *nature has carefully designed infants with a sucking mechanism which enables them to suck on a nipple.* The sucking reflex per se is only one aspect of a fairly complex apparatus. Nature has also cleverly fashioned mothers with breasts which, several days following delivery, secrete milk; with nipples to make that milk available to their babies. When these two mechanisms are functioning at maximum efficiency — that is, when a baby is vigorous enough to suck and when a breast is well stocked with milk — the breast *readily* supplies milk in response to the baby's demand, to its sucking. The baby *easily* gets all it wants and, satisfied, falls asleep — replete. A baby on the bottle, if the mechanics of feeding are properly handled and if the baby is fed as nature intended it to be fed — held closely in its mother's arms — satisfies its hunger in exactly the same way and falls asleep. Both these babies, if they have been properly bubbled, will sleep several hours and then waken again — hungry for more milk. *In my experience sucking is simply a means to an end—satisfaction of hunger.* Furthermore, as soon as a baby grows old enough to satisfy its hunger and thirst by means other than by sucking—by using its hands; eating from a spoon, chopsticks or whatever; drinking from a cup—the infantile sucking mechanism disappears, its usefulness ended. This is straightforward physiology. (See p. 143 on the important relationship between the proper use of the infantile sucking mechanism and dentition.)

Without question the breast-fed baby whose mother doesn't have enough milk, the bottle-fed baby who has to struggle to get milk through a nipple with too small holes, the baby that cries following a feeding because it's still hungry and is offered a pacifier—all these babies will continue sucking in the hope that some good—some food—will come of it. Ultimately, as I see it, these babies, disillusioned and tired, fall asleep—but not for long! There are those, however, who say that these babies continue sucking to satisfy their sucking need. They say, furthermore, that if their sucking need isn't satisfied by this sort of prolonged sucking, *something* will happen; and the "somethings" cited include a wide variety of disturbances, any one of which may beset the child as he grows. Evidence to substantiate the connection between the disturbances and sucking is lacking and, in the opinions of some psychiatrists, the importance of sucking has been greatly exaggerated.

In my experience, the baby *whose mother has loads of milk and to spare* usually gets all it wants in about five or six minutes of sucking on each breast and promptly falls asleep. The baby who is *properly bottle-fed* sucks for an equally short time before falling asleep. Neither of these babies can be kept awake for more sucking. For years I've been following just such well-fed, satisfied babies, and to the very best of my observation no vague "something" happens to them. *As long as they get plenty of food and plenty of loving care, the length of time they suck seems immaterial to their well-being.*

3. I know perfectly well that there are those who say that if a baby is given all the pacifier sucking it wants early in the game, it won't suck its thumb. All I can say is this hasn't been my experience.

4. At ten or eleven months of age — for proper dentition — dentists want babies off all nipples. This includes pacifiers.

5. In using a pacifier you deliberately start and foster a habit that is often very hard to break. In the office for check-ups a depressing number of mothers of year-and-a-half to three-year-olds used to ask how the dickens they could get their children *off pacifiers.* A child that has become accustomed to finding comfort and a refuge in the use of a pacifier isn't easily or happily broken of the habit. You'll find you have plenty of problems to deal with without going out of your way to promote one. *The best way to break a child of using a pacifier is never to give it to the child in the first place.*

If a baby, *right from the start, gets all it wants to eat* — and that means the technique of feeding (breast or bottle) is going smoothly — and if the *schedule is properly balanced*: the sleeping and wakeful periods, the periods of undivided attention and periods of being on its own, the periods of strenuous activity and the quiet periods — I don't believe you'll find any need to use a pacifier.

Fresh Air and Frostbite

Don't feel you *must* get your baby out every day, no matter the weather, hot or cold. Use judgment.

When it's very hot and it seems wise to keep the baby in, watch that the baby isn't in a direct draft from an open window, a fan or an air-conditioner.

When it is cold, having the baby sleep in a room with a window or windows open (out of a draft) is better than bundling it up within an inch of its life to sleep outside.

Most mothers are surprised at how easily a baby develops frostbite. Babies drool and their chins, the area under their chins or their cheeks are so often wet—which increases the chances of frostbite. Frostbite appears as a firm, slightly bluish spot. Minor frostbite isn't serious but is painful. No treatment is necessary other than to keep the baby in out of the cold and possibly give it a little aspirin to make it comfortable. Then try to prevent reoccurrence.

Sunbaths

If you want to give your baby sunbaths—in an open window (out of a draft), in the yard, on the beach—that's fine. Just go at it slowly. Be sure to shade the baby's eyes from the sun.

Start out by exposing the baby to the sun one minute on its front, one minute on its back. Work up gradually to five or ten minutes, front and back, depending on the individual baby's skin. If the baby shows signs of sunburning, slow up!

Don't set out to produce the best suntan in the neighborhood.

Overexposure may coarsen your baby's skin.

Excessive exposure may be even more harmful.

Masturbation

When I was an intern at Children's Hospital Medical Center in Boston, Dr. Kenneth Blackfan was chief-of-staff. He rarely saw private patients but when he did he would call in one of the interns—to give us an opportunity to broaden our clinical experience.

One morning he asked me to be in his office at about ten o'clock. He added, "There's a father coming in from Springfield, in a rush. He's very upset—has something on his mind. I don't know just what."

Dr. Blackfan and I were waiting when the father arrived—almost burst into the office. He didn't stop to take off his coat but started talking at once. The day before he had come upon his little three-year-old boy, masturbating! He knew all manner of terrible things would come of it. He talked on and on, almost beside himself. Finally he came to a stop.

Dr. Blackfan was a very quiet, mild, easy sort of person. He hadn't as yet spoken—he told me later he knew the gentleman was bound to run down, sooner or later. He now suggested the father let me help him off with his coat and that he sit down. Dr. Blackfan leaned back in his chair, paused a moment, thoughtfully, and then spoke. He said that he and his wife had been married about twenty years, and that it was a great sorrow to them that they had never had a child. "But," he added, "if we had been lucky enough to have had a child, boy or girl, and if we had come upon that child masturbating, we would have felt ourselves to be doubly fortunate. Not only would we have been fortunate to have a child, but we would have been fortunate also to have a normal child."

The important thing to realize is that it is quite normal for a small child to masturbate—there is every reason not to be upset or to make anything of it: to allow a youngster to feel concern or distress on your part.

If a child's hands are kept occupied in the daytime; if its day schedule is well-balanced so there are no long-drawn-out periods of boredom; if the sleeping schedule is properly handled so the child isn't lying awake too long before falling asleep or before being gotten up; if, moreover, you make no more of its rocking or of finding it rubbing between its legs than rubbing behind an ear—just move it on to other activities—masturbation should pose no problem.

Shoes

For the tiny baby and the baby creeping around, there's no necessity to put on shoes: booties, moccasins, socks (if you can keep any of them on), or nothing at all will be perfectly all right. Grandmothers are apt to worry over "little feet being cold" and I often find myself siding with grandmothers. I *do* think that if a baby is crawling around over rough terrain it's wise to protect its feet in some way from scrapes and splinters.

However, when your baby starts to walk, or when it spends a good bit of time standing in its pen—in other words, *bearing weight on its feet*—it should be put in shoes, either high or low. I say this on the advice of the orthopedic doctors at Boston's Children's Hospital Medical Center. As your baby starts walking you'll very likely notice that its feet are flat—that is, pronated. In this day and age a good part of a small child's early walking and standing is on hard floors, sidewalks, and paved surfaces, and regular, firm, leather-soled shoes help its arches to come up.

Sneakers, moccasins or bare feet are all right on grass or sand, but orthopedic doctors feel that in this young age group —one- to five-year-olds—playing around in sneakers and bare feet should be kept to a minimum. On hard surfaces, regular shoes provide the support needed to encourage the development of good, sturdy feet. We are no longer treading the soft turf of our American Indian predecessors.

When you put your youngster into shoes, I'd advise high shoes. Granted they look heavy and bulky, but they stay on better. Small children slip out of low shoes very easily—mothers can spend half the day looking for them.

I'm reminded of the mother who by-passed this bit of advice—"high shoes look so awkward on a little girl!" This mother arrived for an appointment one day, hot and embarrassed, 20 minutes late. She apologized and explained that, as they were driving in to the office, her little girl, sitting alongside on her car seat, had suddenly and unpredictably leaned down, plucked off a shoe, and with the speed of light chucked it out the car window.

The mother, knowing a weakness of mine, added. "Hunting in roadside shrubbery for a little brown shoe is as bad or worse than looking for a lost golfball!"

One last bit of advice — again from the orthopedic men — be sure to get shoes at least a half to a whole size larger than seems necessary. Children's feet grow rapidly and a shoe too big is far better than an even slightly cramped foot.

Plugged Tear Ducts

In the first few days and weeks you may notice that "matter" accumulates in the inner corner and along the lids of one or both of your baby's eyes. This is more than likely due to a plugged tear duct — the small passage that runs from the inner aspect of the eye into the nose. Quite frequently in a newborn this duct is plugged or partially plugged, obstructing drainage of secretions from the eye.

This is nothing to worry about — more a nuisance than anything else. I've never known a duct or ducts not to open up with time, though it may take four to six months to do so. If it doesn't clear up by eight months, you should bring it to the attention of your doctor.

For your part, no treatment is necessary other than to wash out the eye or eyes with sterile water as often as is necessary. With the baby lying on its back, head tipped to one side, drip warm, sterile water from a piece of absorbent cotton into the inner corner of the eye on the down side, so that the water runs across the eye, washing off the "matter."

Should the "matter" dry or crust along the lids, or should the lids stick together, wash them off gently with cotton and warm, sterile water — trying not to rub the surface of the eye itself.

Crossed Eyes

Mothers very frequently used to come into the office worried that their baby had crossed eyes. When I would examine the baby and could see nothing wrong I would ask, "Which eye seems crossed?" More often than not the mother would answer, "I'm not sure which. Sometimes it's one eye and sometimes it's the other."

This *appearance* of crossed eyes occurs fairly commonly. Eye doctors refer to it as "simulated crossed eyes." Sometimes as you are looking at your baby from one side, the relatively wide breadth of the baby's nose obscures the white of the far eye, on the inner side, and that eye appears turned in, crossed. If you happen to be looking at your baby from the other side, it's the other eye that appears turned in, crossed. Observe your baby from directly in front and the chances are there will be no crossing of the eyes.

A truly crossed eye will be apparent from whatever angle you observe it. However, if there is the least question in your mind about it, be sure to ask your doctor. *The sooner truly crossed eyes are discovered and treatment started, the better.*

"Lazy Eye"

While speaking about eyes, I want to look ahead and bring to your attention another recommendation of the eye specialists. By three years — or four years at the very latest — your child's eyes should be examined for a condition commonly known as "lazy eye." Inquire of your doctor or the local board of health, as this examination is routinely offered in many communities — *and it should be.*

Here is an excellent example of the effectiveness of preventive medicine. Discovered early and brought to the attention of an ophthalmologist, this is a condition which can usually be corrected with very little difficulty. If allowed to continue until school age — six, seven or eight years — treatment becomes increasingly difficult and less effective, sometimes resulting in greatly impaired or lost vision in the "lazy eye." Moreover, should this happen, there is always the ominous possibility that if, through an accident, the other eye is damaged or lost, a child could be left nearly or completely blind.

L'Enfant Nu by Mary Cassatt. (Courtesy of the Charles and
Emma Frye Art Museum, Seattle, Washington.)

Chapter Four

Nursery Set-up and Equipment

4 — Nursery Set-up and Equipment

Here's a subject that is pretty much out of my field, but I'd like to offer a little practical advice as to your set-up and equipment, primarily with its safety and efficiency in mind. Maybe I can also make a few helpful suggestions based on what I've observed visiting in homes over the years.

A nursery can be a very elaborate affair or it can be a simple, practical arrangement worked into one corner of a room. The baby doesn't care! What counts is to have it comfortable, quiet and safe for the baby and handy for you.

Room. Whenever possible, it's well to have the baby sleep in a separate room.
1. This means better sleep for you parents.
2. Babies don't sleep quietly. They make all sorts of noises, most of them meaningless, and a mother hears them all.
3. You can leave doors open a crack if you wish, but I assure you — open or closed — if the rooms are reasonably close, should the baby need you, you'll hear it.
4. If you have just one bedroom, shift the baby to the living room at night.
5. Temperature for sleeping is, ideally, about 65 degrees.

Bed. This can be a bassinet, basket or car-bed, set up at a convenient height, or you can use a crib right from the start, if you wish. More important than the bed itself is the mattress. You should have a good, *firm, flat mattress* so the baby will be equally comfortable sleeping on its side, front or back.

A *first sleeping arrangement* that makes a lot of sense for a tiny baby is:

1. A waterproof pad, 18″ by 27″, covering the mattress;
2. On the waterproof pad, under the baby's bottom, a 17″ square quilted pad;
3. Across the waterproof pad, under the baby's head, a piece of soft material or a diaper folded lengthwise to three or four thicknesses, stretched tightly so it won't wrinkle, and tucked securely under the mattress.

   This is a very flexible arrangement that permits you to change the "bottom pad" or the "headpiece" separately, as they become wet or soiled, without having to change the entire bed. The waterproof pad will need to be changed a little less frequently. This entire three-piece complex can be placed on top of any other bedding arrangement you happen to like. If you use a crib, you'll have to work out some arrangement to keep the "headpiece" smooth and tight.
4. A sheet or blanket to tuck the baby in comfortably (p. 38).

Changing Table

1. This should be located out of drafts.
2. It can be a *bathinette* with a top that closes over a tub and has its own padded and waterproof cover.

   It can be a sturdy *card table* — though these are low for many women, and a mother spends a lot of time at the changing table.

   As satisfactory as anything, to my way of thinking, is a *chest of drawers* of a convenient height. Someone in the family often has an old one you can paint and freshen up.

   The top of the table or chest should be padded with a folded blanket or a big bed pad, folded, or a piece of foam rubber or some such thing, securely fastened to the top.

Cover the padding completely with a water-proof pad, and you're in business.

3. Some mothers keep a couple of 18″ squares of *smooth rubber sheeting* on hand. These can be placed directly under the baby's bottom when you're changing or cleaning it up; being smooth-textured, this can be wiped or washed clean in a jiffy, saving laundry.

4. It's important to have clean diapers and clean clothes handy, so you can reach them without taking a hand off the baby. (Here's where the drawers of a chest come in handy.)

5. Again with safety and efficiency in mind, think in terms of towel bars, towel racks, hooks, or pegboards beside or over the changing table for such things as face cloth, towels, bottom washcloth, emergency towels or cloths.

6. A well-shaded light for night changings.

7. Think also about hampers, wastebaskets with liners, or ordinary big grocery-store bags standing right beside the table for wet diapers and clothes. For soiled diapers that must be rinsed off in the toilet bowl a diaper pail in the bathroom is handy.

8. Some items to have right at hand:
   a. Box of *tissues; roll of absorbent cotton* or *cotton balls; roll of toilet paper* (small wastepaper bag for disposing of soiled cotton or paper).
   b. *Plastic bowl for warm water and a dish of soap.* After wiping feces off the baby's bottom with the diaper and tissues or whatever, wash the baby's bottom clean with warm water and soap.
   c. *Oil* or *ointment*—apply only on a clean skin.
   d. Container of *sterile water*, if needed, for washing baby's eyes.

9. Bright objects or toys or a mobile hung high over the

table helps cut down on the boredom of being changed.

10. If you like your wallpaper and your baby is a boy, a large piece of plastic or oilcloth to cover the wall behind the changing table is realistic. Some boys have a remarkable range. (I remember a mother who had special feelings about her rug and covered a large area of it under and around the changing table with a big canvas, temporarily borrowed from the family camping equipment.)

Important safety measures where changing is concerned:

1. Before getting the baby from bed or wherever it happens to be, to change it, *check to make sure you have everything you may need right at hand:* tissues, warm water, clean diapers, clothes, and so on. When you change a baby, surprises are the rule!

2. *Always keep one hand on the baby or take the baby with you.* (The strap on a bathinette is good only for limited time use) (p. 40).

3. *Close all safety pins* — a good habit to develop early. Sooner or later everything reachable goes into a baby's mouth. An open safety pin swallowed is a preventable accident.

Bath

1. Give the baby a sponge bath until the cord drops off and the navel is dry (p. 214).

2. Then give the baby a soap-and-water bath in the bathroom, bedroom, kitchen — wherever it works best for you, and where it is warm (about 73 or 74 degrees) and where there's no draft.

3. Use a plastic tub or bathinette, though many's the baby

that's well washed in the dishpan, hand basin or kitchen sink.

4. Have water comfortably warm and about 2 inches deep. A soapy baby is a slippery object!

5. Wash the baby from top to toe with soap — face included (pp. 162, 215).

6. After the baby is bathed and well dried — remember behind the ears (p. 163) — if dry skin is a problem, put on a little baby oil. In hot weather use a little baby powder to keep the baby dry and comfortable.

7. Give a sponge bath when the baby has a cold.

Once again, *be prepared ahead of time* with water the right temperature, washcloth, soap and *towel*. (Having to carry a dripping baby with you while you hunt up a towel is awkward for you and chilly for the baby.)

Feeding

1. In a quiet place — not a lot of talk! If things are quiet the feeding will go better.

2. Comfortable low chair with arms.

3. Temperature of room about 70 degrees.

4. A bubble cloth to go over your shoulder and a waterproof pad for your lap.

5. A subdued light for night feedings.

6. For the *breast-feeder,* a can of powdered Similac, or its equivalent on the pantry shelf. If you have it you likely won't need it, but it may be hard to come by in the middle of the night when the baby is hungry and crying.

   For the *bottle-feeder,* a shelf or table beside your chair with a pan of hot water or a bottle-warmer — and a covered container with sterile nipples.

7. Care of artificial nipples:
   a. Cork with needle and a little plastic container to keep it in (p. 124).
   b. Covered jar or pan for sterile nipples. (I remember one mother using a little one-pint, enameled tea-kettle for this purpose. Once the nipples were sterilized in it and the water poured out from the spout, she had a handy, covered, nipple pail with handle to carry about.)

      As long as a baby is on a bottle, the nipples should be sterilized. A mouth infection — thrush — which occurs most commonly in young infants, is discouraged and usually prevented by boiling the nipples and maintaining a high standard of cleanliness.
   c. After feedings, until time to wash, and to make the washing easier, fill used nursing bottles with water, and put used nipples to soak in a jar of water.
8. In the refrigerator — a bottle of sterile water (water that has been boiled about 5 minutes) with a small amount of sugar in it. Add about $1/4$ teaspoon of table sugar to 8 oz. of the hot sterile water. This can be made up fresh every day — every other day at the most — and kept in the refrigerator, ready to be warmed and used whenever necessary.

   This can also be added to fruit juice when you're offering your baby dilute fruit juice. Don't add boiling water to fruit juice, as that will destroy the vitamin C.

As I said at the beginning of this section, equipment is not really my field. But mothers ask questions, and I used to pass on to them, just as I'm passing on to you, ideas I've picked up here and there from other mothers. You'll come up with many more ideas out of your own experience and that of your friends. The points to have always in mind are *safety* and *efficiency!*

One more suggestion before I drop the subject. When you're going to have a baby, especially a first baby, friends and family give you as gifts many of the things you will need: blankets, booties and baby clothes and so on. However, should you be asked what you need, I wouldn't like to think you would be at a loss for an answer. If the donor is relatively affluent, think big; mention a playpen, stroller, car-seat, highchair, car-bed or sturdy, wooden training seat. If you think you should go easy, more modest suggestions include a good firm teether, infant seat, blanket clips, carriers (back or hip), and harnesses for bed, highchair, stroller, car-seat or walking.

Part Two

Postnatal Views

Introduction to Part Two

I turn to the postnatal section of this book with pleasure and with the feeling of being on home ground. I'll be talking with you here, in these postnatal chapters, in much the same way that I used to talk — day after day, with mother after mother — over the thirty odd years I was in practice. Here, however, there will be one very satisfying difference. The five talks I now plan to have with you will be carried on against the background of all the earlier material in this book. In the old days, when I saw a mother for a half hour or three-quarters of an hour in the office or at home, I couldn't begin to fill her in on all the information I've tried to cover in the prenatal chapters of this book. We did the best we could, but there was always a lot more I wanted to explain to her — as I look back it seems to me that some mothers took a great deal on faith.

Now, however, I can talk with you about your baby — *in the hospital,* before you go home, then when it's *six weeks, four months, eight months* and *a year* of age — and just about every point that's brought up will have appeared earlier in this book at least once, maybe twice or more. It's repetitive, I know — but not, I hope, to the point of being boring. I think you're going to find that taking care of a baby for the first time is so new and different from anything you've ever done before that the repetition will only serve to make things stick.

The theme of this book is *prevention.* I'm convinced that the best way to extend the field of preventive medicine to cover the handling problems and the behavior problems of babies (of children of all ages, for that matter) is to offer parents information *in advance* about "how babies work" and "what is included in their job as parents," then to *help* them *apply* this information as their babies grow and develop.

193

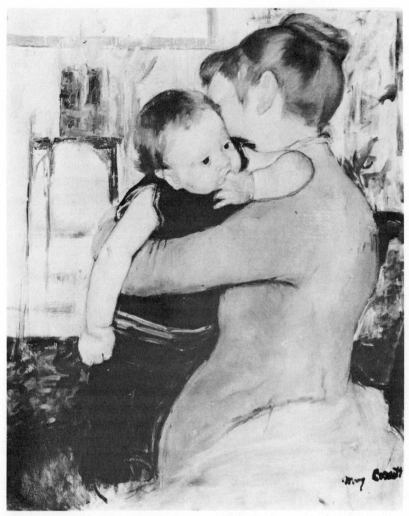

Mother and Child by Mary Cassatt. (Courtesy of the Cincinnati Art Museum.)

Chapter Five

In
the
Hospital

Babies Talk — A New Language
to be Learned

In this chapter I want to talk with you about you and your baby in the period from the time you go home from the hospital to the time when your baby is about six weeks of age. Babies develop and change so rapidly! This tiny, fragile-looking wisp of an infant you're about to take home and are almost afraid to handle will surprise and delight you in just a matter of six or eight weeks by filling out and growing into a very solid chunk of a baby.

The complete care of your baby over this period is more than just a matter of feeding, changing, bathing and making it comfortable, cuddling it and responding to its growing awareness. It's also a matter of getting the family back to normal living and the household running smoothly again. Babies develop securely and happily in a well-ordered setting.

Sometimes the introduction of your baby to its new home doesn't go as smoothly as you would like it to go and certainly, at times, nowhere near as smoothly as I think it should go. Mothers would occasionally show up in the office with a two- or three-week-old baby, saying, "What are we going to do? This poor baby is crying practically all the time! We're about at our wits' end!" This sort of thing shouldn't happen. Now, in the light of all we've gone over, let's consider your first days and weeks at home and see if I can help you get off to a good start — happily for your baby, and with the least possible loss of sleep for you parents, the least possible disruption to your family life.

Let me now make four important points relative to your first days and weeks at home:

1. *Get rested as soon as you can.* This baby is going to be with you for quite a time. Try to conserve and build up your strength.
2. *Be sure your baby, whether on the breast or bottle, gets all it wants to eat!* None of us likes to be hungry.
3. *Work slowly but steadily toward a good schedule,* one that satisfies all the baby's needs, but also one that takes you parents — your working days and nights — into consideration.
4. Each of you, mother and father, has a lot to contribute right from the start. The introduction of this new member of the family into your home requires adjustments, understanding and consideration on both your parts, plus good, open communication.

Schedule

In general, what you are aiming for is a 16-hour day of baby care, housework and as much rest and recreation thrown in as possible, plus close to eight hours of sleep each night — for everyone. For the average-sized baby a good beginning 24-hour schedule is:

> 6:00 A.M. — Feed
> 9:30 A.M. — Bathe
> 10:00 A.M. — Feed
> 2:00 P.M. — Feed
> 6:00 P.M. — Feed
> 10:00 P.M. — Feed
> ? ? 2:00 A.M. — Feed ? ?

To simplify things, this is the schedule to which I refer in this book — see *Training* for possible variations. Once you decide on a schedule that fits your family, stick with it!

Between feedings, most of the time (p. 145), a well-fed baby sleeps! Life for a baby over the first weeks is mainly a matter of eating and sleeping—babies grow rapidly, they need plenty of both food and sleep!

Demand Feeding

It isn't usually possible to start right off with a schedule. For the first few days at home, whether your baby is on the breast or bottle, feed it "on demand"—that is, whenever it cries, feed it; when it sleeps, you get some rest. When it cries shortly after being fed, offer it sterile water with a little sugar in it (p. 188).

1. The reason to do this in the beginning is so that you can get some rest and get your bearings.
2. Discontinue it as soon as possible—as soon as you're beginning to feel rested:
   a. A baby, more often than not, will put itself on a schedule—one that suits it, but takes no one else into consideration.
   b. Given the opportunity to take all it wants at a feeding, the average-sized (p. 54) baby has the strength and capacity to take enough food at a feeding to carry it about three-and-one-half to four hours.
   c. In time, one or more of these three-and-one-half to four-hour periods will expand to maybe five hours or even six hours.
   d. The temptation when this happens is to be grateful, to hold your breath and let the baby sleep as long as it will. But, let me urge you, in the daytime try to resist this temptation.
   e. *Keep in mind that as soon as possible you will want the "expanded" periods to become one good night's sleep.*
   f. So, as soon as you begin to feel rested, take heart, square your shoulders and start waking the baby at four-hour intervals throughout the day for five good feedings. Fill it up!
   g. This is the first step toward eliminating the 2 o'clock feeding.

Feeding

Remember, feedings, breast and bottle, go best when you are rested, when conditions are quiet and comfortable, when your handling of the baby is unhurried, firm and reassuring.

Remember also that the aim of feeding is to see to it that your baby has the opportunity to get all it wants to eat.

Breast-Feeding

Let me suggest that you take a look at the section on Breast-Feeding (p. 105) in Chapter 2, *Technique of Feeding. Be sure you understand what the three Requirements are and how they can work for you* (pp. 108–109).

1. *Never feed your baby longer than ten minutes on each breast.* Babies get milk from the breast very freely. For this reason your baby may get all it wants in five or six minutes on each breast, in which case there is no need to try to keep the baby awake just to take the full ten minutes.

2. *How will you know whether or not your baby is getting all it wants?* There is only one way to know for sure — *your baby, by its behavior, will tell you and keep right on telling you.*

   a. It tells you by the way it behaves during and following the feedings:

      (1) *When, repeatedly, it becomes drowsy and falls asleep in your arms while nursing, and then proceeds to sleep for three-and-one-half to four hours or more, your baby will be telling you, in no uncertain terms, that it's getting all it wants to eat.*

      (2) *When, on the other hand, your baby does not respond in this way to breast-feedings plus frequent offerings of sterile water, it will be telling your very plainly that it's not getting all it wants to eat.*

      Then, by all means, offer formula following the breast-feedings. Just as soon as it is getting all it wants at these supplemented feedings, your baby will let you know by falling asleep and sleeping close to three-and-one-half to four hours.

One way or the other it will be meeting the first two Requirements.

b. *When this happens start feeding your baby every four hours — five good feedings, waking it if necessary in the daytime, letting it waken you for the "2 o'clock."* As it settles into the schedule it will be telling you how well-established and adequate your breast milk supply is.

c. After enjoying this regular kind of existence for a time, your baby will go down after its 10:00 P.M. feeding, full up, and surprise you by sleeping well past the "2 o'clock." *This is when your baby, by its behavior, tells you that it's getting plenty to eat by day — that it would prefer a good night's sleep to another meal* and that it's ready to have you start getting it off the "2 o'clock."

This is the way it begins to meet the third Requirement.

3. Babies on the breast meet the three *Requirements* in different ways and at different times. It depends on how long it takes your individual milk supply to become established; the size of your milk supply; the rate of speed at which your individual baby is growing. However, at some point from two to four weeks after getting home, in one way or another — on all breast, on breast and bottle, or on all bottle-feeding — the three *Requirements* should be met and the "2 o'clock" should be a thing of the past.

4. When I was in practice I had all sorts of opportunity to observe the various ways in which breast-feeding mothers progressed over the first days and weeks.

a. *Mothers with an ample supply of breast milk* — and there were plenty of them — I might not hear from till they brought their babies in for a six weeks' check-up. Things went so easily for them and so happily for their babies!

b. *But there were other mothers whose breast milk either was slow in becoming established or was in short supply.* My aim was to have things go just as easily for them and just as happily for their babies.

At morning "call hour" I used to hear from these mothers —
sometimes just about daily — and, from what they would say
to me about their babies' behavior, I would try to help them
understand what their babies were telling them. By the way
their babies were or were not meeting the first two Requirements, by the way their babies settled into a daytime schedule,
and the way their babies' night's sleep was or was not being
extended, their babies were reporting on whether or not
their mothers' breast milk supply had become established and
just how adequate that supply was. Those morning reports
were just what the mothers and I needed to keep things
going smoothly.

5. *Here then, taken from those morning calls, are samplings of the
kind of reporting you can expect from your baby and suggestions as
to what you can do to keep your baby's days and nights progressing
smoothly and happily.*

   a. *If your baby, by the third, fourth or fifth day home, is meeting the
   first two Requirements, start slowly working it onto a good schedule*—feed it every four hours, waking it if necessary, five
   times a day but not for the "2 o'clock." You should easily
   have it on a schedule at some point in the second week,
   possibly as early as the end of the first week home.

      (1) *If gradually the time it sleeps at night begins to expand* past
      2, past 3 o'clock, you can start getting it off the "2
      o'clock." Breast-feeding for you will be "duck soup!"

      (2) *If, however, the time it sleeps at night does not noticeably
      expand*—if, after ten days to two weeks at home, the
      baby continues to waken at 2 or 3 o'clock at the latest,
      don't fail to question your supply of breast milk. You
      may have sufficient milk for four but not five good
      feedings. I suggest you offer a 6 o'clock bottle — letting
      your baby take all it wants. The length of time it sleeps
      at night should then begin to increase, and gradually
      you too can start getting it off the "2 o'clock."

   b. *If your baby, after three or four days at home, is not showing
   any signs of meeting the first two Requirements, you should*

question your milk supply — it's obviously slow getting established.
I suggest you start offering formula whenever your baby
doesn't become drowsy, doesn't seem satisfied, after ten
minutes on each breast. Let the baby take as much formula
as it wants.

Your baby will respond to these supplemented
feedings in any one of several ways, but, in any case, *it
will now start sleeping longer after feedings* and *you will have
a chance to get some rest* — which is what you need — to build
up a good milk supply. Your baby, getting all it wants to
eat, will now meet the first two Requirements and you can
begin working it onto a good daytime schedule. You should
accomplish this maybe by the end of the first week at
home, certainly by the end of the second.

Keep track of how much formula your baby takes —
this is the way it reports on what your supply of breast
milk is doing.

(1) *If your baby takes only* ¹/₂ *oz. or 1 oz. of formula after an
occasional breast-feeding, and finally no formula at all, you
will know your breast milk has finally, in its own sweet time,
become established,* and you and your baby are off to a
delayed but good start.

A. *If the time it sleeps at night slowly increases,* it won't
be long before you can begin to get it off the "2
o'clock."

B. If, however, by the middle of the second week to
the middle of the third week at home, in spite of
being on a good daytime schedule, *it still wakens at
2 or 3 o'clock at night, you should again question your
milk supply — this time as to size.* You may have sufficient for four but not five good feedings. I suggest
you offer a 6 o'clock bottle, letting your baby take
all it wants.

The length of time it sleeps at night should
then gradually increase. By the end of the third
week or early in the fourth, start getting your baby
off the "2 o'clock."

(2) *If your baby takes and continues to take ½ oz. or 1 oz. after most feedings* but is happily settled on a good schedule, try a 6 o'clock bottle (all the baby wants) *instead* of offering this small supplement after each breast-feeding. It's easier and it *may* prove sufficient to enable you to begin to get your baby sleeping through the night. On the other hand it *may not* prove sufficient (see following paragraph).

(3) *If your baby takes and continues to take 2 oz. or 3 oz. after most feedings, or if a 6 o'clock bottle doesn't prove sufficient to expand your baby's night's sleep* beyond 3 o'clock, you'll know your breast milk supply leaves a good bit to be desired. With large or with additional supplementary feedings you will be able to get the baby off the "2 o'clock." You can go on doing this as long as you wish, but, in my experience, this sort of feeding—half breast, half bottle—isn't satisfactory for either you or your baby. I would advise your facing up to things, weaning and discovering the satisfactions and pleasures of bottle-feeding.

Obviously, the possible variations in the examples I have offered here are many. As I suggested earlier, these are samplings of the kind of reporting you can expect from your baby over the first few weeks—samplings distilled from those morning "call hour" talks with mothers of new babies. *They are intended to show you how to make use of the Requirements, the schedule, the expanding night's sleep—all the things your baby's behavior tells you about your breast milk supply—to work out* your *individual feeding program.* I know how much it means to a girl who wants to breast-feed to be able to do so. I've tried to offer every suggestion I can think of that will prove a help. I would like very much to think that I've been able to improve some mothers' chances of breast-feeding. I would also like to think that I've been able to cut down on the number of mothers who put so much into breast-feeding that they forget they have other responsibilities.

Bottle-Feeding

Let me suggest that you take a look at the section on Bottle Feeding (pp. 102–141) in Chapter 2, *Technique of Feeding*. Be sure you understand what the three *Requirements* are and how they can work for you (pp. 134–135).

In bottle-feeding your aim is to imitate as closely as possible the way a baby on the breast gets its milk. You'll find this something of a challenge.

1. a. *Offer your baby all it wants* — always keeping the supply ahead of the demand, just as nature does. The amount your baby takes may vary from feeding to feeding, but remember on the breast you wouldn't know exactly how much it's taking.

   b. *See to it that the nipples flow very freely and if needed burn an additional hole or holes in the artificial nipple.* Milk should dribble from the nipple when the bottle of formula is held upside down — there should be no need to shake the bottle to get milk out of it.

   c. Unlike the breast the bottle has no valve control to check the flow of milk when a baby stops sucking. Therefore, *when a nipple flows as freely as it ought to, your baby should be positioned almost upright on your lap, tucked snuggly against you, held in the crook of your arm.* In this position you have a degree of control over the flow of milk and *your baby will get its milk as freely as does the baby on the breast.*

   d. Without a breast to close over the openings around and in the corners of its mouth *your baby will very likely swallow a fair amount of air.* Bubbling, therefore, becomes more important and should be done early and frequently.

2. *How will you know when you have the mechanics of feeding going properly?* There is only one way to know for sure — your baby, by its behavior, will tell you. I intentionally repeat here what I said under breast-feeding, the only difference being that here your baby will be telling you — not about your milk supply, which is obviously unlimited — *but about your delivery system.*

    a. When, repeatedly, *your baby falls asleep in your arms while nursing, and then proceeds to sleep for three-and-one-half to four hours or more after feedings,* your baby will be telling you, in no uncertain terms, that you've mastered the mechanics of feeding and that it's getting all it wants to eat. *It will be meeting the first two Requirements.*

    b. When this happens, *start feeding it every four hours,* five good feedings, waking it if necessary in the daytime but letting it waken you for the "2 o'clock." By the way it settles into the schedule it will be telling you exactly how well you're doing.

    c. Living this regular kind of existence, before long your baby will go down after its 10:00 P.M. feeding and surprise you by sleeping well past the "2 o'clock." This is when your baby tells you not only that things are going well, that it's getting plenty to eat daytimes, but that it would enjoy a good night's sleep—*that it's ready to have you start getting it off the "2 o'clock." This is when your baby begins to meet the third Requirement.*

3. Babies on the bottle meet the third Requirement at slightly different times. Primarily this is a matter of the speed with which *you* catch on to the handling and technique of feeding your individual baby. By and large after ten days (it can be sooner) to three weeks (at the outside) the three Requirements should be met and the "2 o'clock" becomes a thing of the past.

4. Once again I revert to my days in practice and my observations of the way bottle-feeding mothers made out over the early days and weeks. The mechanics of breast-feeding proceed simply and naturally as long as plenty of milk is available. The mechanics of bottle-feeding are trickier. Bottle-feeding is a *learned* technique. There is, however, a predisposition among mothers to think that any old way does it—that by virtue of being a mother they know how to do it. Consequently, in my experience, mothers in the process of catching on to how to feed from a bottle tend to run into a number of difficulties.

I used to hear from these mothers at morning "call hour" and from what they would tell me about their babies' behavior — how it had them baffled — I would endeavor to help them understand just what their babies were telling them.

By the way their babies were or were not meeting the first two Requirements, by the way their babies settled into a daytime schedule, by the way their babies' night's sleep was or was not being extended, *their babies were reporting, very plainly, on their mother's delivery system — the nipple holes, the feeding position, the bubbling and the handling.* Now, recollecting those "morning calls," let met sort out the specific difficulties that repeatedly beset bottle-feeding mothers. Following are samplings of the reports you may receive from your baby.

(1) *If your baby takes just a small amount of formula at a feeding and falls asleep only to waken in a couple of hours, hungry* — doesn't sleep anywhere near three-and-one-half to four hours:

A. *Question the size of the holes in the nipple* — your baby may be working so hard to get its milk that it tires — gives up sucking and falls asleep long before being completely satisfied. What's more, in the process of struggling to get its milk it will almost surely be swallowing a lot of air.

B. *Question the position of your baby when feeding.* One reason the holes in the nipple may be too small is that you're afraid the baby will choke if they're any larger. Try sitting the baby up straight on your lap, leaning against you and held securely by your arm. In this position it can handle a faster nipple without choking and you have more control over the speed of the flow of milk.

C. *Question how well you're bubbling* — your baby may have had a stomach full of air and been temporarily satisfied, only to waken, hungry, after a couple of hours. (See *Bubbling Technique*, below.)

(2) *If your baby spits up frequently during, right after or between feedings:*

A. *Question the holes in the nipples* — if they're too small your baby may be swallowing almost as much air as milk and have lots of bubbles that come up, bringing milk with them.

B. *Question your bubbling technique* — bubble early; you may be letting too much milk go down and trap the air.

C. *Question how well you're handling your baby* — *are you rushing the feeding?* Babies are sensitive little things. They don't like to be pushed and joggled around. Spitting up is one way they tell you so.

It's hard to prevent a little spitting up in connection with feedings, but if a baby spits up *frequently* or if it spits up a fair amount with what seems to be the pressure of a good big bubble behind it, check back in your mind to be sure the holes in the nipples are big, the baby is in an upright position, that your bubbling has been consistently *good* and *early*, and your handling unhurried and relaxed.

(3) *If you're having a "lot of trouble getting up the bubbles":*

A. *Make a point of trying to prevent bubbles in the first place.*

Try to have your baby swallow as little air as possible:

Check over the size of the holes in the nipples — remember the mother who snipped the end of the nipple right off (p. 125).

Check the baby's position also.

Check to be sure conditions at feeding time are quiet, relaxed, unhurried.

B. *Bubble early:*

That's when your baby, hungry, swallows the most air. If you allow a lot of milk to go down and trap it, you'll have the dickens of a time getting it up.

Try the "change in bubbling position." (See p. 129.)

(4) *If your baby takes what you think is a good feeding* — *that is, finishes the whole bottle* — *but sleeps only two-and-one-half hours or so:* Once you've checked out the holes in the nipples, the position and your bubbling, *maybe you should update your idea of a "good feeding."* A baby and a baby's appetite grow fast. Some

babies consume an awful lot—more than you'd think possible. Always be sure to offer more than the baby took at the previous feeding—*always let the baby refuse a little*—then, and only then, can you be sure the baby is getting all it wants.

Don't worry that your baby will take too much. If your baby were on the breast you wouldn't know to the ounce how much it was taking.

(5) *If feedings take longer than 30 to 35 minutes:*
   A. Question the size of the holes in the nipples. Is your baby *easily* getting all it wants?
   B. Question whether you're spending too much time bubbling—review *Bubbling Technique* (p. 127).

(6) *If your baby sleeps "most of the day" and "has you up all night":* What about your schedule? Are you interrupting its day sleep every four hours with five good feedings?

(7) *If your baby—on a good daytime schedule—shows no sign of expanding its night's sleep by the beginning of the third week home, you have to say to yourself: "Is my baby getting all it wants to eat by day?"* That means going right back over your feeding technique—the same old things:
   A. The size of the holes in the nipples;
   B. The upright position of the baby when feeding;
   C. Your bubbling technique;
   D. Does the baby, feeding, always become drowsy, refuse a little formula—leaving just enough to show it's had all it wants?

(8) If you'll notice, *I'm saying nothing about the formula disagreeing.* It does happen, but it's just about the last thing to think of (p. 141).

There's a degree of sameness, of repetition, in these examples that may seem unrealistic. But let me remind you, the mothers who used to call at morning "call hour" had had very little chance at prenatal discussion and theorizing about the care and handling of babies. They were learning "on the job"—from scratch. They already had their babies and were emotionally involved. *I know from experience that bottle-feeding isn't always as easy as a mother thinks it ought to be.* The darnedest little problems keep turning up! To help you plug up as many loopholes as possible, I've listed here the ones that used to turn up again and again.

Having read the prenatal chapter on the *Technique of Feeding,* you can appreciate the fact that to bottle-feed your baby properly you can't afford to be casual—you have to put as much care and thought into it as nature has into breast-feeding.

Bubbling

Whether your baby is breast- or bottle-fed, it inevitably swallows a certain amount of air when feeding—the bottle-fed baby, as a rule, swallows more. Bubbling—bringing up as much of the air swallowed as possible—is, therefore, an integral part of feeding. Read over the earlier and more complete section on bubbling (p. 127).

1. *Position your baby up against your chest so it feels secure* and doesn't expect momentarily to crash to the floor. A baby bubbles better if it's firmly held and is, consequently, *relaxed.*
2. *Bubble early in the feeding.* This is when a hungry baby, feeding vigorously, swallows the greatest amount of air—breast or bottle.
3. *If you're breast-feeding,* bubble half way through the first breast, again when you shift from the first to the second breast, and again at the end of the feeding.

   If you're bottle-feeding, bubble after the first ounce or maybe the first half ounce, after the second ounce, half way through feeding and at the end of the feeding.

   The variations are many. Your individual baby will tell you how often to bubble and how well you're bubbling by how much it's spitting up and how much air it passes by rectum.

4. *If you have trouble getting up the bubbles, more likely than not it's because they're trapped under milk.* Try the *"change in position"* — slowly lay the baby across your lap for a minute or two, then slowly return it to the bubbling position.

Remember: it's when you bubble, not *how often or how long, that counts.*

What I have offered here in this matter of feeding and bubbling — breast and bottle — are procedures and suggestions primarily with a view to preventing the many little problems that so often go with feeding. If things are not working out — as in all your handling of your baby — you must show judgment and be sure to seek help from your clinic or doctor.

Vitamins and Fluoride

Your baby needs both vitamins and fluoride — be sure to read pp. 153–159.

Water

Right from the start, *when your baby cries soon after being fed, feel free to offer sterile water with a little sugar in it* (p. 188). However, as soon as you have your baby on a schedule, show judgment as to when you offer it. For instance:
1. *If your baby is crying half way between feedings,* say at 4:00 or 4:30 in the afternoon, warm up a little water and let the baby take all it wants. With something warm filling up its insides the baby may feel comfortable and satisfied — at least for a time.
2. *If, however, your baby is crying closer to a feeding time,* say at 5:00 or 5:30 in the afternoon, slowly get organized and

give the 6:00 o'clock feeding a bit early. (A schedule shouldn't be rigid — feedings on the stroke of the clock. Your baby can't tell time, but it can tell you when it's hungry.)

3. *Water doesn't take the place of food,* however, and repeated crying between feedings should warn you to reconsider either your supply of breast milk or your bottle-feeding technique.

How to Get Your Baby off the "2 o'clock" — How to Meet the Third Requirement

In both the *Breast-Feeding* and *Bottle-Feeding* sections, I've tried to show you that there are a variety of ways by which a baby arrives at the stage where you can begin to work it off the "2 o'clock."

1. The *first step* is to see to it that your baby is getting all it wants to eat — breast or bottle.

2. The *second step* is to get it onto a schedule — interrupting its day sleep at four-hour intervals for five good feedings.

3. The *third step* takes place when the time it sleeps at night begins to increase. This is the reason not to waken it for the "2 o'clock" but to let it waken you. *Slowly but surely, at its own rate of speed, it will extend the time it sleeps past 2:00 o'clock to 3:00, 4:00 or even 5:00 o'clock.*

a. *If your baby wakes at 2:00 or 3:00 o'clock — feed it.* Don't play around with sterile water — water won't hold it till 5:00 or 6:00 o'clock. *Feed it — get it to sleep and you get your sleep.*

(1) If it continues to waken at 2:00 or 3:00 o'clock beyond a week after the time you have it on a good five-feeding daytime schedule, if it's on the breast, you should question your milk supply; if it's on the bottle, you should question your feeding technique.

(2) If you feed the baby at 2:00 or 3:00 o'clock *be sure to*

waken it for the 6:00 A.M. feeding so you won't get your day schedule balled up.

b. *If your baby wakens at 4:00 A.M. or 4:30 A.M., offer it warm sterile water just as you would at 4:00 in the afternoon.* It may be satisfied and sleep until nearer 6:00 A.M.

If the baby is quiet for a time but starts crying again at around 5:00 o'clock, get ready slowly and give the 6:00 o'clock feeding ahead of time—no more fooling around with sterile water.

c. *If your baby sleeps till 5:00 or 5:30, get ready slowly and give the 6:00 o'clock feeding ahead of time.*

If you feed the baby at 5:00 o'clock, try to put off the next feeding till as near 10:00 A.M. as possible and *get the schedule back on the track* by the 2:00 P.M. feeding.

4. The *fourth step* takes place when your baby is sleeping till around 5:00 or 5:30 A.M. *At this point start working on the expanded night's sleep time from the other end:* stop waking the baby for the 10:00 P.M. feeding.

a. Get some rest yourself during the early evening and feed your baby at 11:00 or 11:30 P.M., unless of course it wakens hungry earlier.

b. As soon as the baby—with the benefit of the "delayed 10:00 o'clock"—sleeps through to 6:00 A.M., start gradually working it back, a half-hour at a time, to 10:00 P.M.

c. Your baby will then be sleeping from after the 10:00 P.M. feeding to the 6:00 A.M. feeding.

Believe it or not, it works—even though at times you might question it. I predict that you may be surprised at how soon your baby comes off the "2 o'clock"!

I've spent a lot of time over feeding—what seems to be a disproportionate amount of time when you stop to think of the lengths I went to in *The Responsibility of Feeding* (p. 26 and following) to make it clear to you that feeding is primarily nature's responsibility; that your role is purely supportive. However, *once you really understand what your role is all about—just what goes into making* plenty *of food* easily *available to your baby* (breast and bottle), and *once you get the hang of doing it*—this temporarily inflated and demanding role will, in the matter of two to four weeks, *shrink right down to its proper, subordinate size.*

High time, too, because *Feeding* is just one of the six areas of *Responsibility* that make up your job as parents, and when you go home from the hospital all six *Responsibilities* will be practically breathing down your backs. But before examining them with an eye to where they are heading over the first six weeks, let's consider several specific matters of baby care that may come up over this period.

Bath and Care of the Navel

Usually, when a mother comes home from the hospital, the baby's umbilical cord has not fallen off. To hurry the process along, keep the area around the umbilicus as dry as possible. On leaving the hospital you will be told:

1. To give sponge-baths until the cord has dropped off and the navel is dry;
2. To daub the area daily with rubbing alcohol or to dust the area daily with Dermatol powder. (I tend to favor the powder.)

The cord will very likely fall off around the fourth, fifth or sixth day after you get home. After it falls off, the navel usually remains moist for another four, five or six days. Mothers would often call to say, "The cord has fallen off, but now there seems to be a little pus where it came off." This is quite normal, nothing to worry about, and it's not "pus." Just continue the drying process, using alcohol or powder.

Some mothers worry about pulling off the cord while changing the baby. If, by mistake, this happens, it won't be the first time. It may bleed a bit, but usually no harm is done. Just continue with the alcohol or powder. When the area has dried up, start giving regular tub baths daily.

The only other point to bear in mind is: if the navel becomes *red* at any time or if the navel is still moist after ten days to two weeks at home, get in touch with your clinic or doctor.

Odds and Ends

Circumcision (See pp. 159–161.)

Rashes

    Cheek Rash.   Watch the "headpiece" to be sure it's dry. (See p. 162.)

    White Spots.   Little white spots may appear on the sides of your baby's nose or high up on its cheeks. These aren't anything to worry about. Treatment is simple—just wash the area. Indeed, as I've pointed out under *Cheek Rash*, wash your baby's entire face frequently with soap and water. These little white spots usually clear up very quickly with this sort of care.

    Dry Skin.   (See p. 161.)

Bowel Movements and Constipation

If your baby doesn't have a bowel movement daily, give it a little dilute fruit-juice. (See p. 164.) Be sure, however, that your baby is getting plenty to eat. A baby at this age, if it isn't getting all it wants to eat, often does not have a bowel movement daily.

Hiccups (See p. 165.)

Pacifiers (See p. 171.)

Plugged Tear Ducts (See p. 178.)

Weaning (See p. 114.)

Communications and a New Language

At the outset of this chapter I mentioned that both you parents have a lot to contribute to the care of your baby, right from the start. I referred then, as I have frequently in this book, to the importance of good, open communications between the two of you. Early in practice I ran up against something which, frankly, surprised me — as it may surprise you. However, it kept recurring with sufficient frequency to make me want here, in this first Postnatal chapter, to bring it to your attention, *to underscore its significance.*

Every so often a mother would come into the office concerned because her husband was showing little apparent interest in their baby.

Sometimes a father would call me in the office, bothered because his wife was almost completely ignoring him — thinking of nothing but their baby and not allowing him any part in its care.

If I asked, "Have you mentioned this to him?" or "What does she say when you speak to her about it?" almost invariably the answer would be:

"Oh, I haven't said a word! I hoped maybe you'd speak to him (her)."

Well, here I am, speaking to "him" and "her" — to the two of you. All through this book I've been endeavoring to offer the two of you enough information about your *Responsibilities* and about the *Techniques of Feeding* to enable you to maintain a "hot line" of communication between the two of you. The care of a baby is a joint responsibility — it takes two parents to make a good job of it. Individual reactions differ, male and female reactions differ, but with good communication they can be made to complement each other and help get a baby off to a good start.

For example, you'll find it easier over the first weeks if the two of you can discuss freely and help each other with such things as:

The state of your breast milk supply—not to be looked upon as a mystery but as a physiological condition tied closely to an open and relaxed state of mind.
The progress of the *Requirements*.
The holes in the nipples.
The position of the baby during bottle-feeding.
The "when" and "how" of bubbling.
The schedule.

And as you talk these things over and work them out, you may be surprised to discover that *there is a "third party" talking on the line.*

Many people used to say to me: "Being a baby doctor must be hard!" "How can you tell what's wrong with a baby?" "Babies can't tell you where it hurts—how it feels!" "Babies can't talk!"

Nothing can be farther from the truth! Babies talk very plainly indeed! All through this book I've been pointing out that babies, by the way they behave, tell you exactly what's wrong. They speak clearly and to the point—which is more than some adults do.

You parents are going to have to learn a new language—that's all! You're going to have to plug a new line into your communication system and start listening to your baby. Once you're hooked up you'll find this is fun, and, when things aren't going smoothly, most instructive. For instance, where feeding is concerned, nine out of ten times your baby will be saying one or more of the following:

1. "For heaven's sake—I'm hungry!"
2. "The holes in these nipples are too darned small!"
3. "I've got a stomach full of air! Can't something be done about it?"

4. "Hey! Take it easy! Be relaxed! I'm not going to fall apart!"

I used to suggest writing these out and tacking them up on the wall under the title: "Things to check before calling the repair man."

There's another thing your baby may be saying — and this is the one you're working for. When all your baby does is eat, sleep and seem happy and contented, it will be saying, plain as day:

5. "Mum and Dad — you're doing a good job!"

And it isn't just where food is concerned that your baby will have things to tell you — as time goes on it will be reporting to you in all the areas of responsibility. This brings us back to a look at the six *Responsibilities* and the way in which they will be shaping up over the first six weeks. A review of Chapter 1, p. 17, might help.

Treatment of Infections

Remember, babies usually pick up their infections from exposure to people who either have or are coming down with colds. Be as careful as you can about contacts, especially in winter.

Watch for the "early warning signs" (p. 20) of an infection — another way in which your baby will keep you informed.

Feeding

Before your baby was born, nature saw to it that your baby had all the nourishment it needed; once it's born, just as soon as you've caught on to your supporting role — making *plenty* of food *easily* available — nature will go right on seeing to it that your baby takes all the nourishment it needs. As you get things rolling, feedings will become easy, happy times for your baby and very pleasant, satisfying times for you.

Prevention of Accidents

Prevention of accidents began, I hope, even before you went to the hospital—when you set up your nursery with *safety* and *efficiency* in mind. Always be sure your baby is in a safe place. Remember, this is a responsibility that rests entirely with you.

Training

Training begins as you become rested, as you stop feeding your baby "on demand," as you get the day schedule squared away and work your baby off the "2 o'clock." Helping your baby live happily and successfully in the family and in the world is quite a responsibility!

Discipline

Discipline lies just in the offing. You may be surprised at how early that first bit of fussing occurs, at how soon you find yourselves matching wits with your baby. Don't miss out on those earliest opportunities to help your baby—to make things easier for it as time goes on.

Education

Education begins right from the start as you talk to your baby, as you encourage its growing awareness, as you tuck or hang a bright object at the head of its crib—something to hold its gaze. You both have a lot to offer!

Catching on, right from the beginning, to the significance and importance of each one of these *Responsibilities*—seizing your earliest opportunities—here lies your job as parents. Let me warn you once again: don't dissipate time, energy and emotions over *Feeding* and get off to a slow start where these other *Responsibilities* are concerned.

Mother Feeding Child by Mary Cassatt. (Courtesy of The
Metropolitan Museum of Art. Anonymous Gift, 1922.)

Chapter Six

At
Six
Weeks

6 — At Six Weeks

Don't Turn in the Baby

When time for the six weeks' check-up came round, I always used to enjoy seeing the mother who had gotten her baby's feeding squared away over the first weeks. She would look happy and rested. We would both be pleased to see her baby on the scales — relaxed, pretty well filled out, possibly having put on two or three pounds.

There always comes to mind the mother whose six-week-old baby was doing beautifully and who, when I told her so, heaved a little sigh of relief and said: "Well, *we* thought so, but I *did* begin to wonder. My mother-in-law has been visiting for a few days and when she left she said she'd never in all her born days seen a better baby — *'so good, so quiet, so good-natured — and sleeping all night!'* And she added, *'You are sure the baby is all right?'* So you see, it's good to hear you say so!"

Her baby was very much "all right." That's exactly the way a baby at six weeks should behave.

Now let's talk about your six-week-old baby — what it's doing, what changes are taking place and what these mean as far as your handling is concerned.

Feeding

The thing babies at this age do best is *eat.* Some of them have tremendous appetites — they're gaining so rapidly! Babies, at this stage, are gaining on the average anywhere from 6 to 10 ounces a week. Some of them consume up to 60 to 70 calories per pound of body weight in a day. That's a lot of food! Think

223

of it—for a person weighing 125 lbs. that's over 8000 calories a day! Try that for a diet and see what happens! But for a baby at this stage that's just right. It takes a lot of fuel to get one of these little rockets off the launching pad!

If you are breast-feeding you won't be too aware of your baby's big intake; you won't be concerned.

If you are bottle-feeding you may very well see 6, 7 or 8 ounces of formula disappear five times daily.

Mothers would sometimes come into the office, worried. "Could my baby eat too much?" You don't have to worry. Your baby won't eat too much.

Again, let me remind you—the amount of food a baby takes is nature's responsibility. All you have to do is be sure to give your baby the opportunity to take all the food it wants.

Infections

Around this time you may find you're beginning to get sick and tired of the four walls. Why wouldn't you! You'll want to get your friends in or take your baby visiting. Just keep in mind that babies get most of their infections from contact. Especially if it's winter when lots of colds are about, be on the alert for the possible early signs of infection so you can get treatment started early (p. 20).

Training

Sleeping

Your baby's 24-hour sleeping requirements are going to begin to drop off—though when this starts and how much it drops off vary greatly from baby to baby. Remember, your aim is to keep your baby sleeping all night. To accomplish this I suggest you make a couple of changes in the schedule. When you make these changes and how you extend them will depend 100 per cent on your baby's night's sleep.

1. *In the morning, I suggest you change the bath from 9:30 to 8:00 or 8:30.* Before the bath, give vitamins and fluoride (p. 153).

   After the bath, offer your baby a little warmed, dilute fruit juice — half fruit juice and half sterile water with a little sugar in it (p. 188). This change kills several birds:

   > It effectively breaks into the sleep period from 6:00 to 10:00 A.M.
   >
   > It enables you to push up your baby's liquid intake.
   >
   > It gives your baby — if it wants it — a chance to get in a nap before the "10:00 o'clock" with a little something warm in its stomach.

2. *In the afternoon, I suggest you waken the baby at 4:00 for a playtime.* This breaks into the sleep period from 2:00 to 6:00 P.M.

   If you have friends or relatives who want to see your baby, this is a good time to have them in for a visit. (I offer this merely as a suggestion — sometimes a busy mother finds it difficult to keep her days running smoothly if there are a number of interruptions at odd points in the day.)

   After 30 to 45 minutes of play (always depending on the night's sleep), again offer dilute fruit juice and put your baby down for a rest before the "6:00 o'clock." A good six weeks' schedule is:

6:00 A.M. — Feed
Sleep
8:00–8:30 — Bath
(Before bath, vitamins, fluoride;
after bath, dilute fruit juice)
Nap
10:00 A.M. — Feed
Sleep
2:00 P.M. — Feed
Sleep
4:00 P.M. — Playtime

Dilute fruit juice
Rest
6:00 P.M.—Feed
Sleep
10:00 P.M.—Feed
Down for the night

Time Awake

The afternoon is a good time to start accustoming your baby to being in a playpen. At this age your baby isn't going anywhere. It's just going to lie there, kick its feet, wave its hands, look about and listen. But the playpen offers a change of scene as well as a safe place. It's well to get your baby used to being on its own, awake, for short spells when you have something else to attend to.

Prevention of Accidents

By this time, always having your baby in a safe place and always keeping one hand on it when it's out of the crib—especially when it's on the changing table—should have become second nature. Remember to watch out for telephone conversations—they have a way of stretching out. Let me remind you that there are far too many preventable accidents in the first year.

Discipline

At some point around six to eight weeks of age your baby, when you put it down, will very likely start fussing. Your baby is growing up, it's becoming aware of the good things of life. Time was when all it wanted to do was eat and sleep; now it's beginning to enjoy your company and quite naturally may put up a fuss at the idea of losing it. Check the baby carefully to be sure there's nothing wrong: if it stops fussing the minute you pick it up and starts again as soon as you put it down, give it the benefit of a second check, and then put it down and ignore any further fussing. This is your first opportunity to teach your baby that you will not respond to unnecessary fussing. This is your first opportunity to help your baby learn it can't always have its own way. *Don't miss out on these early opportunities when a little discipline will accomplish so much.*

Education

Take time in all your handling of your baby to talk to it, sing to it, respond to it. Hang bright objects over the crib, changing table and playpen — place them in strategic spots for your baby to gaze at. At playtime you will have a wonderful opportunity to observe your baby and encourage its responses to motion, sound and color. All this is fun and comes naturally to parents.

Changes are Tricky — Comparisons are Risky

Changes are taking place — you're going to find that you'll be put to it to keep up with the changes. Your baby is growing at a great rate. You no sooner catch on, get things going smoothly, get settled into a good schedule — than your baby is off on a new phase of its development, and it's time for a schedule change. Mothers over this six weeks' to four months' period are forever behind the eight-ball — more often than not trying to fit the 12-week-old baby into the 8-week-old pattern.

If something your baby is doing has you puzzled or worried, don't ask yourselves, "What under the sun is wrong with this baby?" Don't consider "turning it in!" Ask yourselves, "*What are we doing that is wrong for this particular baby at this stage of the game?*"

Always remember that as parents you are dealing with your individual baby. Once you start getting out, seeing your friends and their babies, it's so easy to be thrown off by what you see and hear. *Beware of making comparisons!*

I remember a mother coming in with her small baby—her first—and this mother's confidence had completely broken down. Her baby wasn't doing what any of her friends' babies were doing—none of their advice worked with her baby. The day before a friend had told her that something she was doing would get her baby into "terrible trouble." She was so close to tears I didn't think that pointing out that *all babies are different* would offer much in the way of help. I *did* know, however, that she was a close friend of a mother whose four youngsters I'd been seeing over a number of years—a mother whose feet were pretty firmly on the ground. So I asked, "What does Mrs. N— say about your baby? What's her advice?"

The mother paused a moment and a queer look came over her face. Then she said, "You know—she's never said anything at all! She's the only friend I have who's never tried to give me any advice!" She thought a moment and then added, "That's what you're trying to get at —isn't it?"

Well it was, and I was just thankful she worked it out all by herself. The best-meaning friends in the world can give you advice based only on their relatively limited experience with their own babies.

Odds and Ends

Now, let's consider some of the bothersome things, the often not serious things, that crop up at this stage of the first year—from six weeks to four months. Some of them you have already encountered, some start and taper off over this period, some continue on beyond. *These are things that become problems only if you are unprepared for them and allow them to get out of hand.* Most of them I have dealt with elsewhere in this book, so I will simply point out their special applicability to this stage of your baby's growth and then refer you to the more detailed discussion.

Circumcision

If your boy has been circumcised, by now the end of the penis should be well healed and presenting no problems. Before long, however, you should be on the lookout for redness around the opening of the penis — the early sign of an ulceration developing. The sensitivity of your individual baby's skin is a factor here. So too is the concentration of the ammonia in the urine. You will reduce the concentration of ammonia as you increase your baby's fluid intake by offering dilute fruit juice following the bath and playtime. This will cut down on the likelihood of an ulceration forming — as will also frequent soap-and-water washings of the general area. I assure you that prevention is, as usual, far easier than treatment of this nuisance problem. (For treatment, see p. 160.)

If your baby has not been circumcised, be sure at check-up times you ask your doctor if you are taking proper care of the foreskin. It's important to have all the normal adhesions broken by the time the baby is about six months old so you can easily wash under the foreskin. (See p. 161.)

Rashes (See p. 161.)

Here are problems that vary greatly from baby to baby — again depending on the sensitivity of the skin.

1. *Dry skin.* (See p. 161.)
2. *Cheek rash.* (See p. 162. See also *Teething*, p. 166.) Be sure to keep the "headpiece" *dry*, and keep the baby's cheeks clean with soap and water.
3. *Bottom (diaper) rash.* (See p. 162.) Frequent washings with soap and water are the best treatment for diaper rash. *Use ointment only on a clean skin.* Your individual baby's bottom will tell you how frequently it should be washed.

 As I suggested under *Circumcision*, by offering dilute fruit juice after the bath and at the end of playtime you can cut down on the concentration of ammonia in your baby's urine. The more liquids you offer your baby, the more you cut down on the concentration of ammonia in the urine — the less trouble you will have with diaper rash. *There's a direct relationship between your baby's fluid intake and diaper rash.*

4. *Heat rash.* (See p. 163.)
5. *Rash behind the ears.* (See p. 163.)
6. *Cradle-cap* (See p. 164.)

Bowel Movements and Constipation

 Your baby should have one or two soft movements every day — another reason to add dilute fruit juice to your baby's diet at this time. Movements should not be "formed" and, if they are, apple and prune juice are the best laxatives for a baby. The amount needed varies greatly from baby to baby. Don't worry about giving too much — if you do, your baby will just have a few loose movements and you can cut back. (See *Bowel Movements*, pp. 164–165. Note particularly *Special Precautions* and the reference to *Treatment of Infections*.)

Fresh air (See p. 174.)

Frostbite (See p. 175.)

Sunbaths (See p. 175.)

Lopsidedness

Something to watch at this stage of a baby's growth is the shape of its head. If your baby sleeps on its stomach — a position, by and large, most babies seem to prefer — you will have no problem; but if your baby prefers to sleep on its back, watch the shape of its head. Until the bones in a baby's skull fuse together, at about seven or eight months, a baby's head may become flattened on one side or the other depending on the position in which it sleeps. Babies tend to fall asleep facing in the direction from which their mother will come. If your baby sleeps on its back, you can prevent lopsidedness by having it sleep with its head at one end of the crib for one week: while it is looking toward the door, the pressure is on one side of its head. Then shift it so that its head will be at the other end of the crib the next week: it will still be looking toward the door but the pressure will be on the other side of its head. If the baby continues to sleep on its back, continue this shifting back and forth until it is six or seven months of age.

An amusing but pertinent footnote:

A mother brought her four-month-old baby in for a check-up, and in the course of the examination I pointed out that her baby's head was a little lopsided. Her baby slept on its back — the crib opposite the door. Once I brought the flattening to her attention the mother could easily see it. I made the suggestions I have just made here and the mother went home and shifted her baby so its head was at the other end of the crib. She was pleased to observe that her baby did indeed fall asleep with its head on the other side.

She called a few weeks later to say: "It's not working anymore! You know the wallpaper in the baby's room has those big red roses on it? Well, the baby's taken a shine to the red roses—falls asleep staring at the wall. She likes the roses better than she likes me! Now what?"

So, from then on, the shifts were made on the basis of her baby's preference for red roses.

The point is that, if your baby sleeps on its back, it's well to observe the position in which it falls asleep and to keep an eye on the shape of its head. You have a degree of control here in the toys and bright objects you hang over the crib and around the room as well as in the positioning of the crib.

This is certainly not a serious matter, but you will want your baby at seven or eight months to have a nicely rounded head.

Plugged Tear Ducts (See p. 178.)

Crossed Eyes (See p. 179.)

Weaning

At this time the question of how long a mother should continue to breast-feed often arises. This is entirely a personal matter. Many mothers at two, three or four months find they are getting up tired, and going to bed tired, and would welcome the suggestion that weaning would lighten their load.

I think that if you have nursed two to four months you should feel quite free to wean whenever you wish. You've given your baby a good start and it will continue to do well. What's more, you're every bit as good a mother as the mother who feels fine and prefers to continue nursing right up to ten months or so.

If you decide to wean, bear in mind that it should be done slowly. The speed depends entirely on your comfort. If your breasts are full, be sure to nurse—going slowly you can't get into any trouble (p. 114). Remember, wean to a bottle—either formula or, if your baby is close to three-and-one-half to four months of age, whole milk. Don't wean to a cup at this age (p. 144).

Responsibilities from Six Weeks to Four Months

This 6-week-old baby is very different from the one you brought home from the hospital. It's also different from the four-month-old baby that is the subject of the next chapter. Let's run through the *Responsibilities* and see how they will be affected by your baby's continuing growth and development.

Feeding

You should continue to trust nature to see to it that your baby will take all the food it wants. But there are pitfalls ahead that you will want to avoid at all costs. (To comprehend them fully I suggest that you turn back to the chapter on *Feeding*) (p. 31.)

At six weeks most babies are eating like regular little pigs, but at around two-and-one-half to three months their caloric intake will drop from 60 to 70 calories per pound of body weight daily to about 30 to 40 calories (pp. 31–32). This drop-off manifests itself in a loss of appetite—though the *degree* and the *time* of loss vary considerably from baby to baby. The appetite of the baby that's had plenty to eat right from the very start will surely drop off at this time. But for the baby that got off to a slow start the drop-off will take place correspondingly later.

Here's where any number of mothers fall into a trap and

start doing a thing that can lead to all kinds of problems — *coaxing their baby to eat.* In a matter of only a few weeks, the very same mothers who came to the office worried because their babies were eating too much would be right back in the office worried because their babies were "not eating enough." Let me assure you, as I used to assure them — *I have never seen a baby, given the opportunity to take all it wants, get into trouble from "not eating enough." The babies that get into trouble are the ones that are coaxed to eat and who develop a feeding problem which, in turn, leads to all manner of other problems* (pp. 32–34).

Solid Food

At about three months I suggest starting a little cereal and fruit — *after* the 10:00 A.M. feeding. Remember, a baby's principal food is its milk (source of calcium and protein); so be sure to offer the solids after the formula or breast-feeding. The reason to offer solid food at this young age is *partly* to introduce your baby to food of a texture different from that of milk, and *partly* to accustom it to taking this food from a spoon. Even if your baby takes only one-fourth of a demitasse spoonful, these things will slowly be accomplished (p. 56).

Since you don't want the introduction of solid food to cut down on the amount of milk your baby takes, how much solid food should you offer?

Bottle-Fed

1. If your baby is taking less than 24 to 26 ounces of formula a day, *offer very little solid food.*
2. If your baby is taking 26 or more ounces of formula a day, offer all the solid food it wants one, two or three times a day.

   I used to suggest that when a baby is taking the contents of a can of evaporated milk or a can of prepared formula in a day, rather than break into a new can for a day's feeding, it's easier for the mother to fill the baby up with as much solid food as it wants.

If, however, the baby starts cutting back on the amount of milk it takes, be sure that you cut back on the amount of solid food you offer.

Breast-Fed

1. If you have to offer solid food two or three times a day to satisfy your baby's appetite, be sure to question the adequacy of your breast milk supply. Remember, milk is your baby's principal food. Solids are introduced at this time primarily for educational reasons (pp. 141–143).
2. A good way to check your breast milk supply is to offer a 6:00 P.M. bottle instead of a breast-feeding. If your baby gobbles up 8 ounces of formula at 6:00 P.M. and is still hungry for solids two or three times a day, you should seriously think of weaning, as your breast milk supply is almost surely limited.

Treatment of Infections

As your baby grows, the number of contacts with those who have an infection or are coming down with one is bound to increase, especially in winter. Your baby is almost sure to have a few colds—you can't prevent them all—but try to keep them to a minimum. There's no reason to expose a baby unnecessarily. It is true that with each infection a child builds up a certain amount of immunity, but at this young age don't rush things.

Watch for the early signs of infection and start treatment as soon as possible (pp. 20–22).

Training

Sleeping

As your baby's appetite drops off, another change takes place. Around three months of age, and this varies, your baby will very likely tell you that it is ready to come off the 10:00 P.M. feeding. Now, how does it tell you?

1. You begin to have trouble wakening it for the "10 o'clock."
2. Your baby is obviously not interested in the feeding.
3. More often than not it takes a poor feeding.
4. But in spite of the poor feeding and to your great surprise, it sleeps through the night and has to be wakened for the "6:00 o'clock."

When this happens you can drop the "10 o'clock." If the baby is on the bottle, distribute the amount of formula in the 10:00 P.M. feeding among the remaining four bottles. Life really seems almost back to normal again!

You can continue on the 6, 10, 2, 6 schedule if you wish, but one that is just as good for the baby and easier for you parents is:

> 7:00 A.M. — Feed
> 8:15 to 8:30 A.M. — Bathe
> 10:30 A.M. — Feed
> 2:15 P.M. — Feed
> 4:00 P.M. — Playtime
> 6:00 P.M. — Feed

With this schedule you sneak up a little during the day. You mothers can get in an extra hour's sleep in the morning, and the two of you parents still have a chance for a quiet supper.

Time Awake

Your baby is now sleeping through a long, uninterrupted night. To keep the baby doing this its daytime waking hours may have to be increased even more, though the amount babies have to be kept awake in the daytime varies tremendously (p. 67). Don't use the crib as a play place. Cribs are for sleeping.

After breakfast you can put your baby in the playpen till bathtime, and in the afternoon you can lengthen the playtime. This is when the playpen begins to become invaluable for short periods. It's a safe place to leave a baby for a short time to interest and amuse itself. You mothers have housework and all sorts of things to do. Babies can be very happy playing in their pens. But you should be careful to balance these periods in the playpen with time out of the pen when you give your baby your undivided attention. Don't abuse the use of the playpen!

Education

Over this period education becomes, as it were, two-pronged: on the one hand, *teaching your baby to be independent and resourceful alone in its playpen;* on the other hand, *stimulating its growing responsiveness and dexterity in the times when you give it your undivided attention.* Gradually you can encourage its early attempts to reach for things, grasp them and hold on to them.

Prevention of Accidents

As your baby becomes increasingly active, your safety measures and safe handling are constantly being challenged.

1. Watch the changing table and always keep a hand or harness on the baby.
2. You can no longer count on the baby's staying put on a big bed or on a pad on the floor. I've already talked about the value of a playpen.
3. Remember there's always a first time a baby rolls over or moves around or hitches itself along!
4. Watch where you place an infant seat — the center of a big table or the floor are about the only safe places. Babies tip over infant seats surprisingly early.

Discipline

I have already mentioned *how much just a little discipline can accomplish if started early.* This is the time when *your opportunities to ignore unnecessary fussing* as you put your baby in its bed or playpen continually increase. You will have other opportunities as you *change it, wash its face, wash out its eyes, give it nose drops* and *take its temperature.* It's most important, right from the start, that with a *firm hand* holding it down and a *calm, explaining voice* you let your baby know that you are going to carry out necessary procedures. *If you do this consistently,* your bright baby will catch on very quickly.

From six weeks to four months family life should be going along easily. A contented baby on a good schedule at this age is as close to the equivalent of "no child in the house" as you'll ever have again. Awake periods are relatively short and mainly cleaning-up and feeding times, which are happy and satisfying times for mother and baby. The lucky father is the one who learns early how to involve himself in some of the care and handling — first thing in the morning, when he gets home evenings, certainly on weekends.

This is fun time for everyone! Your baby is shaping up into a nice little bundle to play with and is beginning to respond good-naturedly to your attempts to amuse it. You begin to catch glimpses of its personality. You begin to discover interesting and delightful things about it, and you can be sure it's learning a lot about the two of you.

The Bath by Mary Cassatt. (Courtesy of the Los Angeles County Museum of Art. Bequest of Mrs. Fred Hathaway Bixby.)

Chapter Seven

At
Four
Months

7 — At Four Months

Look Out! Changes Ahead!

This four-month-old baby of yours is quite a handful and quite a little person. No question but that it's grown. It has very possibly doubled its birthweight and has stretched out maybe four or five inches.

It is gaining more control over its actions all the time — over its arms and legs. It holds its head up well and turns it from side to side as it wishes. It can very likely roll over.

Everything it does it does with more vigor — including crying.

It's becoming increasingly conscious and observant of its surroundings — bats out at things, is beginning to reach for them and occasionally hangs on to them.

It's graciously responsive: rewards your efforts to amuse it — your very presence — with a smile.

From the way it's drooling you know that a tooth is slowly working its way through the gum and may appear anytime over the next month or so. I'd just as soon have you hold the baby at this time. I've learned not to trust babies at this stage of the game; they think absolutely nothing of spitting up a bit of the drool they're constantly swallowing.

In line with all this growth and development, let's take another look at the *Responsibilities* — nature's and yours — that we discussed in Part One of this book, now with an eye to any changes to be made at four months.

Feeding

Remember, milk is still your baby's principal food; it provides protein and also the calcium needed for growing bones. As we shall see shortly, under *Schedule,* your baby at about this time is ready to go on three meals.

If you are bottle-feeding I suggest you start offering your baby whole milk. Formula is milk with a sugar added. By shifting to whole milk you eliminate the added sugar and, as a result, the calories in the milk are reduced. This encourages the baby to satisfy its appetite by taking other essential foods.

Offer an 8-ounce bottle at each of the three meals — before offering solids. Since there's no 'added' sugar in whole milk, feel free to put a bit of sugar on cereals or wherever you yourself would like some.

If you are breast-feeding offer the breast before offering solid food. Remember to watch the amount of solid food your baby takes (p. 235).

If you decide to wean at around this time, wean to whole milk *from a bottle — not from a cup* (p. 144).

Solid Food.   Your doctor will advise you, very likely give you a diet list. At four months a baby is ready for and needs a more varied diet, new foods. I used to suggest, in addition to fruits and cereals, offering:

> Crushed graham crackers and milk — a change from cereal, also a mild laxative.
>
> Strained vegetables.
>
> Egg yolk — the yolk of a 20-minute boiled egg, mashed finely with a very small amount of milk slowly added to make a smooth consistency. Offer a little of this three or four times a week, *if* your baby likes it. If not, offer a little strained baby meat. *Egg yolk or meat adds iron* to your baby's diet.

Vary the meals; *offer small amounts.* You're introducing your baby to new foods, so do it gradually — there's no hurry!

Don't coax — you must be sick and tired of hearing this by now.

Just as important—*don't camouflage* foods to try to get your baby to eat them. This is just coaxing in a different guise.

I remember a mother bringing in her baby a couple of weeks after making the diet additions I've suggested here. Her baby had a rash behind its knees and in the bend of its elbows. I inquired about meals, and the mother volunteered the information that her baby hadn't seemed to take to the egg yolk—had refused to eat any. She added, "But I didn't let him outsmart me! He loves mashed banana, so I mixed some egg yolk with the banana and he took it well—for a time. Now he's beginning not to like it so much."

I hope, by now, you see what I'm driving at! Her baby *didn't like egg yolk; he was sensitive to it.* He did his best to tell his mother so but she wasn't about to listen to him. She tried to fool him—to camouflage the egg, to coax him. So her baby told her again, in no uncertain terms, that egg was not for him, by breaking out with a little eczema.

Babies very rarely like a food they're sensitive to. However, it was obvious that I hadn't done a good job of making it clear to this mother just what coaxing is. In any case, she discontinued the egg yolk and offered a little meat to provide iron instead. The baby's eczema cleared up, but it left its mark—on the mother!

Feeding is primarily nature's *Responsibility.* She assumes responsibility not only for *how much,* but also *to a certain extent for what* your child eats.

Training

Schedule

At the time of this growth and development on the part of your baby, I suggest some *changes in schedule.* At around four months, most babies are ready for three meals. Here's a possible schedule—but bear in mind that schedules should bend and flex to meet your family requirements and habits. (See pp. 52–53.)

7:30 *Breakfast,* breast or bottle, followed by cereal and fruit. Down in a playpen: a safe place, a change of scene — maybe some exercise, maybe a cat-nap.

9:00 *Bath.*

Before the bath — vitamins and fluoride. Make sure your baby is getting all it needs of these, especially when you change to whole milk (pp. 153–156).

After the bath — I suggest you start offering your baby straight fruit juice, perhaps with a little sugar in it, from a cup. *This is your baby's introduction to a cup — so go slowly!* Your aim is to slowly accustom your baby to this new way of taking liquids with an eye to the time, half a year away, when dentists think babies should be off all nipples. (See pp. 142–144.)

Naptime — if your baby wakens much before dinner, a short playtime, either with your undivided attention or in its playpen.

12:00 *Dinner,* breast or bottle, followed by solids — a variety depending on your baby's appetite: vegetables, maybe egg yolk (or meat), and fruit.

Naptime — the length depending on your baby's night's sleep.

3:00 *Playtime* of an hour, more or less. A time when you should
to give your baby plenty of undivided attention. Finish
4:00 off with a good drink of dilute fruit juice *from a bottle* — as much as your baby wants to take.

Quiet time — asleep in crib or just resting on its own in the playpen.

6:00 *Supper,* breast or bottle, followed by cereal and fruit.

Down for the night. If bottom rash is a problem, up at 10:00 or so for a bottom wash and a diaper change.

Time Awake

With your baby's steady growth and development, the length of time it's awake in the day will slowly increase. The amount it increases should be based solidly on how your baby sleeps at night, *not* on how much your girl friend's baby sleeps or is awake.

This means *planning ahead* each day: cutting naptimes short if your baby isn't sleeping through the night; *keeping a sensible balance between the amount and distribution of the undivided attention you give your baby and the times you leave it to amuse itself in its playpen.* Locate the playpen where your baby can watch you going about your housework and you can talk to it. Your baby will like having you stop frequently to play with it or give it a pat as you go by. Babies thoroughly enjoy company.

Education

As your baby becomes increasingly responsive and observant and exhibits greater dexterity, your opportunities in this area will be forever growing.

Discipline

This stronger, louder more vigorous baby of yours will be offering you plenty of opportunities to apply the brakes as it fusses on being left in its playpen or put to bed—as it takes exception to your carrying out necessary procedures. Just remember to think of your disregard of this kind of fussing as opportunities to help your baby at a time when helping is relatively simple and can accomplish so much, and also be sure to credit your baby, even at this tender age, with the capacity to learn. (See pp. 73–75.)

Prevention of Accidents

Playpen. This is becoming increasingly useful in so many ways—for *Training, Discipline, Education,* as well as for safety. I hope by this time you are beginning to savor its potential.

Sleeping Harness.   I suggest you reread the section on the sleeping harness in *Prevention of Accidents* (pp. 42–44). Four months is the time to start to accustom your baby to a sleeping harness. At this age a baby accepts one without a murmur. From this age on to the time, at 9 months and older, when a sleeping harness becomes really meaningful in terms of preventing accidents, a baby learns to associate it with that good feeling of being tucked snugly in bed, tired out, ready for sleep; or that equally happy time when, well rested, it bobs up as you unfasten the harness, all primed for the next bit of fun.

As time goes on, it becomes progressively harder for a baby to adjust to a harness easily and happily. While four months may not be absolutely your Last Chance Gasoline, *don't think for a moment* that, on cold nights when you worry about your eight-month-old baby being covered, you'll find it easy to start using a sleeping harness! *It won't be easy! Don't think for a moment* that when you worry about your one-year-old or year-and-a-half-old climbing or falling out of its crib, you can get it to accept a harness happily. *That's expecting a lot of a small child!*

In practice, time and again, parents faced with these worries would ask, "What can we do? ' "How can we keep our baby in its crib?"

Some parents, over a period of a week or two, by making a point of putting their baby down too dog-tired to struggle against the contraption—occasionally with the help of a little mild sedative—would manage to get their youngster to settle into a harness. Other parents would find the adjustment so miserable and unhappy for their baby that they would give it up.

At such times my own inner, unexpressed reaction always was: Why wasn't I able to get the logic of starting the use of a sleeping harness across to these parents when their baby was around four months old? I no doubt slipped up.

How does one pass on experience?

I remember a mother coming in distressed because her year-and-a-half-old boy had fallen out of his crib two nights running. He had doped out how to stack up in a corner of his crib the toys he *had to have* in order to go to sleep, and he used them as an assist in climbing up and *out.* Well, at this point it isn't easy to come up with helpful suggestions—though I've had plenty of opportunities to observe how different parents have tried to cope with the problem: a mattress on the floor to bounce out on or to sleep on; bars on the windows; a Dutch door to lock a child in but permit parents to see and hear; and there were other methods. As you can readily see, all these become, in the last analysis, a matter of restraint of some sort. To this particular mother, whose boy was a little toughy, I half-jokingly suggested she put him down in a football helmet and shoulder pads. That pleased her!

She called two days later to say that a friend in the next apartment had phoned during her boy's naptime with the information that her "little football player" was draped out over the window sill of his bedroom, watching the kids playing in the courtyard four floors below. Did I have any other suggestions? My logical next suggestion was: bars on the window.

Let me add a personal note. Mrs. Turtle and I have brought up three children using sleeping harnesses. We now have seven grandchildren sleeping in them or grown out of them. In our experience a sleeping harness securely fastened on *any kind of bed, anywhere*—at home, visiting, traveling, camping, out for the evening—means sleep and security for the baby and peace of mind for the parents. As one of our daughters says, "When we go to the home of friends for dinner and the evening, we sometimes take our baby with us, and my husband carries the crib—rolled up in his pocket."

Mrs. Turtle and I enjoy having these grandchildren left in our care because when we put them down we know they are happy, comfortable and safe!

The youngest—just past two—refers to her sleeping harness agreeably as "*my* night." Christmas afternoon, tired out by all the excitement, by trying to keep up with the big fellows, she asked to have "*my* night" pinned down on an unaccustomed bed. Then, contentedly, she resigned her weary little self to its familiar comfort and security.

Four months is the age to get a baby used to a sleeping harness. If you hope to prevent accidents in the future, you have to think ahead.

Odds and Ends

Let's now take a look at the various odds and ends of problems that may crop up over the period ahead—from four to eight months.

Circumcision

If your boy has been circumcised, watch for redness at the opening of the penis—this can be the forerunner of an ulceration. Let me refer you to the suggestions I made about prevention in the *Six Weeks* chapter (p. 229) and about treatment should an ulceration develop (p. 160).

If your boy has not been circumcised, be sure adhesions are slowly being broken (p. 161). This should be accomplished by around six months or so. Thereafter, be sure to push back the foreskin and wash whenever you bathe the baby, just as you wash every other part of its body. Cleaning under the foreskin isn't what causes masturbation—some mothers worry about this unnecessarily.

Rashes

Cheek Rash. Your baby is drooling more and more, and everything goes into its mouth, drawing saliva out over its cheeks. See p. 162 on cheek rash, and especially p. 167 on teething. Be sure to keep the headpiece *dry* and wash the baby's cheeks frequently with soap and water.

Bottom (Diaper) Rash. Around 6 to 8 months, when you go in mornings to get your baby up, you may notice the odor of ammonia in the room. You will almost surely notice it as you change the baby.

1. When the urine becomes more concentrated and the ammonia content higher, diaper rash can become more of a

problem. As your baby's waking hours increase, however, frequent offerings of water and fruit juice will help keep the urine dilute. 2. Remember, soap and water washes first, then ointment *only on a clean skin.* (See p. 162.)

Heat Rash. (See p. 163.)

Rash Behind the Ears. (See p. 163.)

Cradle Cap. (See p. 164.)

Plugged Tear Ducts

If, at six months or so, "matter" continues to accumulate in your baby's eyes, or if it is troubled by crusting around the eyelids, be sure to bring this to your doctor's attention. (See p. 178.)

Bowel Movements and Constipation

Movements should still not be formed. You can control their firmness by using nature's laxatives. (See pp. 164–165. Note particularly *Special Precautions* and reference to *Treatment of Infections,* p. 165.)

Fresh Air (See p. 174.)

Frostbite (See p. 175.)

Sunbaths (See p. 175.)

Teething (See pp. 166–168.)

From four to eight months is teething time, the time when the advanced signs of teething peak:

Drooling and cheek and chin rash;
Spitting up;
Slimy, frequent stools and bottom rash;
Night cough;
Crying out at night as if in pain.

Thumb-Sucking

From four to eight months, babies are really feeling their teeth and trying their best to do something about it. Everything goes into their mouths — fists and thumbs included. Don't try to stop this; just have plenty of safe things to chew on readily available. Understanding why a baby chews on things may make it easier for you not to have a conniption fit every time your baby's thumb or fingers go into its mouth. (See pp. 168–171.)

Growth

Many mothers wonder around four or five months if their baby is getting too fat — should be put on a special diet. In my experience, if a baby is on a normal diet, it would be most exceptional to have to put it on a diet to reduce its weight.

1. At around three to four months babies normally stop gaining as rapidly as they did at first.
2. Babies, *early*, tend to grow proportionately more in *breadth* than in *length*. Then, just about the time mothers start to worry that their babies are getting too fat, their babies start lengthening out and gradually distribute their fat. At about a year of age, these babies are just right.

If a baby under a year of age is on a normal diet, it's unnecessary to worry about its getting too fat or to take steps to hold down its weight.

Overpossessiveness

Around four to eight months it is well to think about this and to accustom your baby to being handled by others, as well as to accustom yourselves to *enjoy* seeing your baby handled by others.

Babysitters

This is about the time babysitters come into your lives. If your baby is going along smoothly on a good schedule, is becoming accustomed to being handled by others, and is slowly learning that unnecessary fussing doesn't work, you will feel more comfortable on leaving it, and I assure you that you will find it easier to get a *good* sitter who will be willing to come back a second time.

Responsibilities from Four Months to Eight Months

From some of the problems that are beginning to enter your lives, you can see how rapidly changes are going to be taking place over this four- to eight-month period. At four months your baby is still so cuddly, amiable and adaptable, its fussing is still so relatively mild and inoffensive, its activity is still so circumscribed, that it is next to impossible for you parents to envision what lies ahead. What seems so simple and easy at four months will be something quite different at eight months. This baby of yours is beginning to emerge as an individual. Your job as parents is just shaping up. This is the time to establish as "second nature" patterns in the *Safety, Training, Discipline* and *Education* of your baby that can grow and develop as your baby grows and develops.

Let's have a look at the *Responsibilities* as they will figure in your baby's development from four to eight months, and try to calculate where they are heading.

Feeding

Here your role continues the same as it has been right along — *to provide* food and *to offer* food to your baby. You'll be offering new foods, and it will be up to you to vary them and make the meals attractive. But here your supporting role begins and ends. Nature, as always, is right on deck carrying on with her responsibility to see to it that your baby *takes as much food as it needs.*

Appetite.   As I've already pointed out, at around two-and-one-half to three months, babies' big early appetites begin to fall off; and from four to eight months, *very few babies eat as much as their mothers would like to see them eat.* Moreover, the amount they eat begins to vary greatly and unpredictably from one meal to the next. This is new and different, so be on your guard! *Don't allow your emotions to get mixed up in how much your baby eats.*

Milk.   Over this period babies often begin to get tired of and bored with their milk; they've been taking it for such a long time! But they continue to need the nourishment in milk, so it's up to you to vary a bit the way in which you offer it.

1. You may find it reasonable to *alternate* offerings of breast or bottle with the solids.
2. If your baby begins to cut down to less than a pint of milk a day, this need be no problem. There are other ways to introduce milk into its diet. Offer junkets, milk puddings, soft custard, milk soups and similar items.

Put plenty of milk on cereals; add a little to vegetables or fruits; crushed graham crackers take up a lot of milk. Just do your best, one way or another, to have your baby take at least a pint of milk a day.

If you're breast-feeding it isn't always easy to be sure of your milk supply, which makes things tricky. (See p. 235.)

New Foods. I used to suggest, at around seven or eight months, adding variety to a baby's diet by the gradual introduction of meats, potatoes, rice, spaghetti, cottage cheese, soft boiled eggs and so on. It doesn't matter so much *what* you offer, as *how* you offer it!

Vary the meals;

Keep them small—you can always offer more;

Make them attractive.

You're introducing new foods:

Some your baby may take to;

Others it may not like right off the bat;

Some it may never like.

Remember, your baby is another individual and will have tastes of its own. Go slowly!

Above all, you've got that spoon in your hand, and there's always the temptation to try to get just one more bite into your baby, or to have your baby finish what's in the dish (you probably shouldn't have put so much in to begin with). Read over pp. 32–36 on what coaxing is and, whatever you do, leave the *amount* of food your baby takes to nature. *Stay on your side of the fence!* (p. 90)

Highchair. Up to four months of age most mothers feed their babies while holding them on their laps. Some mothers, bottle-feeding, start to use an infant seat fairly early; but I feel that being held in its mother's arms is, for a small baby, an important part of the process of being fed.

However, at some point from four to eight months, with the introduction of additional solid foods, you may find it easier to start feeding your baby in a highchair. As soon as your baby can sit up, or is happy being propped up, this works well.

Always use a harness in a highchair—babies slide under the tray and slip to the floor easily.

The highchair has an added advantage as a place to feed a baby. In time the tray can be taken off and the chair pushed right up to the table, thus, as the child gets older, making the transition from highchair to eating at the table an easy one for the child.

Infections

Remember, as your baby gets older, contacts with people who either have or are coming down with infections constantly increase. Try to minimize unnecessary exposures.

Watch for the early signs of infection—especially if there has been a known exposure. Get treatment started early. (See pp. 21–22.) It's better to start treatment early even if an infection doesn't develop—a day's rest and extra liquids are never amiss—than to be late in getting it started.

Training

Sleeping

Naturally, as your baby gets older, its 24-hour sleep requirements drop off.

Your primary aim is to have your baby sleep all night.

Your secondary aim is a short morning nap and a longer afternoon nap.

Looking ahead, a night's sleep plus a long afternoon nap make a good distribution of sleep time. By eight months the morning nap may have to be completely eliminated. You and your baby will have to work this out between you. (See p. 62.)

Time Awake

As your baby's sleep falls off, you will have to assume increasing responsibility for its time awake. (See pp. 67–69.)

Discipline

Bear in mind the importance of a firm hand and an explaining voice, both of them used consistently and with inner conviction. Babies differ, but over this time you parents will almost surely find that your baby is *louder, more determined, less patient* and *more persistent* in fussing at procedures that annoy it—diaper changing, face washing—and at being left in its playpen or settled in its crib. If, over this rather crucial period—four to eight months—you carry out necessary procedures with *firmness*, with *disregard of fussing*, with a *cheerful "let's get it over with" manner and tone of voice*, your baby will catch on and these procedures can—believe it or not—continue to be fun for both of you.

However, firmness and disregard of fussing are simply canceled out if you show annoyance, exasperation or anger at your baby's protests, squirming and fussing. (See pp. 76–81.)

Prevention of Accidents

Here's where looking ahead becomes all important! At four months a playpen isn't *absolutely essential,* but it's becoming more and more so. By eight months it *surely will be! Don't lose the use of it!* From four to eight months your baby *will accept it, become accustomed to it,* and *be very happy in it,* for reasonable periods. Don't misuse it! When, at eight to ten months, your baby begins to creep, to get itself about one way or another, unless your baby has become accustomed to the playpen, I don't see how you can prevent accidents, without giving your baby your undivided attention most of the day.

If you are really *thinking ahead*, you will start at four months to prevent accidents that can happen at eight months and older (pp. 45–48).

> A mother brought her seven- or eight-month-old baby in to the office. Creeping around, it had managed to pull a toaster off the dining-room table. We patched up its head and when we were through the mother said, "What am I going to do? I can't watch him every minute! He's so quick!"
>
> I knew this mother had stopped using the playpen a couple of months earlier — *her smart baby had fussed his way out of it!* No use looking back! What could I say? I know how hard it is at eight months to get a baby back in its playpen! This is the pickle parents get into if they aren't helped to or if they fail to look ahead.

Education

Fun for everybody!

Offer a variety of stimuli and draw responses from your baby. Encourage its growing perceptions: sense of touch; looking at things; listening to things. Fathers have a lot to offer here. If they want to, they can *find the time* — in the morning, when a busy mother is trying to get the day organized; in the evening; weekends.

A point I'd like to make here is that *changes are taking place,* your baby is *growing!* While you parents may be gazing on your baby with pride and indulgence, your baby is almost surely quietly observing and appraising you. If you just sit back, which is so easy and tempting, your baby, by six to eight months, will be quite capable of beginning to take advantage of you in innumerable little ways. *Education works both ways and parents can sometimes be slower than babies to learn!*

I consider the period we have covered here — four to eight months — an instructive, learning time for parents.

May I suggest that, if you keep up with your homework — your part of the job — *this is the time when you parents can establish attitudes and approaches to the handling of your baby that will carry you through the first year and well beyond and make life so much easier for your baby.*

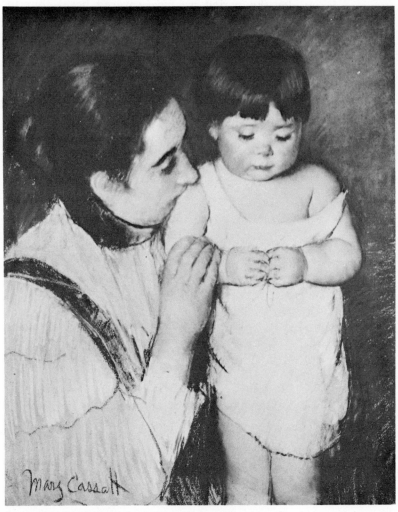

Young Thomas and His Mother by Mary Cassatt. (Courtesy of the Pennsylvania Academy of the Fine Arts.)

Chapter Eight

At
Eight
Months

8 — At Eight Months

Who's Smarter — Parents or Baby?

At eight months, figuratively though not necessarily physically speaking, babies are getting ready to stand on their own feet. They are becoming *somebody* — one more person in the world to be reckoned with, as I'm sure you parents are finding out.

By this age most babies have tripled their birth weight. They have added maybe seven or eight inches to their length at birth. Around this age they tend to stretch out and distribute their chubbiness.

They are almost surely sitting up. Many of them can pull themselves to their feet but, as a rule, most of them have only one way to get down again — to fall. (Watch out for hard or sharp objects in the playpen.)

Some babies at this age are creeping, some rolling, some hitching themselves about in remarkable ways, but, one way or another, they are on the move. *Watch out!*

All the time they are getting stronger and more assertive. They bang their toys about. They are experimenting with their vocal apparatus, trying to produce sounds other than crying. They can be noisy!

They continue to grow ever more observant of and responsive to their surroundings, and to attention from those around them — from you! They smile and gurgle and have a good hearty laugh when you play with them.

The changes you can see are equaled, very likely surpassed, by the changes you can't see — the changes going on inside their little heads.

They're beginning to contemplate purposefully, to cogitate, to put two and two together. You're going to have to keep your wits about you to keep up with your baby's nimble, expanding mind.

From here on, generally speaking, the time at which things happen, at which changes take place, varies anywhere from a matter of weeks to a matter of months from one baby to another. Babies have their own inner timetables: they may be advanced in one area and pokey-slow in another — no comparisons, please! What is "normal" differs so widely at this point that it makes sense to consider in one chunk the entire 8- to 12-month period, without bothering to break it down. This period differs from the 4- to 8-month period mainly in that everything is just *a little more so* — it offers you parents a testing time of sorts, a chance to see how well you have your responsibilities in hand.

Training

Schedule

From 8 to 12 months there aren't many schedule changes. The principal one involves naps, and here the variations from baby to baby are great. (See *Training*, pp. 62–63.) It's well during this period to keep getting up, going to bed and mealtimes *fairly regular*. In between times, because babies are usually increasingly awake and active, the schedule should be *fairly flexible.*

7:30 — *Breakfast*
> Through the morning it is well to alternate periods in a playpen or some other safe place with periods when you give undivided attention.

Bath or sponge bath

Juice from a cup
Vitamins and fluoride

All these can be timed to offer strategic breaks throughout the morning.

A short nap, depending on night's sleep

12:00 or possibly 11:30 — *Dinner*

> If your baby takes no morning nap, it may begin to tire — in this case, the noon meal can always be pushed ahead a little.
>
> *Afternoon nap* — the longer, possibly the only nap. Its length depends on how your baby sleeps through the night.

3:00 to 5:00 (approximately) — *Playtime*

> 1. *A good part of the time on the loose with your undivided attention. The remaining time divided among short periods spent in its playpen or propped up in its highchair or in some other safe place* — time by itself.
>
> 2. Offer dilute fruit juice at some point, from a bottle or, once the baby is weaned, offer straight fruit juice from a cup, at intervals.

5:00 to 5:30 — *Bath or sponge bath*

> Crawling around, babies get dirty — at this stage of the game they make good dry (often good wet) mops. Toward the end of the day a bath can be relaxing.

5:30 to 6:00 — *Supper*

> Chance for a short, quiet time with father. Watch out — don't get your baby *too* worked up just before bedtime.

7:00 (approximately) — *Bedtime*

> Although it may vary a bit, summer to winter, this early bedtime gives parents a chance to have a quiet supper and evening together.

Awake Time

From eight months to a year most babies are awake the greater part of the day. A baby at this age:

> a. *Is more active* — not active enough to really wear itself out, but plenty active enough to sometimes wear you down and out;

b. *Is more of an individual* — beginning to have a mind: some notions and ideas of its own;

c. However, *its attention span is short.*

At this age, *your job becomes increasingly and differently challenging.*

a. It takes ingenuity, flexibility and above all a good sense of humor to keep things on an even keel. No two days will be alike!

b. You should be prepared to juggle various possibilities about. To shift and balance your baby's needs and schedule against the needs and schedules of the other members of the family.

There will be *periods when the baby is on its own,* in a safe place, with you in the background — observing and ready to break in as needed:

a. With offering of juice or water; with a wash or wipe off; with a diaper change and so on.

b. With a change of scene: shifts from playpen to high-chair; shifts in location of playpen or highchair from room to room, from indoors to outdoors.

c. With momentary chances for you to get off your feet, sit down and play for a few minutes, admire and encourage its ingenuity.

d. With shifts of toys — a few toys at a time, changed as the need for a new stimulation is indicated.

This is the stage when weariness or boredom, unobserved, unanswered, unprevented, encourages thumb-sucking (pp. 168–171) *and masturbation* (pp. 175–176).

There will be periods when you give your baby your undivided attention:

a. When your baby has a chance to creep, roll, hitch itself about, occasionally balance itself, stand or take a few steps — a chance to get about, explore, investigate — indoors, outdoors — always with your undeviating attention and involvement.

    b. Times when, your baby in the stroller, the two of you take walks, times when you go shopping, visiting, out in the car.

You will learn to switch things around at the drop of a hat— just keep in mind that:

    a. *Times on its own are just as valuable as times when you give completely of yourself.*

    b. You should offer variety always within the framework of a fairly regular schedule—*you and your baby will derive satisfaction and a feeling of security from a certain degree of sameness in such things as "going down," "getting up" and "sitting down to meals."*

    c. *Everything goes on with your baby's safety in mind.*

Feeding and Eating Habits

You'll find your baby's appetite continues to vary greatly from meal to meal, day to day. Take it in your stride—*this is no concern of yours.*

One of your principal jobs as parents is to teach your baby good eating habits. Eating everything and anything with hands and splashing food about are not my idea of good habits. I think finger food should be food that is always eaten that way:

> crackers
> toast or bread and butter
> zwieback
> cookies
> carrot sticks
> celery sticks
> apple or fruit chunks

but, not as a rule, meat, potatoes and cooked vegetables.

Don't be in a rush to turn the spoon over to your baby. Do so slowly — occasionally try it out toward the end of meals.

It's important to keep meals under control: When your baby starts playing with the food — throwing it on the floor — that should mean the end of the meal.

Don't let bad habits that will have to be changed later get started!

All babies are different. Try not to make comparisons. *Don't worry about how, how much or what the baby across the street is eating. You're feeding your individual baby.*

Bowel Training (Not Bladder)

1. *Many babies by 8 to 12 months are ready to begin bowel training.* You mothers are so close to your babies you often sense when this is a possibility. (See pp. 65–66.)
2. As I've suggested, a shelf rigged up or a small table that straddles the toilet seat and all helps to keep a toy or toys immediately accessible and, for the boy baby, may help to keep the level of trajectory within bounds.
3. Five minutes allows time enough for nature to work — if she's about to do so.
4. If this training venture isn't working, drop it — *try it again in a month or so. Watch your emotions.* Don't allow your desire or your determination to be successful in this area filter through to your baby. And here again — *no comparisons!* Have I made the point that *all babies are different?*

Infections

Keep in mind the importance of minimizing contacts so as to prevent infections. Be alert to nature's early warning of infection and get in on the ground floor with treatment. (See pp. 20–22.)

Odds and Ends

Constipation

Your baby's stools may be more "formed" than they have been, but they should continue to be soft and the baby should continue to have a bowel movement daily. Should stools tend to become hard, rely on nature's laxatives: juices, fruits and so on. (See pp. 164–165.)

Teething

Throughout this period your baby's back teeth — the big molars — are erupting. They don't, as a rule, seem to trouble a baby as much as did the earlier teething. Sometimes a good rub along the gums with a clean finger is comforting.

Thumb-Sucking

1. A baby may still be chewing on its thumb, fist, fingers or knuckles because of the discomfort of teeth. Have readily available plenty of good things to chew on and plenty of toys to keep hands busy.
2. Watch the day and night schedule. Your baby, left too long in its crib or pen, may become bored and, for lack of something more interesting to do, resort to sucking on a thumb.
3. This is the beginning of a period that stretches out for almost a year or so, when there may be a gradual, barely noticeable change-over: A baby who has been sucking or chewing on a thumb because of the *discomfort of teeth* may continue to suck or chew out of *boredom, weariness or stress* — seeking comfort or consolation. As the thumb, or whatever, slips into the mouth, you can quietly and unobtrusively offer a toy, a new interest or a change of location.

4. Your control over the schedule has much to offer here. *So does your control over your emotions.* Don't let your baby sense for one moment that its sucking has you disturbed. (See p. 170.)

Weaning

Somewhere from 10 to 12 months, give or take a month either way, your baby should be weaned from the breast or bottle, as recommended by the dentists (p. 144). (See *Weaning, Breast,* p. 114; *Bottle,* p. 136.) Remember to go at it slowly! *When you shift to the cup your baby's fluid intake may fall off, so between meals offer your baby all the juice, dilute fruit juice or water it wants.*

I want to repeat—be sure your baby is off all nipples by about a year of age.

Prevention of Accidents

From eight months to a year and onward most babies are exceedingly active. Left to themselves they are all over the place. They are unpredictably and often incredibly fast. A mother can't possibly be watching them every minute and do anything else at the same time.

For this reason it becomes increasingly important that you do—better yet, that you have by this time built into yourself the importance of doing—everything possible to prevent accidents.

Mothers used to bring their injured babies in to the office to be patched up, and so frequently the mothers seemed to be trying to convince me that somehow or other the accident was the baby's fault. "I don't know what I'm going to do! This baby is just 'accident prone,' that's all!"

Babies aren't "accident prone"! At this age babies are simply bursting with energy and curiosity—and they should be!

It's parents that are all too often either unaware of or un-
conscious of the risks and dangers in their babies' daily lives — or,
regrettably, *prone to be casual about such things.*
Let me put into the record once again:
   When you are unable to give your baby your undivided attention,
when you are doing your housework etc.
   a. *Be sure your baby is in a safe place:*
      A playpen;
      A highchair with harness;
      A baby-proofed room with gate;
      A fenced in play yard with gate.
   b. *Be sure to use harnesses in the* highchair, stroller, crib,
      training seat, and car seat.
*There are far too many accidents in the first year — let's keep them to a
minimum!*

The end of the first year sees the beginning of the second phase
of your responsibility to prevent accidents. This is when you
begin to teach your baby safe ways of handling itself. This is
when your responsibility in *Discipline* merges with your responsibility in *Prevention of Accidents* and you begin to teach your baby
the obedience that will make it a safer child. (See pp. 49–50).

Discipline

Between eight and twelve months discipline takes on a
new look. *You are no longer dealing with a baby, unable to do a little
thinking for itself. You're dealing with a developing individual.* At
this age babies often become very absorbed in what they are
doing. They're having fun playing. They resent having their
play interrupted by what they consider ridiculous routine procedures. Quite naturally they fuss! *This requires understanding,
tact and good humor on the part of parents* as well as *firmness and consistency.*
   Also, because babies are beginning to get about, there are
more *untouchables* and *restrictions.* Therefore *the words "no" and*

"don't slowly enter the picture. (See p. 77.) Said meaningfully and firmly they gradually become warnings a baby learns to respect. Sometimes, to get the point across, *the words have to be backed up with a little discipline,* which may mean the *loss of freedom* or the *loss of your undivided attention. Back in the playpen a baby senses your disapproval even at a very young age.* Use of the words must be carefully rationed—don't keep repeating them meaninglessly all day long.

By this time—eight to twelve months—*babies know a great deal about you parents:*

1. *They know when your firmness may give way to their persistence.*
2. *They know when you are tired and may give in.*
3. *They know you are not always consistent—when something just may be worth "another try."*

If at this pliable stage you establish certain *definite limits* to your baby's action and behavior, *you will slowly convey to your baby the meaning of obedience.* As time goes on this will make things happier, easier and more secure not only for your child but for you parents as well.

Education

Because babies at this age have developed a fair amount of coordination, they are better able to handle themselves and to manipulate objects. And because their minds are really beginning to tick, they soak up new impressions, make associations and begin to relate cause and effect. So there's no end to what you can offer to stimulate these growing accomplishments— which means letting yourselves, your ingenuity and your imaginations go.

This is when you invent games and surprises— encourage skills by putting things together and taking them apart, by piling things up and knocking them down, and by putting tops on and taking them off. This is the period when you have roughhouse times as well as quiet times with picture books, nursery rhymes, and music.

And just as important for your baby's development and as fascinating for you to observe—this is the time when you leave your baby on its own—in a safe place—to entertain itself, to repeat simple procedures over and over, to try out growing skills, and to become absorbed in its growing perceptions, its own creativity.

All this adds up to *fun and education for baby and parents.*

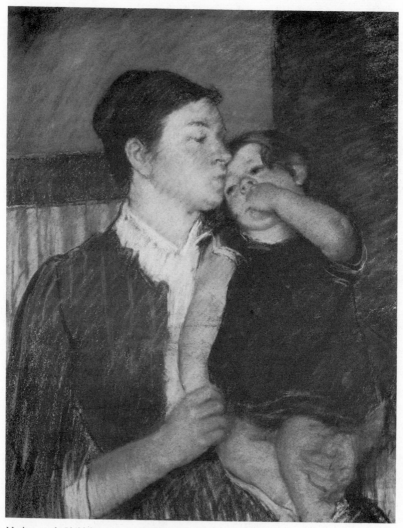

Mother and Child by Mary Cassatt. (Courtesy of The Art Institute of Chicago.)

Chapter Nine

At
One
Year

9 — At One Year

The Season on Parents Now Definitely Open

A mother came to the office bringing in her baby for its first-year check-up. I was happy to see them. I had enjoyed all my contacts with this family over their baby's first year — in the office, phone calls, house visits. From the start this woman had been anxious to do a good job of handling her baby. She'd been easy to help: receptive to ideas, conscientious in following through on suggestions. Now I was pleased to go over her baby.

He was healthy and solid, skin clear, color excellent. He had stretched out a good nine inches, he weighed in at better than triple his birth weight. I took him out of the scales and held him up high; he chortled and beamed down on us — no trace of apprehension. I proceeded to vaccinate him as, relaxed and confident, he sat on his mother's lap — he hardly even bothered to screw up his face.

I mentioned one or two things to be on the lookout for and then asked the mother if she had any questions. She thought for a moment and then said, surprisingly: "You know what I was thinking? I should think this baby would be tired!"

"Tired!" I exclaimed, wondering what on earth she could mean.

She went on, "Well, I was thinking as I came in today. You know, I used to teach school and I worked hard at it and by the end of the year I'd be dead-tired — worn out. Well, *this baby has taught us so much over this year*, that I should think *he'd* be tired — just about worn out."

Well, that's the way the first year goes when you know what your job consists of and stick with it — when you listen to and learn from your baby.

If over the course of these *Postnatal* chapters, by stressing the *Responsibilities,* I've made them seem demanding and time-consuming, made the first year seem difficult, a lot of work, let me say right now that that is just what the first year isn't — shouldn't be, at any rate. In Chapter Seven, *At Four Months,* I pointed out that four to eight months is the time when you parents can establish attitudes and approaches to the care and handling of your baby that become an integral part of you, that grow and develop *in you* as your baby grows and develops.

What happens is that as the year goes along you begin to find that you instinctively guard against unnecessary exposure to infection and keep an eye out for nature's early warning signs. You get in the habit of offering small, balanced meals, of not worrying about the amount your baby eats, of just making sure it gets all it wants. The safety of your baby stays uppermost in your mind at all times — thinking in terms of safe situations becomes practically automatic. You keep the days running pretty much on schedule because that's the way days go best and the way your baby is happiest. The playpen for your baby becomes just that — a good place to play for a short time. Encouraging good habits is easy because, surprisingly, babies like to do things well — they love to hear your praise. When they wave a hand and get a pleased response, they, in turn, respond with pleasure. You ignore fussing, and fussing ceases to be worth it. The limits you set are — gradually, sometimes — observed. Nothing is more fascinating than to watch a baby crawl to an off-limits spot, look at it speculatively, turn to consider you, and then move on. Again, it's not worth it. Is this baby learning? Is this baby primed to learn all the other things you have to offer?

Sure, I suppose you can think of the first year as I've suggested you carry through with it as "work." Caring for, observing, constantly thinking in terms of a baby — some might, I suppose, consider this "work." To a certain extent the Responsibilities *are demanding, time-consuming.* But what job that is worth it isn't work? And what do you come out of this first year with? Let's take a look:

I would like to think that, having read this book *prenatally,* and having been able to take advantage of the opportunities the first year has to offer, you will find yourselves living with a baby whose physical systems are running smoothly, whose nerves are not jangled, a relaxed baby, slowly and happily adjusting to living *in* this world and *with* the people in it.

I would like to think that over the course of the year you parents will have developed patterns in the care and handling of your youngster that will stick by you and continue to be a help.

I would like, moreover, to think that you will be way ahead of the game: that you will have anticipated and prevented many of the nagging problems with which, when I was in practice, I used to see so many parents struggling — primarily because they had gotten off to what seemed to me a poor start. To live with a two-, three- or four-year-old youngster who is completely out of hand, running you ragged, ruling the roost — this is strenuous, frustrating business. To try to correct solidly entrenched handling problems at age two, three or four is easily *twice as much 'work,' twice as demanding, twice as time-consuming* as anything this book has to suggest.

Here are a few examples of the sorts of things that used to come up in the office — examples with which by now you should be quite familiar, which you should readily recognize, either as vigorous extensions of the mild fussings I hope you will learn to ignore early in the game or as that often hard-to-resist temptation to try to take over nature's responsibility for the amount of food a baby eats, to try to coax more food into it.

I think of the little mother who came in with her sturdy two-year-old boy. He seemed almost as big as she. She heaved him up on the examining table and said, "What *am* I going to do? He is *so big* and *so strong* I can hardly handle him! And when I try to change him he kicks so with *those shoes* — just look!" Her arms had black-and-blue marks up and down them. In a wrestling match between the two I'd have bet on the boy anytime! *Babies grow big so fast!*

I think of the endless numbers of mothers who used to say such things as: "What *am* I going to do? I can't spend the whole day with her! I take her out to the play yard and play with her for a bit in the sandbox but she watches me like a hawk! The minute I so much as stand up or start to edge toward the gate she lets out the most awful yells and screams! You'd think I was murdering her! I just can't get anything else done!''

I think of the hectic mothers on the telephone: "I don't know what his temperature is. He won't let me near him with a thermometer! I'll see if I can get the girl next door to come in and help me hold him. I'll call back if I manage to take his temperature—otherwise I'll have to wait till my husband gets home.''

And always, heaven help me, I think of the remarkable number of remarkable mothers who, when I would weigh their child and say that it was gaining quite satisfactorily, would exclaim; "But I can't believe it! How *can* she have gained? She eats next to nothing! I spend hours trying to get enough food into her! She has me so upset and worried!'' Sometimes it used to seem to me that mothers who succumb to this particular worry and upset would, if laid end to end, stretch the length of Boston's Circumferential Highway!

This book isn't intended to help you treat handling problems such as these in your two-, three- and four-year-olds. All it can, hopefully, do is help you prevent some of them. If from the start you know what your job is and stick with it—carrying on with your four Responsibilities, assisting but not interfering with nature as she carries on with hers—you will, I believe, find imbedded in you patterns in the care and handling of your baby that will continue to bolster you as your child grows.

I would like now, for the last time, to take a look at all six Responsibilities—at where they stand at year's end, and where they go from here. I would like to reflect upon how those by now second-nature attitudes and approaches will help you in the next months, year or so.

Treatment of Infections (Nature's Responsibility)

1. As your child grows nature will continue to provide you with the early warning signs of infection.

2. When your child has a cold your job will continue to be: to *keep him in bed, warm and quiet, increase his fluids and watch his bowels* — to support nature in her treatment of infection.
3. I hope I've made it clear that infections are *almost always the result of contact.* As your child begins to play with other children and starts school, he or she is bound, for the first few years, to have an increased number of infections. Nature will continue to do her part; with each infection a child develops a little more immunity. Colds are not an entirely losing game.

However, once your child starts school, if he has repeated infections, don't ever question the wisdom of taking the child out of school for a couple of weeks' rest — a couple of weeks in which to be free from constant exposures.

Don't ever push nature too far. There might just be a time when a combination of circumstances — such as overtiredness coupled with repeated infections — could result in a child's having not just an ordinary cold but a cold with complications.

As children get older, infections other than colds enter the picture. Very commonly they start as colds. If your child has a cold but *it is not straightforward, if you are puzzled, if there is anything out of the ordinary* — a rash, severe headache or abdominal pain — don't try to diagnose it yourself! Don't ask the girl across the street!

Call your doctor!

I always think of the mother who called me in one Monday morning to behold her little girl liberally sprinkled with the rash of chicken pox. The mother said: "Well, Saturday she seemed fine! Her nose was a little drippy and she had a few funny red spots on her, here and there, but she wasn't complaining of a thing! I asked my friend next door and she said, 'They look kind of like flea bites to me. Maybe your dog has fleas!' So I let my little girl go to a birthday party in the afternoon. Boy, am I embarrassed! Now I'll have to call all those mothers!"

You should be aware that your child not only can pick up colds but *can also spread them.* Don't be thoughtless about the spread of infection, in or out of the home!

Don't let the child who is sick to her stomach in the night and then wakens with only a very slight temperature talk you into letting her go to the school picnic.

When your boy doesn't admit to a sore throat because he doesn't want to miss football practice — and then has to miss not only the next day's practice but Saturday's game as well — maybe you can help him understand the importance of giving in to an infection early, both for his sake and for the sake of the other guys on the team.

As your family grows you have the opportunity to slowly pass on to them your responsible attitude toward the treatment and spread of infection.

Be sure to see to it that by around the end of the first year, your baby has had all the necessary immunizations. Remember also that check-ups are most IMPORTANT! Don't be casual about them!

This is when possible defects, diseases and conditions of one sort or another can be picked up early and treated or corrected far more easily than if allowed to go on — things such as flat feet, poor posture, anemia, and sugar in the urine and many others. This too is when handling problems can be caught and checked.

This is good *preventive medicine.*

Get the advice of your dentist about teeth care and check-ups. Dentists feel that most parents are pretty casual about this.

Be sure to have your child's eyes checked for "lazy eye" between the ages of three and four years. (See p. 179).

Hearing should be checked by at least the first grade.

These check-ups should educate you and the family to the importance of family check-ups yearly.

More preventive medicine!

Feeding (Nature's Responsibility)

I've talked a lot about feeding, but this is an area of responsibility in which those early built-in attitudes and approaches have a great deal to offer both parents and growing child. If, by at least four to eight months, it becomes firmly wedged in your head that you can safely leave to nature the amount your baby eats, and if you steadfastly carry on with the concept, coaxing, for you, will be "out."

At a year of age most children are on pretty much of a house diet: whatever is being eaten, cut or ground or chopped up to size can be offered. But the feedings should still be kept well under control. At this age a child can hold a cup and wield a spoon, but not reliably or to much useful purpose.

I remember stopping in at a home one noontime. Beckoning me to the kitchen door to see her year-old boy, the mother said delightedly, "Look! He's just about learned to feed himself!"

Well, there was easily as much food on the boy's face, hands and hair, on his bib, highchair and floor surrounding the highchair, as there could possibly have been inside him!

Nothing is gained by being in a hurry. Don't ask too much of your child. Keep the eating of meals within the range of his competence and understanding.

As your child gets older and can sit at table, he will still need your help in understanding that meals are not for dreaming, or for jumping down from the table and running around; that eating a meal is something that can be accomplished in a reasonable time. These are things that will require time and patience on your part. Your own eating habits and standards enter in here. As you can readily see, this is a place where two Responsibilities — feeding, the offering of food, and training, helping a child slowly develop good eating habits — overlap.

A few points to bear in mind as you go along:

1. Your job is to offer *well-balanced meals, vary them, make them attractive.*
2. Don't pile food so high on a plate that your child is discouraged before he starts. Give small — sometimes very small — helpings. You can always give more. But in a world where many children go to bed hungry, it's well to start early to discourage wasteful eating habits.
3. Remember, appetites vary tremendously from meal to meal, from time to time, and from child to child. Don't make comparisons!
4. For any number of children meals are just a matter of refueling. They come in hungry and want to get back to whatever they are doing.
5. If a child wants only a particular food or a particular part of the meal, just keep that particular helping reasonably small. Don't be upset or worried lest the child starve. Long before he does that, he will begin to broaden his diet to include other foods.

A mother came into the office one day. I had never been able to convince her that she didn't know exactly *what* and *how much* her children should eat. *She had always coaxed!* Her two children were the age when meals are a family affair. This day she came in plumb discouraged. "Eating at our house is just one big fight! It's getting so I dread the next meal! My husband becomes so upset he often gets up and leaves the table, disgusted!"

This is the bitter end of coaxing.

Meals should be pleasant. The following suggestion may at first sound absurd, corny, but it's worth thinking about. If you can accustom yourselves to thinking of your child as "a guest at your table": someone to be offered a good meal but not someone to be criticized for his or her tastes, for the size of his or her appetite—someone, moreover, from whom you expect courteous appreciation for your efforts and hospitality—this may offer you some long (very long) range attitudes and approaches toward this business of feedings and mealtimes.

Prevention of Accidents (Your Responsibility)

I've given you figures that show there are far too many accidents in pre-school years. Ninety percent of these could have been prevented.

I've constantly stressed the importance of always keeping the possibility of accidents in mind, of thinking and planning ahead in order to prevent them. Always knowing where small hands and fingers are before slamming a door in a car, in a house, anywhere, is a case in point.

Playpens, gated areas, harnesses are still very much in order for your year-old child. Their use will slowly taper off over the next few years.

Parents sometimes worry unnecessarily that a child may become too dependent on safety devices. I'm reminded of a grandson who, at age two-and-a-half, when a baby brother came along and was put into a sleeping harness, decided that he, for his part, had arrived at man's estate and could get along quite well without one. His sleeping harness was duly eliminated and all went well for a matter of several weeks, until he happened to come down with a cold. Feeling pretty mean and apparently wanting comfort in his misery, he asked to have his sleeping harness put back on his bed where it remained in use for the duration of his cold. Recovered, the harness was once more discarded— this time for good.

As I've been at pains to point out, your responsibility to prevent accidents goes right on as you teach your creeping, climbing, beginning-to-walk-and-run child safe ways of handling himself:

To sit rather than stand in high places—beds, chairs, walls and fences.

To slow down, not race around, in a house full of sharp edges and corners.

To stay in one's own yard.

To stop at a curb and look both ways.

To learn to read *stop* and *go* lights.

Encourage your child's obedience to simple, carefully rationed rules of safe conduct. It takes constant supervision, repeated warnings, rewards and punishments to build up the obedience that makes a child a *safer* child. This is a slow process but as your child grows it can develop into a family pattern of responsible behavior where safety is concerned—a regard for safe play, safe games, safe activities and situations. In due course your attitude as adults toward safe, responsible conduct, your attitude toward traffic rules, policemen, laws and law enforcement can become your growing child's attitudes.

Your child's increasing ability to get about brings up another angle of your responsibility in prevention of accidents.

1. Keep well out of your child's reach materials for cleaning, spraying, painting and dusting that are marked POISON or that you question.

Paint used before 1945 on the inside and outside of apartment houses and homes often contains *lead*. So does some exterior paint used today. *Lead is a poison!* If your child develops the habit of eating chips of paint, or of plaster that contains lead paint, if he starts chewing on sills or railings or any surfaces that might have been painted with a lead paint, he could get *lead poisoning*. Check promptly with your clinic, doctor or hospital.

2. Keep medicines well out of reach, preferably under lock and key.

   Small children are unbelievably agile! They can climb from the toilet seat to a hamper to the washbasin *quite easily*, remove a bottle of, say, aspirin or thyroid pills from the top shelf of the medicine cabinet, then climb down, open the bottle and proceed to eat the pills.

3. A bottle of syrup of ipecac should always be on hand where small children are about—but JUST AS IMPORTANT—*always call the doctor to see whether it should be used, and if so in what dosage.* Having it available can save precious time!

I suggest that you obtain from your doctor or clinic information on how to proceed in case of an emergency. This is an aspect of *Prevention of Accidents* that goes well beyond the scope of this book, but may I advise that you have, pinned up beside your phone the number of:

> Your doctor;
> The hospital;
> The Poison Control Center;
> The Rescue Squad.

Your clinic or doctor will advise you on helpful pamphlets. A good one, *How to Prevent Childhood Poisoning, A New Approach,* is offered at ten cents per copy by The Department of Health Education, The Children's Hospital Medical Center, 300 Longwood Ave., Boston, Mass. 02115.

> The edge of the road is where two ways meet,
> One is for wheels and one for feet,
> And I must stop and look to see
> Whether wheels' way is safe for me.
> I look to the left and I look to the right
> And I scamper across if no wheels are in sight.

But if wheels' way is a busy street
I hold a hand to guide my feet.
Or watch the lights turn green and red
And wait till they signal WALK instead.
Or keep my eyes on the friendly cop
Whose white-gloved hand tells the wheels to stop.

When I grow up from feet to wheels
I'll always remember how it feels
To have to stand and wait and peer
Right and left for wheels' way to clear.
I'll roll to a stop and signal to feet,
And smile and wave as they cross the street.

LPT

Training (Your Responsibility)

When I first discussed this area of responsibility I suggested that there are two aspects to *Training*: your baby's physical maintenance, and its social adjustment. Let's see where they both stand at the end of the first year and where they are heading.

Physical Maintenance

I'd like first to consider the question of keeping your baby's physical system — its motors — running smoothly and efficiently.

Schedule

If you have kept your baby's days and nights going pretty much on schedule you will, by the end of the first year, come to appreciate the advantage of continuing to maintain a fairly regular, well-ordered existence for your growing child.

Feeding

Well before the end of the first year, feeding becomes a matter of three meals a day. In time, one by one, your child's mealtimes can become the same as your mealtimes; but don't be in a hurry to have all your meals together. This is something to grow into slowly: don't ask too much of a small child too soon; don't ask too much of yourselves. "At times" and for "special occasions" does it for quite a while!

Sleeping

This will continue to be a matter of keeping your particular child sleeping through a good night.

a. Naptime will have to be trimmed down and finally discontinued.
b. An hour or so rest period should take the place of a nap, following the noon meal. An accustomed, quiet time, alone, in a room or on a bed with a few specially chosen toys, offers a youngster a change of pace. It's equally valuable for a mother—a well deserved "coffee break." In my experience, the mothers who learned to take advantage of this bit of respite complained less frequently of their patience wearing thin toward the end of the day.
c. Gradually bedtime will have to be moved along to keep a child sleeping through the night.

Bowel Training

Your child should have a bowel movement daily. Here's a place where maintaining a regular schedule pays off as time goes on. Let me refer you back to *Training* (pp. 65–66) and *At Eight Months* (p. 268).

Bladder Training

Bladder Training can usually be started at around two-and-a-half to three years of age. The time to start it and the length of time needed to accomplish it vary greatly from child to child. Watch your emotions!

Try to establish firmly in your mind the fact that there is a simple, very direct relationship between a child's fluid *intake* and *output*: between the time and the amount a child drinks and the time or number of times it has to go to the bathroom. Learn to accustom your child always to go to the bathroom *before* setting out on any enterprise.

Carrying this concept forward to the question of bed-wetting, it is neither practical nor fair to cut down a child's liquids, say at four o'clock in the afternoon, so he will stay dry at night, unless at the same time *you* make a deliberate effort to effectively increase the amount he drinks throughout the morning and early afternoon. Over 24 hours a child needs lots of liquids. At four in the afternoon a youngster, to stay dry all night, should be fairly bursting with fluids. He can then go through the late afternoon and evening, voiding frequently, needing very little to drink to keep from being thirsty and, in consequence, stand a chance of making it through the night. Small children can't waken easily from a dead sleep to go to the bathroom, and they often may not be able to wait till you are ready to get them up.

Exercise

Exercise inevitably take place as your baby gets about more and more. Gradually you can assist your child to develop coordination and motor control in walking, in helping dress himself, in rolling and tossing things, in climbing, jumping and running. Play out of doors in the fresh air goes much better if you enter into it from time to time, offering incentive, direction and companionship.

Social Adjustment

Now let's consider your baby's social adjustment. This sounds big, but it's a matter of helping your baby learn how it fits into the family, first of all, and then into the scheme of things beyond. Social adjustment also includes giving your child some of the useful equipment—good habits, good manners—that will enable him to accomplish the "fitting in" process as painlessly as possible.

Fitting in begins as you gradually apportion the time you give your baby on a practical basis, allowing for:

a. Plenty of undivided attention time: times when you are together having fun, times when you have an opportunity to offer a wide variety of experiences, to start teaching your baby all manner of things.
b. Plenty of time for your baby to become accustomed, with you in the background, to being on his own. When he learns to accept the fact that you have other matters to attend to, when he learns to amuse and interest himself—to be resourceful.
c. Times when your baby becomes accustomed to being left in the care of some other member of the family or a babysitter.

It's valuable for a baby to get the feel early not only of how precious and important you are to each other but of how temporarily independent of each other you can be.

Equipping your child with good habits, a few good manners, I've already touched upon briefly under *Feeding.* This also begins as you teach your baby to accept others, to go to others, to be friendly, to smile. This sort of thing takes place best against the background of your own cheerful, agreeable approach to other people. As time goes on you have at your disposal some everyday, useful tools to help your baby relate to others:

Learning to wave a hand;
Learning to say "Hi!," "Hello" or "How do you do";
Learning to say "please," "thank you," "you're welcome";
Learning to share, to take turns;

Learning to shake hands—either one will do as a starter;

Learning to speak to people by name, to reply to a question.

These are simple expressions or acts of friendliness, but with your *example, help* and *encouragement* they can become solid props in your youngster's encounters with others. Saying or doing them over and again, becoming familiar with them, slowly helps to bolster a child's confidence. So too does the response they prompt in others.

It takes time to teach them and time to learn them, but I've watched parents use them effectively to help their youngsters gain some self-reliance and assurance. Just don't expect too much too soon. Robert Louis Stevenson's little verse says it with complete understanding:

> A child should always say what's true
> And speak when he is spoken to,
> And behave mannerly at table;
> At least as far as he is able.

The logical extension of these attitudes and approaches to your baby's early training is that in time (hopefully before he's through high school), your child, growing up in a warm, well-ordered, responsible home environment, will end up:

1. With some idea of the importance of keeping his physical systems in good running order—a reasonable amount of sleep, something approaching regular and balanced meals and adequate exercise.
2. With some idea of the importance of a sensible amount of time apportioned to school, jobs, recreation.
3. Finding it no very great problem to get along with others of all ages.

Discipline (Your Responsibility)

Your earliest approach to discipline should be based on respect—on the recognition of your baby's ability, even at the tender age of six to eight weeks, to catch on to the idea that you intend to ignore unnecessary fussing (p. 73). Your baby's response to this relatively mild bit of discipline should serve to increase your respect. In time, however, as you unfailingly, unflinchingly, maintain this attitude toward unnecessary fussing, your baby will, in turn, come to respect you for your firmness and consistency. In this way, quite simply, your beginning discipline becomes solidly rooted in mutual regard.

Unnecessary fussing you will undoubtedly have with you for a considerable time. A baby or a child is not about to give it up easily. Every time fussing works it is given a new lease on life. However, if you do your best to disregard it and do so consistently, your child at a year of age won't resort to it as frequently or keep at it with the same degree of intensity and determination as does the child whose parents only begin to apply the brakes at around a year or a year and a half.

As the first year goes along and you continue to carry out procedures essential for the care of your baby, steadily and cheerfully ignoring its occasional attempts at unnecessary fussing and, furthermore, as you firmly insist on maintaining the restraints needed to insure its safety at all times, you will generate an atmosphere of respect and trust that should help greatly to cut down on the amount of discipline needed over the next stages of your baby's growth and development.

For now, as your baby begins to get about, the "no's," "don'ts" and "no-no's" pile up. Increased activity and freedom inevitably bring restrictions for your growing child just as they do for the rest of us. You have to keep the pressure on the brakes when your creeping child is on the loose. When your child starts to walk and then to run, when it becomes increasingly independent, with notions of its own and the agility and strength to pursue them, limits will have to be set to its behavior and actions.

The limits must be reasonable and understood.

The limits will involve both *tolerable conduct* and *safe conduct.*

You must see to it that the limits are obeyed, you must enforce them consistently and firmly so that your child will have the security of knowing where it stands. The little child that persistently repeats the same small naughtiness seems to be pleading for the reassurance and security that a bit of discipline affords.

To accomplish these things you will almost surely, at times, have to resort to further disciplinary action.

1. Your earliest form of discipline, based as it was on recognition of your baby's ability to catch on to the idea that unnecessary fussing is something to be ignored, is something unbecoming, something beneath it, something not to be put up with, should continue to set the tone of all your discipline.

   Your steadfast, good-humored disregard of such unbecoming behavior over the first year should effectively reduce the need to resort to much in the way of more forceful disciplinary action as time goes on.

2. Your next form of discipline, as your baby starts creeping, is a matter of buttressing the "no's" and "don'ts" by temporary loss of freedom and temporary loss of your undivided attention, both reinforced by expression of your disapproval — something a baby senses very early in the game.

3. For some children this form of discipline often continues for a time, sometimes for good, an effective and adequate form of punishment.

   To be sent for a brief time to sit on a "scold chair";

   To be sent to one's room for a short time;

   To be temporarily "an outcast";

   To be temporarily in "disgrace";

for any number of children these remain sufficient forms of reproof.

4. For some children, as time goes on, this may not be enough.

   a. Before the end of the first year the baby that fusses, that puts up a struggle when you change its diapers, may, after a couple of warnings, need a sharp little smack on its bottom.

   Surprise coupled with hurt — both added to the tone of your voice expressing good-natured disapproval, making clear that this is not the way to behave, making it clear that this is not behavior you will put up with, can serve as a very effective deterrent to this bit of misbehavior. If you do this early in the game, as the need for it becomes apparent, if you administer this mild corrective measure without any show of emotion, anger, annoyance, exasperation, you may be surprised at how exceedingly reasonable your baby will be in return.

   The bright, appraising, rather wicked glint in the corner of the eye of a year- to year-and-a-half-old youngster as it surveys you, grimly calculating the risks involved in setting up a bit of a ruckus, in kicking out, should help you to retain both a healthy respect for its mental acumen and a sense of humor in your dealing with it. Furthermore, if you will forgive me, this is the satisfaction and good feeling that good discipline, started early and persisted in steadfastly, engenders between baby and parents over the first year or so.

   b. To enforce observance of the limits you set to actions and behavior, some three-, four-, and five-year-olds will almost surely have to have an occasional well-administered spanking. By "well-administered" I mean not with the hand but with an impersonal paddle of some sort or other — preferably with something specially reserved for the purpose — not through layers of clothes and diapers but on a bare bottom. The procedure should be made a formality — not allowed to be spur-of-the-moment reaction. Emotions should be held at a distance.

c. Indiscriminate slapping of a hand, wrist or face I consider questionable and usually ineffective forms of discipline.

One tends to slap impulsively, when one is angered or irritated, without time for reflection—irresponsibly. In no time at all a child may be slapping or kicking back. When this happens your discipline simply degenerates into a free-for-all. Emotions, uncontrolled, can wipe out the effectiveness of your discipline. At once the cry goes up: "Aren't parents entitled to show their feelings?" "Shouldn't children be made aware that mothers have feelings too?" I can only suggest that feelings and emotions, usefully channeled, are too valuable for all concerned to be squandered in this fashion.

Your own self-control in matters of discipline can, in great measure, help foster in your child a little of the self-restraint toward which all your efforts at discipline are directed.

In all your handling of your child, but possibly a little more so in discipline, it is important that you parents present a united front. When you differ, as you are bound to do, do so behind the scenes:

No arguing or wrangling to confuse, to disconcert your child and leave it feeling at a loss, insecure.

No chinks left open for it to put its fingers into and play one of you against the other.

Your earliest attitude and approach to discipline, way back at six to eight weeks, maintained perseveringly and good-naturedly throughout the first year, as time goes on will mean less time spent on a "scold chair" and fewer spankings; will mean a happier youngster playing with his little friends; will mean an easier adjustment to those first days in school.

> Sometimes when I've been awful bad,
> And "they" call a halt, I get fighting mad.

And Mum says, "Whoa! With a frisky horse
You have to shorten rein, of course!"

"When the car gets rolling all it takes,"
Dad says, "is an extra shove on the brakes!"

So, then, alone in my room
They give me lots of time
To see that the "hand on the reins"
And the "foot on the brakes" *are mine!*

LPT

Education (Your Responsibility)

Here's an area of responsibility which, after about the first year, gets pretty well out of my competence. Once a baby reaches the point where it can put little boxes into bigger boxes in the proper sequence it's about come to the end of my qualifications as teacher or educator. Fortunately so much is being done, written and talked about in this field that you'll have plenty to turn to.

This is a thoroughly challenging and enjoyable responsibility. You parents will find yourselves drawing on all your own experience, imagination, ingenuity and education—and wish you had more. Babies and children love to learn. Your baby and child will soak up all you have to offer to stimulate and direct its growing perceptions and comprehension.

I would like, however, to remind you of what I referred to earlier as your baby's "complete education," which I tend to think of as the education parents and home have to offer. This involves its training, its discipline, the measures you take to keep it safe, as well as all you offer to direct and stimulate its mental capacity and energy. If, over the course of the first year, you manage to maintain a good sensible balance among your four *Responsibilities,* I think you will find it works well for all concerned to go on with more of the same. In my experience very little children, the one-, two-, three-year-olds, come along most happily and develop the greatest degree of self-reliance when they lead a fairly regular, low-keyed existence; when you are able to alternate periods of undivided attention with periods when they are on their own, in a safe place, indoors or outdoors, well within your range of hearing and occasional observing.

Small children in a secure, familiar environment live pretty much in a peaceful world of their own. They trot back and forth, intent, full of engrossing pieces of business — constantly learning. As you parents emerge from the background from time to time to initiate a different kind of play, to offer a drink, occasionally to apply the brakes, to look at picture books again and again, to sing or say nursery rhymes over and over, to bring play to an end at routine intervals with a satisfying meal, a fun bath, a customary rest or sleeptime; as you provide change and excitement with an excursion into the outer world, to the corner, to the playground, to the grocery store, around the block, to the park; as you welcome people in, as it were, from outer space — friends old and new — to invade for a time your peaceable kingdom; as you take off once in a while, leaving an aunt or a babysitter to do all the usual things just a little differently; as you keep your child's world running securely, on an even keel, you are offering it a sort of extension course in its "complete education."

Never underestimate what you and home have to contribute to your child's education. You have much to offer: your tastes, your standards, your insights, your humor and imagination — all manner of things that add immeasurably to your child's individuality. If you have the choice don't feel that you *must* start your child in school or nursery before, I'd say, five years — four at the earliest. Long years of schooling lie ahead. Your youngster won't miss out — in my way of thinking it will be ahead of the game.

Obviously, as time goes on, a child needs the companionship of other children, needs to learn how to get along with other children. But as long as other children are available to play with now and again — in the home, in the neighborhood, or imported—that's good for a start. Adjusting to getting along successfully with one's peers is much the same as that earlier adjustment to getting along with one's family. It takes time and a bit of doing. Hopefully, all your *Responsibilities,* properly carried forward, can make this second adjustment an easy one. Exposure to other children, repeated, encouraged, gradually increased—geared to your individual child's responses—should slowly do the trick.

I would like to suggest that the upshot of this extended "complete education" is that your youngster will start school, at whatever age, ready to absorb and enjoy what its teachers and school have to offer. Youngsters who are exposed to discipline and training for the first time when they hit school have some unhappy and rocky first weeks and months—ask any first grade teacher. The child with some notion of what it means to be obedient, and self-controlled, who doesn't expect always to get his own way, who can be resourceful and independent for a short time when the situation demands, who has the added advantage of having acquired a few good habits and manners— this child is all set to have fun and to learn. This is quite a contribution to make to your child's education.

Mother and Child by Mary Cassatt. (Courtesy of The Art Institute of Chicago.)

Appendix

Parent
Education

Appendix — Parent Education

Parenthood is a mixed bag of responsibilities and blessings, of joys and jolts; and the road you two are preparing to take stretches a goodly way. This book can give you a glimpse of what lies ahead only as far as the first bend. Before you shoulder your pack and take off on your "Parents' Progress," I'd like to speculate briefly with the two of you on what lies around the bend and beyond. I've been accompanying parents over short stretches of that road for some years now. I know something of the disconcerting talk you may hear, something about where to look for encouragement and assistance on the way. I also know that this is a journey that can be very satisfying and a lot of fun!

Over the last few years there's been some talk — much of it fairly loud and articulate — tending to belittle the role of a mother and homemaker. According to such talk, a capable young woman would seem to be wasting her time if she merely takes care of her children and manages a home. She would seem to be settling mindlessly, complacently, for a job that is inferior, second-rate alongside all the exciting, interesting, liberating careers open to women.

I would like to take exception to this attitude, though first let me make one thing quite clear. If a mother is free to choose, and wishes to turn the care of her children over to others and pursue a career outside the home, this, like her decision to breast- or bottle-feed, is entirely up to her. I've known and respected many young women who have done just this, have seen them make significant contributions to society and reach high levels of personal achievement. What I take exception to — what I strongly object to — is the idea implicit in the attitude that bringing up children from infancy to adolescence, creating an interesting, stimulating, satisfying home environment, constitutes a second-rate job, is a waste of time. That young women who settle for it lead, as it were, more or less wasted lives.

After 33 years in the practice of pediatrics, involving close contact with considerable numbers of this so-called "wasted human resource" and their families, I can only conclude that if that attitude is correct I have been looking through the wrong glasses all these years. It has been my impression that the majority of mothers and homemakers are working hard at something they want very much to do and to do well, that they are doing so with very little outside recognition, just about no help, but with a great deal of satisfaction. Through my wrong glasses all these years I've been seeing them in their homes at all hours of the night and day, "doing their thing," completely submerged in it and by it. I've seen them pursuing what I consider a calling so challenging, so demanding, that I often wonder if some of those who choose the career out of the home may not be ducking out on a tough one.

I've seen them taking care of their kids, sick and well, good and naughty, day and night, year in and year out. I've seen them keeping their homes running, a job which, with or without modern labor-saving devices, is plain hard work. I've seen them using their ingenuity and creativity to make their homes comfortable, beautiful and meaningful for children and husbands; sharing with their husbands the problems and pleasures of children and home; pooling with them experience, skills, effort and education to provide the richest possible background for their growing youngsters. I've seen them filling by native capacity and preference a supporting—but by no stretch of the imagination a secondary—role: succeeding as their husbands succeed, as their children succeed. Their sights are set very high!

As I've been observing them over the years it has seemed to me that most mothers are inherently fitted to bring up children and make a home for them to grow in. Unfortunately, largely, I suppose, because motherhood is a calling that goes back in the mists of time, it has been allowed to muddle along on the basis of something "more or less instinctive" which in part it is; The "just plain everyday common-sense," which in part it is also; and, regrettably, the "once a year sentimental" approach. What seems to have been almost completely lacking is any critical awareness of the long-range impact of this taken-for-granted calling; any thought of equipping mothers with the training to enable them to carry on with something approaching the degree of competence and confidence most of them feel the need of, and, as their children grow, come desperately to want; any attempt through special training and improved general education to upgrade the vocation of a mother and homemaker to the level of a skilled profession — which, it seems to me, it should be considered.

This book is a modest attempt to offer, prenatally, a little of the knowledge and understanding of the way babies work that I have come to realize most mothers-to-be want. As I see it, only some such sort of early education can enable more mothers to prevent the handling problems that even before the end of the first year may result in behavior problems. Only with the aid of some such beforehand picture can more mothers acquire the attitudes and approaches that can help make things go smoothly as their children grow and develop. My hope is that this book will provide a sense of direction and dignity to a timeless but woefully underestimated and misjudged profession.

Much more is needed! I would like to see all mothers who wish to remain in their homes working in their chosen field, encouraged, financially assisted when necessary. It seems to me that, with a little insight and imagination, training for it — prenatally and postnatally — could be provided. Continuing education is offered, frequently required, in other occupations and professions. I would like to see something of the sort made available to mothers, and to fathers who wish to take advantage of it.

In my opinion the pediatric branch of the medical profession has a great deal to offer here. It has always seemed to me that the pediatric profession could avail itself far more effectively and efficiently of some of its trained personnel — the men and women who have been in practice or working in the field of pediatric nursing, and who have been dealing with babies, children and parents, for at least 20 or 25 years. It is my feeling that many of these doctors and nurses would be pleased to slow up a bit from the daily round of practice if they could at the same time direct their accumulated knowledge and experience into more widely productive channels. To make partial use of their time and experience to conduct group sessions for mothers, for parents, in conjunction with practicing pediatricians, would both lighten the load of the younger pediatrician and broaden what he has to offer. The group approach makes it possible for participants to ask the questions they so often hesitate to ask in a busy doctor's office; and, furthermore, it enables them to see that their experiences and problems are, more often than not, shared in common with others. In this way, handling and behavior problems could be brought within the scope of preventive pediatric medicine.

New methods and techniques and collaboration with other branches of the medical profession and with educators could make continuing education of a high quality available to parents of pre-school, grade-school and high-school children. No single group is more involved than parents in the problems of children and young people. What better approach to today's youth problems could there be than coordinated effort on the part of all those most involved: trained parents, the medical profession and educators?

Increasingly treatment in a variety of forms is being made available to deal with behavior problems, adolescent problems and the problems of young adults. But treatment is difficult, often discouragingly slow, often incomplete and disappointing. Moreover, it is unquestionably costly. On the other hand, unsuccessful treatment or the failure to provide necessary treatment can result in serious and ugly consequences, and can prove far more costly in terms both of the individual and of the community at large. Let me again say what I have been saying throughout this book—that in my experience prevention of behavior problems is far easier than treatment. Let me suggest that, in the long run, prevention has far more to offer everyone concerned and should prove far less costly from every angle.

Providing parents, right from the start, with training to help them anticipate and prevent some handling and behavior problems would greatly cut down on the need for treatment, and would assist in reducing some of our more grievous and pressing social ills.

Forgive me if I have walked ahead too fast and too far on the road of "Parents' Progress." It is a long road, and I would like very much to see you get all the help possible. I hope I've given you some added understanding of the significance of the job you're tackling, and of the importance of availing yourselves of, actually pressing for, the training and help — begun prenatally and continued throughout your child's growing years — that will enable you to do your job to the best of your abilities, to do everything you can for your baby and child. Without question you mothers learn much as you bring up your babies but a little advance training has certain fairly obvious advantages.

I remember a mother coming into the office with her baby, her fourth, for a routine check-up.

After I'd gone over the baby and we'd sat down to talk, she started in asking questions about the baby — all sorts of little questions, one after the other. For some reason I couldn't quite fathom she seemed unsure of herself. Finally I said, "Wait a minute! Hold the phone! You know the answer to that one as well as I do! What's the matter? This baby is doing well, going very smoothly! What is it that has you bothered?"

She paused a moment, smiled, gave her baby a little hug, and answered, "I know she is — I hope she is, anyway. But I *do* wish I knew *now* just about *half* as much as I *thought I knew* when I had my first baby! Being a parent is a very humbling experience!"

Beyond any shadow of a doubt there is a lot to be learned on this job, but it has always seemed to me that more or less the same lessons should not have to be learned all over again by each new mother — all too often the hard way and frequently at the expense of her baby.

I'd like to leave you with a few thoughts to mull over. First of all, anything and everything the two of you bring with you on this journey: experience—no matter how humdrum, how bizarre; education—no matter how standard, how advanced, no matter the field; everything and anything, often when you'd least expect it, can be turned to account.

I was called one night to see a six-month-old baby. The parents, Canadians, were new to Boston. I had never seen them before. The baby had a temperature of over 105 degrees—when I arrived he was jittery, close to convulsing.

I gave him a rectal sedative and in a short time he relaxed and dropped off to sleep. The parents relaxed too and the mother gave me her account of the day. It had been quiet enough—everything as far as she could recall pretty close to normal. Her baby had eaten a small supper and been quite willing to be put down. An hour or so later she thought she heard sounds and went to have a look. The baby appeared flushed and felt hot to her touch. She took his temperature and it was close to 105 degrees.

Now—as we sat there—she was still incredulous. "It's hard to believe! It happened so fast! You know, I'm a chemist. I used to work as an industrial chemist. I worked with dynamite. But dynamite is at least predictable! Handling dynamite is simple compared with handling a baby!"

There's a comparison for you! This mother had a rather unusual vantage point from which to gauge and learn to respect a baby's potential.

However, in addition to what you bring with you on this journey, you, like all parents—and over my years of experience this has included parents from Boston's north and south ends, from the core city to the outermost suburbs, from all sides and levels of Beacon Hill—the two of you will receive at the hands of your babies and growing children the same ungrudging, leveling. learning opportunities.

Once, when I congratulated a mother on how well she and her husband were handling their three-year-old boy, after thanking me she re-

marked: "But you know, Dr. Turtle, what my husband says is true. Only
last night when we had tucked this fellow in bed and I was telling my
husband all that had gone on during the day, he said to me, 'Boy, oh
boy! I just hope this kid is learning half as much from us as we are from
him!' "

These are the opportunities that parents, closely involved in
the care of their youngsters, can enjoy. This is what they're
entitled to! However, it's the value, the importance of these
opportunities for continued growth and development, for added
learning and maturing which, it seems to me, the zealous pro-
ponents of day-care centers or of the "two-career family" completely overlook.

Obviously, not everyone develops in the same way, but as I
see it, those of you who wish to take some years out to bring up
a couple or more youngsters won't find that you've wasted your
time, that you've failed to realize your full potential, that
you've stepped outside the mainstream of existence. On the
contrary, in the process of going through the steady day-after-
day assumption of responsibility for the care of your babies and
growing children; of living outside of and beyond yourselves;
of catching occasional glimpses of the world through the candid,
unclouded eyes of your youngsters, it is my impression that you
will find that everything the two of you possess in the way of
native ability or acquired knowledge will come out broadened
and deepened. Bit by bit, as your children grow, with the understanding and cooperation of your husbands, you mothers who
wish to will find that you can get back to careers or professions,
that you can complete or continue your education. There will
be those of you who will discover new openings for your talents
and energies, in your homes, in your communities — schools,
hospitals, welfare, politics — in innumerable ways. In my experience, anything you turn to stands to gain from the added
perspective, tolerance, awareness of human needs and concerns
that family life generates. You won't have lost any ground!

I once took care of the baby of a young mother who was an intern at Children's Hospital. She'd bring her baby in to the office and half the time we'd talk about the baby and half the time about her work in the hospital. I felt that in the back of her mind she was wondering about her future.

One day she brought her baby in for a check-up and told me her husband had finished at the business school and they were moving away. "Frankly," she said, "I'd like you to give me some help. Should I start practice now, or should I stay at home?"

Well, I wasn't in a position to tell her what she should do. I could let her talk. I could listen to her think out loud. I could and did suggest that, if she decided to do so, she would find staying at home and taking care of her baby a rewarding experience.

*   *   *   *

She came in a few years later. I was very pleased to see her. By this time they had a second child. Together we went over the children. When we were all finished, she said, "I'm not sorry I put off practice for a while. I don't know how I could have made better use of my education! What's more, I'm learning such a lot!" Then she added, "It's been fun. I'm so glad I didn't miss it."

❧Index

Note: This index is intended as a guide to the principal discussions in the text, but it should be borne in mind that inevitably there is a good deal of overlap—many of the subjects, necessarily, are discussed under other topics. Also, specific ages mentioned (weeks or months) are intended to be only rough approximations. Remember, babies of the same age may differ in many ways!

The detailed Table of Contents will also aid the reader in search of specific information.

W